OLD AGE IN ART

OLD AGE IN ART

LARRY **SILVER**

REAKTION BOOKS

Published by
REAKTION BOOKS LTD
Unit 32, Waterside
44–48 Wharf Road
London N1 7UX, UK
www.reaktionbooks.co.uk

First published 2025

EU GPSR Authorised Representative
LOGOS EUROPE, 9 rue Nicolas Poussin, 17000, La Rochelle, France
email: contact@logoseurope.eu

Printed and bound in India by Replika Press Pvt. Ltd

A catalogue record for this book is available from the British Library

ISBN 978 1 83639 051 0

Contents

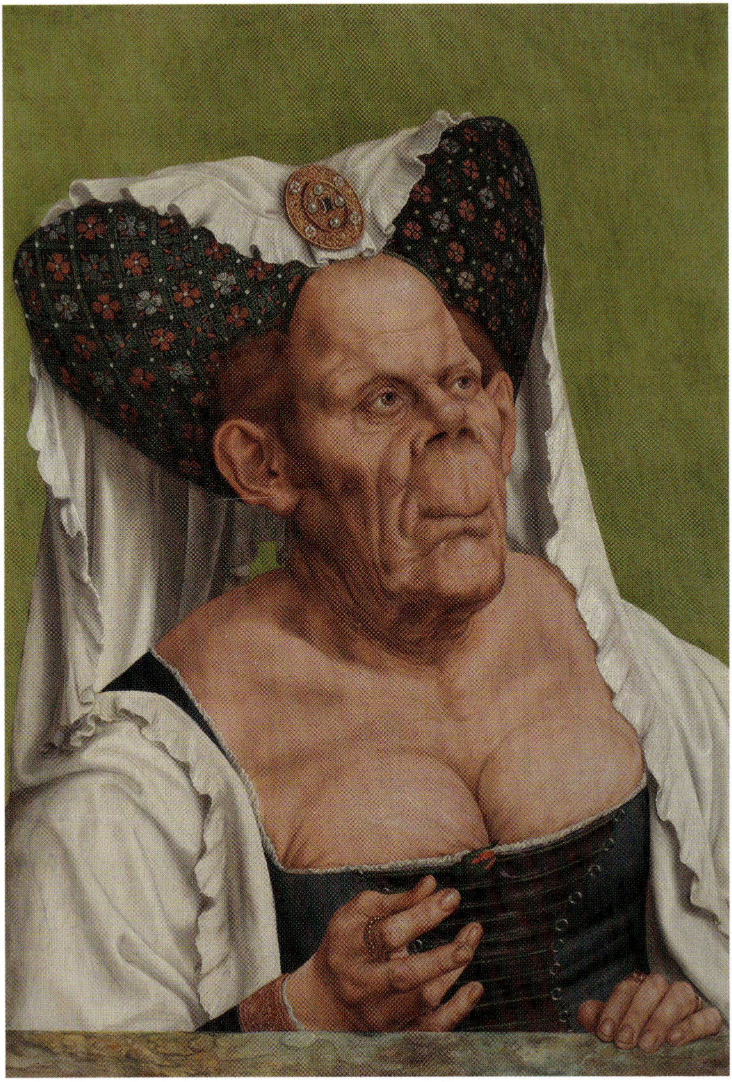

Frontispiece: Quinten Massys, *An Old Woman (The Ugly Duchess)*, *c.* 1513, oil on panel.

Preface

Ars longa, vita brevis

I am a part of all that I have met;
Yet all experience is an arch wherethro'
Gleams that untravelle'd world whose margin fades
For ever and forever when I move.
How dull it is to pause, to make an end,
To rush unburnish'd, not to shine in use!
As tho' to breathe were life! Life piled on life
Were all too little, and of one to me
Little remains: but every hour is saved
From that eternal silence, something more.

ALFRED, LORD TENNYSON, 'Ulysses'

Time present and time past
are both perhaps present in time future.

T. S. ELIOT, 'Four Quartets'

The Child is the father of the Man;
And I could wish my days to be
Bound each to each by natural piety.

WILLIAM WORDSWORTH, 'My Heart Leaps Up'

> Grow old along with me!
> The best is yet to be,
> The last of life for which the first was made.
>
> ROBERT BROWNING, 'Rabbi Ben Ezra'

Nothing lasts forever. Human life is always subject to age. Recent times, however, have been marked by attention to what Robert Harrison Pogue critically calls 'juvenescence', the seeming ability and desire of the species to preserve a more youthful vitality into later years.[1] The common phrase 'Forty is the new twenty' sums up this outlook, which seems to celebrate greater, more healthful longevity, as well as the concomitant opportunity to bring maturity and experience to pursuits normally associated with younger years.

On the other hand, the discipline (in all senses) of history seems to be waning in its role as a guidepost or guardrail for contemporary considerations. Even leaders of the Academy, such as the American Historical Association, warn of the heightened stress on 'presentism' – examining past events through the lens and values of the moment – rather than taking a more period-based, research-driven, historical perspective on our various heritages.[2] Pogue echoes this sentiment: 'The greatest blessing a society can confer on its young is to turn them into the heirs, rather than the orphans, of history.'[3] After all, ever since the technology of writing was invented (not to mention modern transmissions through digital technologies), humans have had the capacity to bequeath stories and accumulated wisdom to later generations, whether within families or across societies. To a certain extent, the explosion of computer-related technologies now in the hands of today's young has created the feeling that all information and social contacts can be accessed in a single hand-held digital device. As a result, historical consciousness is itself becoming a thing of the past. Pogue poses the contemporary conundrum: 'Can a society . . . lose its historicity and still possess a future? Can we consign our cultural memory to oblivion and continue to understand what drives our actions, decisions and the stories we tell ourselves about who we are?'[4]

Attitudes towards the past can also emerge from the contemplation of ruins – particularly the remains of the surviving grand structures from ancient Rome, which inspired Edward Gibbon in 1764 to begin his famous history – as the ultimate form for remembrance of things past, called forth from their remaining fragments.[5] Of course for ruins, the dominant mood is an awareness of transience, reading back to their lost antique splendour, whether ravished by nature or by deliberate human destruction. Already in the mid-sixteenth century Joachim Du Bellay writes of their enduring survival in his *Antiquités de Rome*:

> And though your frames do for a time make warre
> Gainst time, yet time in time shall ruinate
> Your works and names, and your last reliques marre . . .
> If under heaven anie endurance were
> These moniments, which not in paper writ
> But in Porphyre and Marble doo appear
> Might well have hop'd to haue attained it.[6]

In visual terms during the same century an inscription on Herman Posthumus's *Landscape with Roman Ruins* (1536) shows a small visitor taking the measure of a massive capital within a vast array of other fragmentary ruins, beside a Latin inscription from Ovid's *Metamorphoses* (15:234–6), *Tempus edax rerum tuque invidiosa vetutas omni destruitis*: 'Time devourer of all things, and you envious age destroy all.'[7] Certainly the endurance of ruins, including signs of their damage or loss, can evoke their accumulated age as well as their disintegration.

Consequently, contemplation of building remains conjures up a ready analogy to the process of human ageing in the life cycle.[8] In effect, this direct encounter of a present-day witness with surviving ruins results in a dialogue between present and past. Such reveries can occur even with what is thought to be the oldest living thing in nature: a bristlecone pine, almost 5,000 years old.[9]

In similar fashion, a painted or sculpted representation of old age focuses viewer attention (as it once did for the artist who made the representation of agedness) on that visible trace of a personal history, a life story. Old age does not emerge merely from biological change, that is, the inevitable decline of the organism over time. Certainly, there is natural truth in the riddle posed by the Sphinx to Oedipus: we walk on four legs in the morning and two legs at midday, but come the evening, we eventually depend on three (an added cane). However, old age additionally embodies its own accumulated culture, value added, which leads to a tested set of judgements and wider perspectives about human behaviour and achievements. To have lived through momentous changes and events also provides a person with numerous comparisons to the immediate present. Memory and lived history inevitably leave their mark on older people, some of whom can be likened to ruins, while others can be seen as profoundly affected by the events of their life.[10] Like the difference between a culturally saturated, specific 'place' in contrast with uniform, extensive 'space',[11] advanced age also provides a positioned, historically situated place in time, whether measured within an individual life or in biographies unfolding across centuries. While time might not heal all wounds, it does provide additional experience and a cumulative learning process. Even repeated rituals acquire additional layers of meaning and memory for those who have experienced them across a span of years. Obviously, individuals and their particular eras occupy their own sited culture in time, affected by many conditioning elements (increasingly examined by contemporary humanists): gender, race and class, and, of course, regional geography with their own specific cultures.

Historically, old age has been assessed with conflicting evaluations. In one respect, a kind of positive cleverness, even slyness, acquired through experience enables older people to rely on their ongoing experience to shorten routines or size up situations previously encountered. The wisdom of elders is time-honoured, appropriate for service as judges and a source of instruction for younger generations. Old age can bring accumulated honours as well as the virtues of prudence and moderation. But of course physical strength and flexibility decline steadily with age, and mental acuity declines alongside, so that eventually negative conditions, senility or diminished attention, also creep into responses to circumstances.[12] Old age brings eventual decrepitude.

On one hand, old persons are often associated with heightened piety, or a kind of reasonable wisdom gained through reflection in the twilight of life. But such consciousness of mortality can have negative aspects, the opposite side of the same coin. It might prompt a grasping desire to hold on to worldly possessions in a form of greed, or to behave as if age has imposed no limits on youthful passions or impulses towards over-indulgence, such as lust, giving rise to the stereotype of the 'dirty old man'. Old people as a group can also be socially marginalized from younger segments of society, seen as socially unproductive or even distinctly different in kind, with faces marked by ugliness and bodies by deformity. Women beyond child-bearing years often suffer greater stigmas and isolation, being represented as procuresses for younger women or even as witches who corrupt young acolytes. All these stereotypes about the character of the aged recur throughout history.

One direct way of seeing the situated aspect of old age as interpreted by previous centuries is to examine depictions of old age in the visual arts. This short book will examine pictured instances of old age and its associated values in images ranging across historical periods on a span from ancient Rome to twentieth-century Europe and America. Examples include media as diverse as sculpture, painting, printmaking and, occasionally, photography. Chapter One considers old age within related concepts, beginning in ancient and medieval eras: formulations about the Ages of Humanity. Those in turn are tied to other systems, which extend to clusters of temperaments or humours, seasons and even planets, viewed within the dominant framework of astrological thought. Chapter Two takes up some specific images with contradictory valences: some that value old age; others that satirize old-age infirmities and follies (including the diabolical sin of witchcraft, usually associated with old women). Chapter Three turns to specific narratives, beginning with the Bible and extending into Graeco-Roman mythology before concluding with literary fiction. In contrast, Chapter Four focuses entirely on portraiture of the aged, including numerous self-portraits.

Chapter Five takes up a theory advanced by a number of scholars – namely, that certain artists have what can be termed an 'old-age style'. This exclusive group comprises painters and sculptors who enjoyed very long careers, most of them living to be more than eighty years old yet still actively producing innovative and moving works in their latter years. Several of them produced candid old-age self-portraits among their creations, and almost all of them intensified the visible marks of their creative practice. This emphasis on facture might be the result of several potential causes: an increasing confidence in their overall mastery of a specialized craft (or of several crafts, since many of these artists worked in multiple media); a late-career freedom that they had already achieved after a lifetime of success; and/or the inevitable physical decline of those fine motor skills necessary for the subtler finish usually visible in their earlier works. The reader can judge whether the very phenomenon of old-age style is convincing, especially in its validity for any or all of the chosen case studies (admittedly selective in a book of this size). But this focused study itself makes a fitting finale for the previous chapters. Not only does it include old-age self-portraits (with the exception of two landscape artists, Turner and Monet), but the artists' chosen subjects extend their earlier preferred topics into experimental new directions.

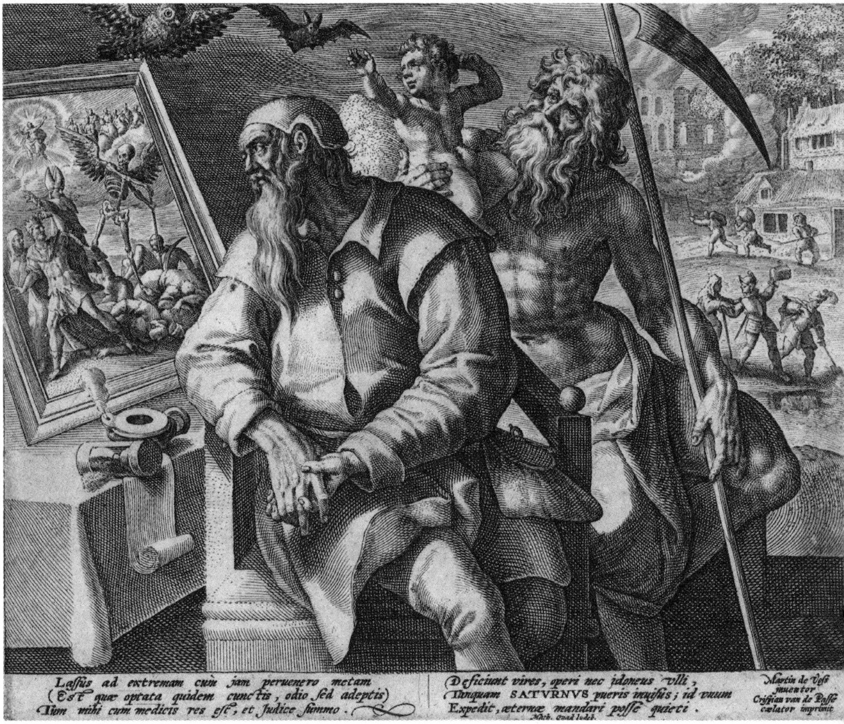

1 Crispijn de Passe after Maarten de Vos, *Senectus dolori*, 1596, engraving.

One

Old Age Is Relative: Age and Stage as Concepts from Antiquity to the Renaissance

> Our span of life is divided into parts;
> it consists of large circles enclosing smaller.
> One circle embraces and bounds the rest;
> it reaches from birth to the last day of existence.
>
> SENECA, 'Letters to Lucillus', XII

> Thou hast measured all things in measure
> and number and weight.
>
> WISDOM OF SOLOMON II:20

> Medieval man . . . was an organizer, a codifier,
> a man of system.
>
> C. S. LEWIS[1]

As health care improves and lifespans extend, one begins to hear such phrases as 'Age is just a number' or 'you are only as old as you feel.' What this sliding scale reveals is that old age – like any measurement – is relative to other ages and appears at the far end of a sliding scale. While the concept of stages in childhood development was a twentieth-century insight by Jean Piaget ('The child is only going through a stage'), this same kind of insight remained fundamental to older classification systems that dominated European thought from antiquity to the Middle Ages (and even well into the early modern period). Such systems within natural philosophy are ultimately based on cosmological beliefs about the heavens and earth, as well as their intimate relationship, and the same systems also pervaded literature and the visual arts.[2]

First, old age must be situated in relation to other stages of the life cycle.[3] When age was considered as a stage, a culmination of the life process, it often formed that last step in a numerical sequence already tied to a larger notion of cosmic order and harmony between heaven and earth. In the broadest terms, three stages of life comprised the sequence: youth, maturity and age, with finer numbers derived from subdivisions of each segment. Already Aristotle's *Rhetoric* (2:12–15) divided life into three phases – youth, maturity and old age – and Horace's *Ars poetica* (ll. 153–78) described life as unfolding in Four Ages.[4]

Maarten de Vos (1532–1603), a later sixteenth-century painter and designer of prints, produced a series, engraved by Crispijn de Passe the Elder, that set forth the Four Ages of Humanity: Adolescence, Love; Youth, Labour; Honorable Virility; and, finally, Senescence or Old Age, Pain (*Senectus dolori*, 1596; illus. 1).[5] His image of old age shows a white-bearded man clasping his hands and contemplating a painting, in which skeletal Death with his scythe is driving a bishop and a king before him as bodies pile up, while in heaven a judging Christ and saints are enacting the Last Judgement. In front of the picture an hourglass and a smoking lamp rest on the table, both symbols of transience, and above it fly two negative creatures, an owl, usually understood as an ominous bird of night, and a bat of death.

Behind the man is the figure of Father Time holding a baby,[6] but he is not noticed by the old man, whose gaze is fixed firmly on his picture. The print is accompanied by Latin text that reads:

> Since I am now exhausted and arrived at the ultimate
> goal (It is indeed what all have wished, yet viewed
> with revulsion by those who have reached it), since
> now doctors concern themselves with my interests,
> plus the highest Judge. Strengths disappear, and –
> no longer fit for any work – I am resentful like Saturn
> towards his children; only this is still useful, to be able
> to leave off to the eternal – to rest.

One obvious correlation tied the ages of humankind to the four seasons, with old age linked to the cold of winter and the death of flora, in opposition to the springtime renewal of warmth and life. Divisions were marked astronomically by solstices and equinoxes across the year. Thus childhood resembled spring, youth summer, maturity autumn and old age the finality of winter. Linked to the ancient philosopher and mathematician Pythagoras, this connection between ages of humanity and seasons of the year was also repeated by Aristotle and, later, by medieval scholars.[7]

When artists began to make images of the Four Seasons, particularly during the period of printmaking across the sixteenth century, they inevitably likened old age to winter and youth to springtime. A good example of the fusion of winter with old age is a print from *The Four Seasons* by Hendrick Goltzius (1558–1617), a Dutch printmaker, on the eve of the seventeenth century (illus. 2).[8] Winter's personification is a stooped old man in a cloak and hood, who warms his hands over a brazier that he carries. He walks through a snowy landscape filled with bare trees and ice skaters. Ancient authors already linked the seasons to the Four Winds of the cardinal directions, so the cold north wind (Boreas) blows more snow onto this landscape. In the sky zodiacal symbols of the three winter months appear: Capricorn, Aquarius and Pisces. Accompanying verses along the outside of this roundel composition underscore the connection between winter and old age:

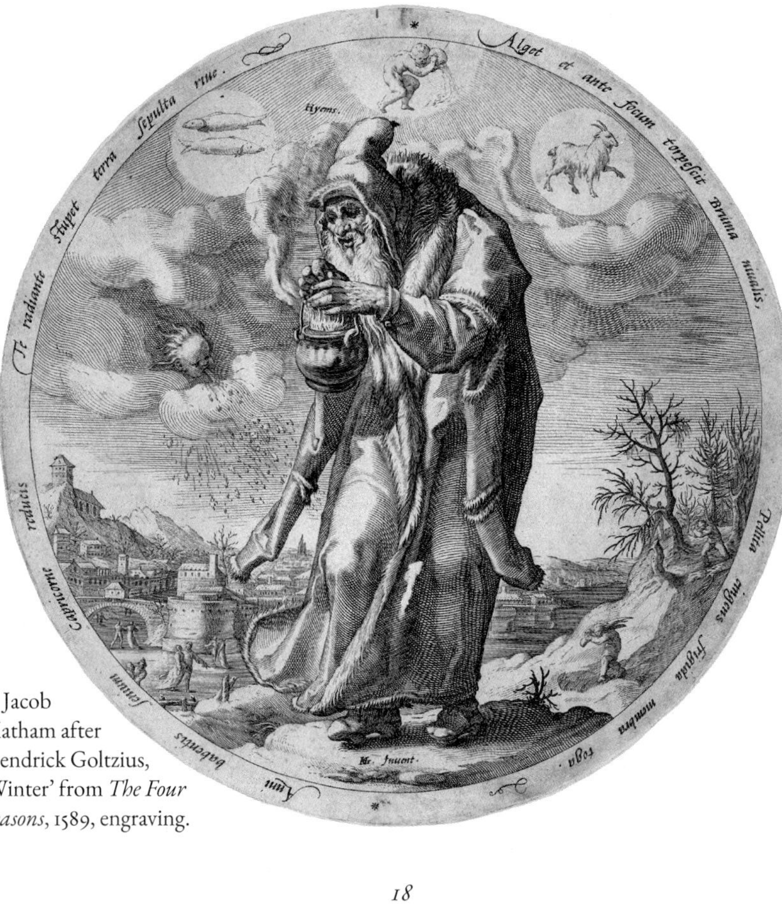

2 Jacob Matham after Hendrick Goltzius, 'Winter' from *The Four Seasons*, 1589, engraving.

> He is cold, snowy Winter, and sits rigid before the fire, his freezing limbs wrapped in a fur coat. And as you, Capricorn, transform the age of the departing old year [to the youth of the new], the earth lies buried in snow while you shine down.

In a disturbing tall, narrow panel Hans Baldung (1484–1545) painted a four-part image of a woman's lifespan from infancy to death, with death represented by a standing skeleton that holds an hourglass and a clock without hands that resembles a eucharistic wafer (1547; illus. 3).[9] Death is shown as male, with vestiges of hair still on his body. But the three figures are intertwined. Already Death's legs crowd together with the old, tanned woman who stands beside him, and she in turn pulls at the cloth that veils the sex of the pale young woman at left as she places the other hand on her shoulder. (For the old woman, Baldung also made a related half-length study from life of an aged individual with a cap and an exposed breast; *c.* 1535.) A tear slides down the cheek of the young female figure as the two women turn their heads together. In the foreground of this bleak landscape, painted in subdued earth tones, stands an owl of night. The bird is placed beside a sleeping infant, whose ambiguous reclining form already anticipates the state of death. But that same infant also touches the lance held by Death, which is already broken, so there may be here a suggestion of eventual Christian consolation in salvation. Certainly the painting's wintry setting accords with old age and reinforces the suggestion that the theme of death dominates here after life's warmer, earlier phases. Close inspection of the icy landscape reveals small, Bosch-like demons who grab naked humans for hellish torments in the background ruined tower structure.

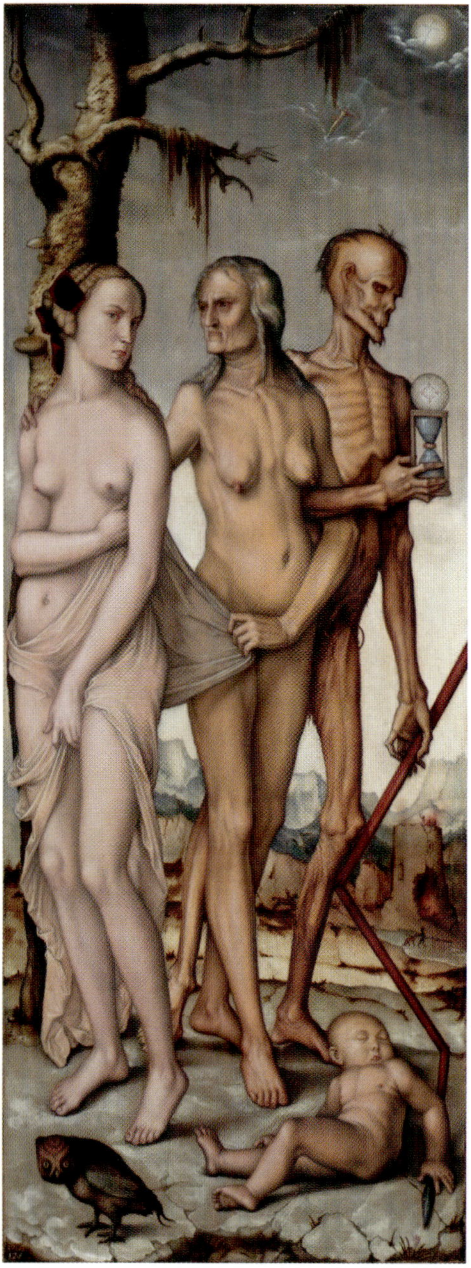

3 Hans Baldung, *Ages of Women*, 1547, oil on panel.

But from the soft light aureole in the upper right a crucifix is descending, a promise from heaven of conquest over death that reinforces Death's broken lance.[10]

A rosier image of the Ages of Humanity is provided by the great Venetian painter Tiziano Vecellio, or Titian (*c.* 1488/90–1576), in his painting *The Three Ages of Man* (*c.* 1512/14; illus. 4).[11] In the left foreground of its verdant landscape sit two lovers, a naked man and his clothed female paramour, who plays shepherd's pipes and wears a wreath of myrtle, the herb sacred to Venus.[12] They gaze into each other's eyes in a suggestively erotic interaction. Beside them lies a trio of infants, one of them winged, and thus marked as Cupid, who tries to rouse the two sleepers, who may be dreaming of their potential future. Behind them at some distance sits an old, white-bearded man holding two skulls for contemplation – that is, introducing death into Arcadia – with a numerical echo of both the sleeping infants

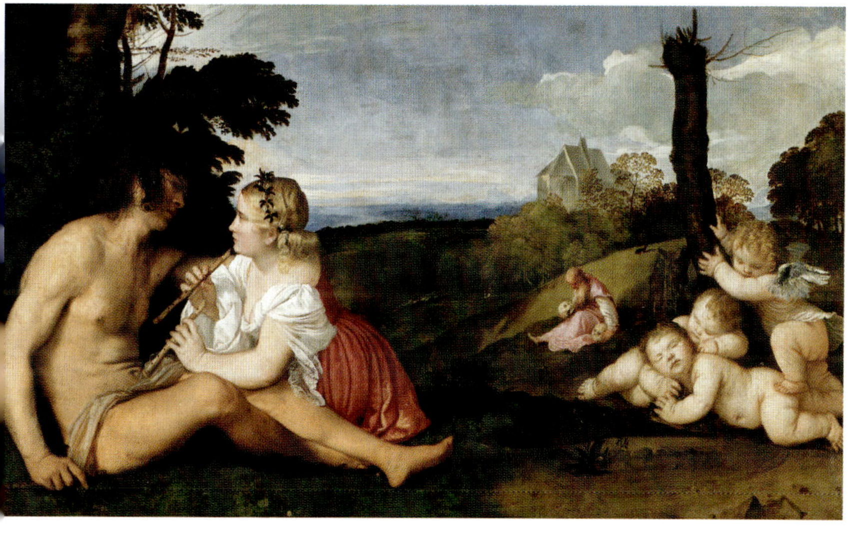

4 Titian, *The Three Ages of Man*, *c.* 1512–14, oil on canvas.

and the two lovers.[13] He echoes the young woman with pipes through both his seated pose and his pink garment with white sleeves, which inverts her colour scheme. By implication, then, the skulls foretell the ultimate destiny of both seemingly oblivious, self-absorbed pairs, in a kind of memento mori reserved for the viewer. In Titian's image, the Ages of Humanity are three: infancy, maturity and old age, or senescence.

Another version of the Ages of Man was projected onto the Three Magi, those kings from 'the East' who followed the star of Bethlehem to come and adore the Christ Child (Matthew 2:1–2). Artists showed a triad of monarchs with their followers at the manger, with the oldest given precedence and placed closest to the Child, as in a later painting by Quinten Massys (1526; illus. 5). Here the oldest king in profile (whose face probably derives from a Leonardo da Vinci caricature) kneels with hands clasped in prayer before the seated Virgin and Child. Massys also incorporates the presence of a Black king as the youngest magus at the far right, thus aligning the subject of the Three Magi with the three continents of the Old World: Europe (given precedence with a white man, because it was the first to adopt Christianity officially under the Roman emperor Constantine), Asia and Africa.[14] In between a swarthy man completes the image of Asia, but without distinctive dress or features, compared to Africa's facial attributes. Another triad of youth, maturity and old age appears in a painting by the Venetian painter Giorgione (*c.* 1478–1510), *The Three Philosophers*, the subjects of which are often viewed as the Three Magi, guided by a bright sun, but also as more specific philosophers.[15] The central figure wears the turban-like headdress of a Moor, but these isolated figures, clearly embodying three stages of the ageing process, remain outside the context of the Adoration experience of the Magi.

The tetrad of Four Ages and Four Seasons was readily analogized in turn to other quartets. The four cardinal directions, symbolized by the Four Winds, also correlated with the Four Ages, so (as Goltzius already indicated) the cold north wind, Boreas, obviously mapped onto winter and old age. And the Four Elements – earth, air, fire and water – comprised the universe through their varied combinations of oppositions: heat/cold and wet/dry qualities. Already Plato's *Timaeus* made the claim that creation began with the opposites of fire and earth, with the middle terms of air and water. Educationally, another tetrad, the *quadrivium* (arithmetic, geometry, music and astronomy), included the four branches of calculation and ratios in medieval teaching. Ancient and medieval medicine, stemming from Hippocrates and Galen, identified four humours, fluids in the body essential for proper physiological functioning: blood; phlegm; yellow bile, associated with anger; and black bile, associated with melancholy.[16]

Pulling together many of the tetrads that echoed one another, Crispijn de Passe the Elder created his own series of the Four Winds, culminating in the north wind, Boreas (*c.* 1600; illus. 6).[17] Atop clouds sit the Olympian gods who represent the cold, outermost planets: Jupiter with his eagle and thunderbolts, and Saturn with his scythe as Chronos (Father Time), holding an inverted baby (his own offspring, whom he will eat to avoid being overthrown). From the cloud the wind blows fiercely as storms lash the land. Above them a pale moon shines beside their planetary symbols (along with Mercury). Beneath Saturn, a flying weather witch brings a hailstorm that sinks ships, while

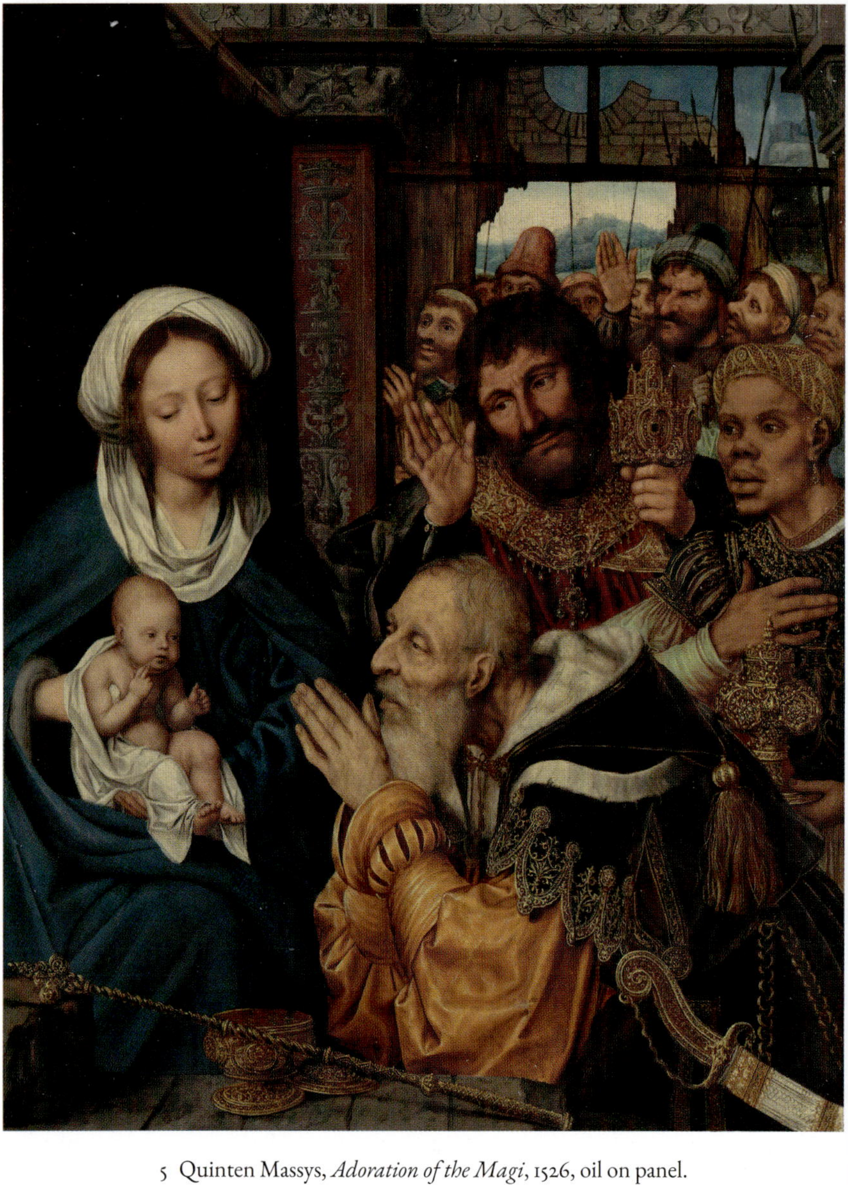

5 Quinten Massys, *Adoration of the Magi*, 1526, oil on panel.

the personification of Winter (Hyems) sits with a torch and bridle on the barren landscape below Jupiter. Northern hostile geographies are labelled below: Nova Zembla on Russia's Arctic Ocean as the site of a bear hunt; the Lapps of northern Scandinavia; and the Sarmatians, related to the Scythian nomads of the steppes and Urals (described by Herodotus (Book IV), who are warming themselves in a tent. The text declares: 'Fiercely the north wind blows from the pole. Saturn and Jupiter are lords of this benumbing part of heaven. It falls first in Scythia, then Sarmatia receives its traces. It rages in these northern fields, an icy storm.'

Perhaps the most compact image to suggest both the complex interactions and the fundamental relationships of these

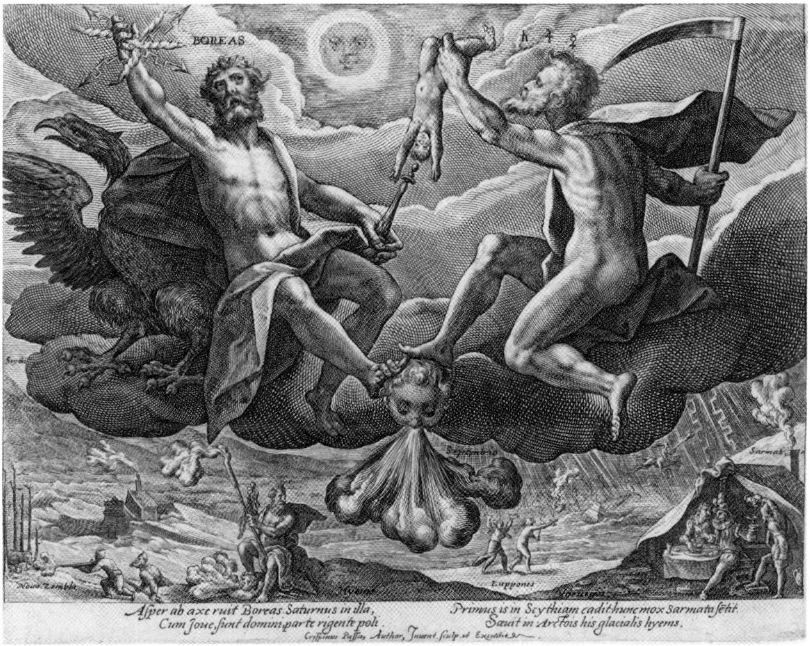

6 Crispijn de Passe, *North Wind* (*Boreas*), 1589–1611, engraving.

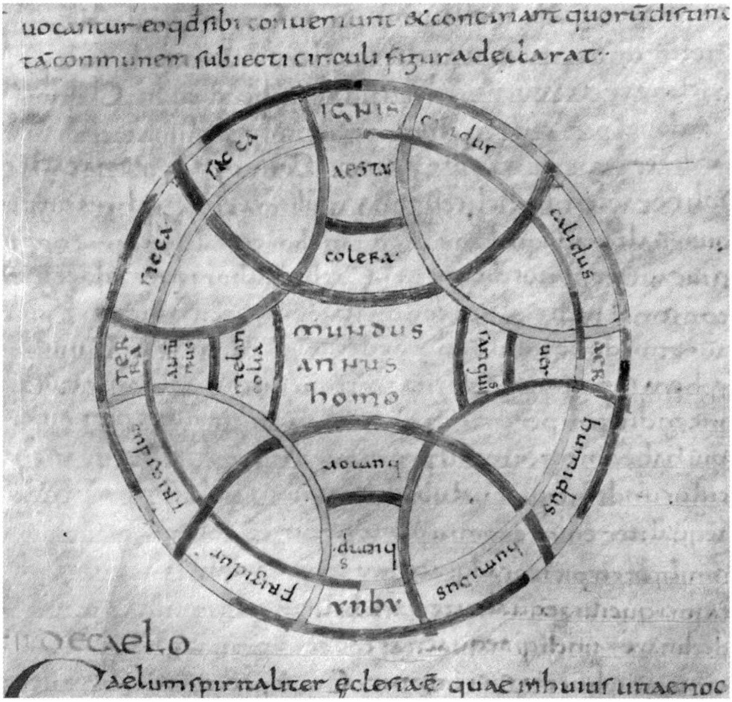

7 Cosmographical tetrad, diagram from Isidore of Seville, *De natura rerum*, late 8th century.

tetradic concepts is a cosmic diagram, ultimately stemming from association with Pythagoras, but for the most part codified during the Middle Ages and illustrated in manuscripts. This graphic image – also the logo of the Warburg Institute, University of London – derives from Isidore of Seville's *De natura rerum* (613 CE; illus. 7).[18] Though without express indications of the ages of life, it juxtaposes various concepts to fit them into four groups around a circle, the centre of which signals the topics that interrelate: *mundus* (world), *annus* (year) and *homo* (humanity). Each element shares qualities with its neighbours, arranged according to the poles of cold/heat and dry/wet. Thus, at the top, Fire (*Ignis*) is measured by its qualities of heat and dryness and correlates with Summer (*Estas*) and the humour of yellow bile (*Colera*). Following the circle clockwise, Air (hot and wet) produces Spring and blood. Then Water at bottom – thus opposite in its wet and cold from Fire – is linked to Winter and phlegm. Finally, Earth matches up with Autumn and black bile, or melancholy. This diagram also corresponds to the ancient claim that the body is a microcosm of the greater cosmos, or macrocosm.

Just as the world system in this model consists of four elements and four seasons, humanity is composed of four humours and four seasons, or ages. Thus a simple addition of the Four Ages of Humanity corresponds to the overall sequence and oppositions to be found in greater nature. Old age was sometimes given two phases: cold and dry old age (*senectus*); and decrepitude with memory loss (*senium*) – cold and wet, as on the diagram. Moreover, it was easy to group the months and their accompanying signs of the zodiac within the four-fold scheme, with groups of three months in a row comprising the season, but other clusters of zodiacal signs also corresponding to the four humours, so that earth, air, fire and water signs would recur in turn within each season that shared their qualities. Thus the cold and wet water signs associated with winter and old age would be Cancer, Scorpio and Pisces; the hot and dry signs of summer are Aries, Leo and Sagittarius. Astrology, based on the study of zodiacal signs for their influences at birth and potential for prophecy, formed another major ancient and medieval branch of knowledge, extending into the Reformation era.[19]

To complicate the harmony of tetradic diagrams further, one could introduce the effects of planetary influence, starting with the seven known planets within Earth-centred astronomy:

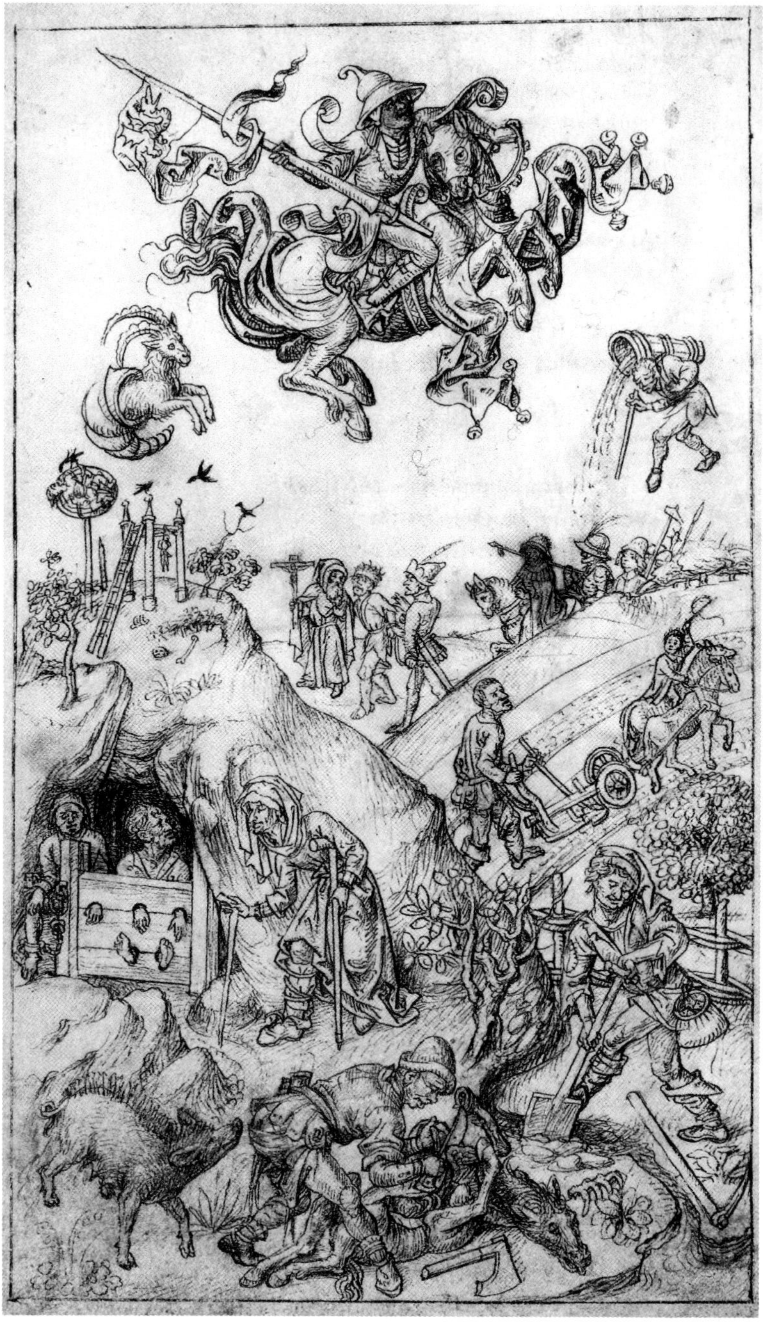

8 Saturn and his children, miniature from the 'Housebook' of Wolfegg Castle, *c.* 1480.

the Sun and Moon as well as Mercury, Venus, Mars, Jupiter and Saturn. The same seven-part harmony also pertained to other clusters of seven: seven days of creation; seven days of the week; seven sacraments; seven liberal arts in courses of medieval study (by merging the *quadrivium* with the *trivium* of grammar, rhetoric and dialectic).[20]

Moreover, the influence of planets could affect individual psychology. The planet Saturn was strongly associated with melancholy, Venus with amorousness.[21] Visually this powerful, shaping celestial influence found representation in its own series, the 'Children of the Planets', popular in print ensembles of the early modern period.[22] In that concept each of the seven planets is shown in flight at the top of the image, and the earthly followers dominated by that planetary influence appear below, pursuing their various job aptitudes.

A good example of Children of the Planets is a cluster of drawings by an anonymous German master in a manuscript called the 'Housebook' (illus. 8).[23] Saturn appears first in this series, bringing a deleterious influence from the furthest, coldest planet. The planet itself carries a banner with a dragon as he rides a horse ornamented with bells, the common attribute of a fool or madman. Below him are the zodiacal symbols of Capricorn and Aquarius. His influence, linked to cold, dry earth, is described as pale, hard, cold, sad and old in the accompanying poem. The depictions of planetary 'children' below Saturn include numerous activities: farmers who dig ditches and plough fields; a crippled woman on crutches; a prisoner in the stocks or manacles; and a convict heading for execution on a hillside gallows. In the foreground another ragged peasant has slaughtered his old horse. Saturn's world is filled with both hard labour and criminality.

By contrast, other planets create different settings and occupations. Not surprisingly, Venus, riding side-saddle, overlooks happy followers, both rich and poor, including nude couples in bath houses and the pleasures of music. Mars is armoured and leads his followers to violence. Perhaps most productive is the scene of Mercury, patron of the visual arts and professions of intelligence and industry, including writers, goldsmiths and clock and organ makers, as well as painters and sculptors. As noted, Sol, or Sun, is the warm and dry opposite of cold, moist Saturn. Crowned, he rides with a regal sceptre alongside the zodiacal lion of Leo, and his children are happy, noble, strong and handsome. The poem notes that they serve God in the morning, and the image features a small chapel. In a walled garden, the preserve of nobles, young courtly lovers listen to music at leisure, while beyond their yard sturdy young men in a meadow compete as athletes.

De Vos's version of the Seven Planets includes 'Saturn' (*c.* 1580; illus. 9), with the same Children.[24] Dragons reappear, but here a pair of them pull the chariot of the god, who wields the scythe of Chronos (the very spokes of his chariot are blades) as a child cowers before him. Symbols of Capricorn and Aquarius occupy the upper corners. Below, a forbidding landscape of crags and coastline resembles the northlands in de Passe's *Boreas*. The accompanying text provides some explanation of these scenes:

> Saturn rules over the continents of the West and over mines and bestows sinister gifts to magicians, generates magic with ungodly powers like the god of skills. And since his metal is lead, weighty and rigid, his subjects are heavy in heart [melancholic] and stiff in conduct.[25]

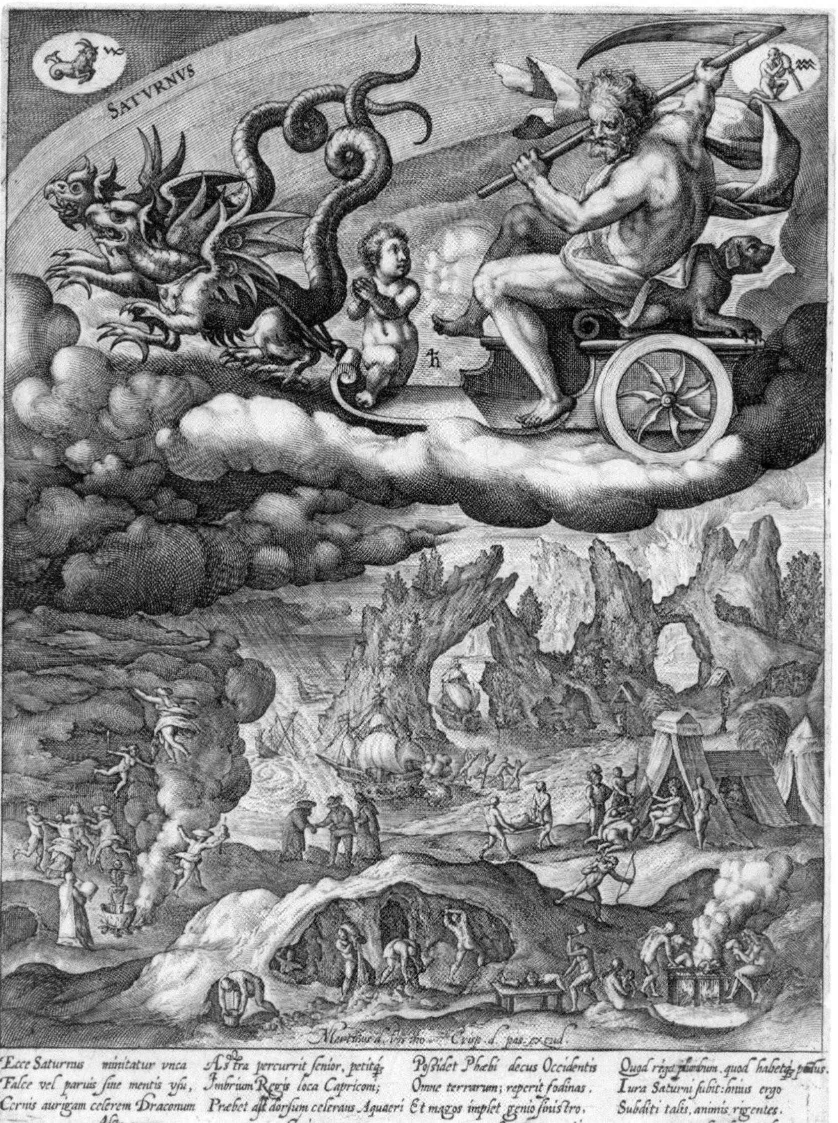

9 Crispijn de Passe after Maarten de Vos, 'Saturn' from *The Seven Planets*, 1589–1611, engraving.

Generated by a witches' sabbath (see illus. 28) in the lower left corner, storms assail ships, though one of them uses cannon to attack naked natives on the shore. At the bottom centre miners have replaced the ditch diggers of 'Saturn' in the 'Housebook', and in the lower right naked cannibals are roasting human limbs. These are all scenes taken from the most extreme accounts of life in the Americas, whose exploitative silver mines were administered by Spanish colonials but whose native peoples were accused of cannibalism.[26] Under a tent, a feathered Amerindian leader, backed by armoured Spanish soldiers, receives ore from the mines and kneeling obeisance from subjects or captives.

Once the concept of seven was associated with the Ages of Humanity, because of the planets, a variety of ages unfolded. Some versions showed each phase as a ten-year interval up to age seventy; others kept the division of seven for the number of years, with ten segments.[27] Shakespeare's fool in *As You Like It*, Touchstone, follows up the speech of Chapter Four's epigraph with a seven-part division of the phases of life in his famous lines, starting with 'All the world's a stage.' After declaring that 'one man in his time plays many parts, His acts being seven ages' he goes on to characterize those ages as mewling infant, whining schoolboy, sighing lover, quarrelsome soldier and then justice. He continues:

> The sixth age shifts
> Into the lean and slippered pantaloon,
> With spectacles on nose and pouch on side;
> His youthful hose, well saved, a world too wide
> For his shrunk shank, and his big manly voice,
> Turning again toward childish treble, pipes

And whistles in his sound. Last scene of all,
That ends this strange eventful history,
Is second childishness and mere oblivion,
Sans teeth, sans eyes, sans taste, sans everything.
(II.7, 139–66)

One other way to show the passage of time with either units of seven or ten is to adapt the Wheel of Fortune of Boethius's sixth-century *Consolation of Philosophy* to form a Wheel of Life, with the Ages of Humanity arrayed along its rim. Youths ascend, maturity stands on top and old age descends to the right when the image is read clockwise. Each individual gets one turn of the wheel.[28] The most impressive example is an early fourteenth-century English manuscript, the De Lisle Psalter (*c.* 1310; illus. 10).[29] It features ten episodes around its circumference with Christ at the centre ('I perceive all at once, I govern the whole with reason'). Rhyming Latin couplets define each stage – from the meek, milk-drinking infant to the decrepit, aged men, until at the very bottom of the wheel we see the casket with ashes of death ('I have been turned into ashes, life has deceived me'). Atop the wheel sits an enthroned, ruling king in his prime, but as the wheel descends the images and the texts tell a story of decline: 'I take up a staff for myself, at death's door,' followed by 'Given over to decrepitude, death shall be my lot.' Then 'Given over to feebleness, I begin to fail,' and 'I thought that I would go on living, life has deceived me.' In the images the individual dies in the eighth age, and this sequence balances the four corner figures, who summarize the stages of life in the four traditional phases: *Infantia*, *Iuventus*, *Senectus* and the most infirm, reclining *Decrepitus*.

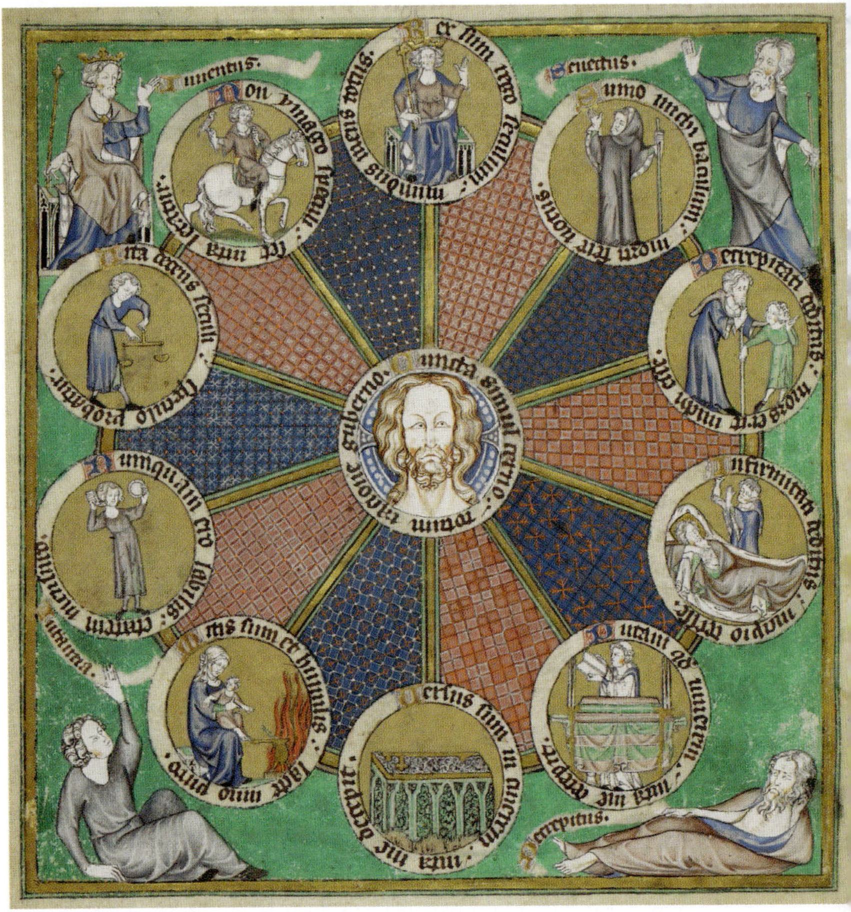

10 Wheel of the ten ages of man, miniature from the Psalter of Robert de Lisle, *c.* 1310.

We see the new organization of the Ages of Humanity in a sixteenth-century print that visualizes the stages of life as a series of steps, ascending from infancy to maturity and then descending. In Protestant Augsburg in 1540 Jörg Breu the Younger designed a woodcut (illus. 11).[30] Here, nine steps, with a tenth place for skeletal Death above, mark the seven-year intervals from cradle (shown on the first step) to grave, and below the structure itself the Last Judgement unfolds with open tombs and naked souls being separated towards heaven and hell. In contrast to Baldung (see illus. 3), Breu shows the ageing process through males rather than females. On the highest step at midlife a scholar unfolds a scroll. On the four declining steps of increasing age, the men are all bearded, and the final figure, following an old man with a walking-stick, stoops to embrace a grandchild as he leans on a book. Thus is the circle of life, like the Wheel of Fortune, affirmed, just as a closed coffin rests at the lower right beside the open tombs of the resurrected figures.

Also depicting ten steps in the ageing process, a Dutch woodcut (*c.* 1545/55) by Cornelis Anthonisz. of Amsterdam essentially

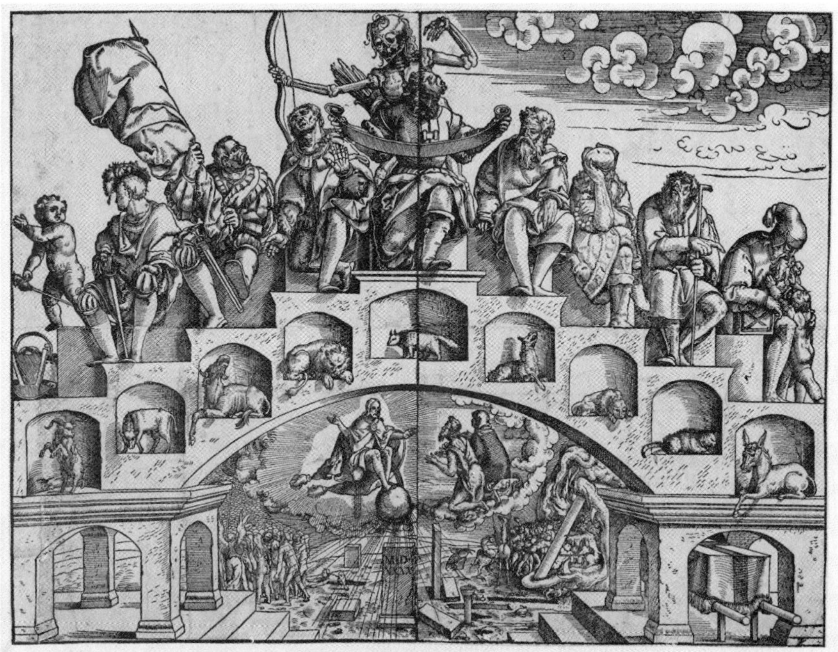

11 Jörg Breu the Younger, *The Steps of Life*, 1540, woodcut.

presents a variation on Breu's earlier imagery, including the animals of the decades.[31] Here the basic structure is a triumphal arch under the hourglass of Time and ruled by skeletal Death with his arrows; both appear above a scene of the Last Judgement, visible through the central portal. Accompanying texts mark the decline of later decades: 'Look what I show/ The 80-year-old/ He rides the ass/ It saddens him/ To live longer.' And for the final figure, aged ninety: 'The 90th year/ One sees it clearly/ You're all old ware/ A living death.' Flanking trees reinforce this point, with living branches at the side of youth and dead ones opposite. Songbirds and musical instruments adorn the branches of youth, but the ominous owl, spectacles and crutches accompany old age. There is a cradle left and grave at right, with a central coffin pointing the way to the Last Judgement.

Ancient and medieval concepts of the Ages of Humanity still pertain in the mid-sixteenth century: truly Old Age is relative, and an extension of all that has gone before.

Two
Wisdom and Folly

Upon the supreme theme of Art and Song:
Bodily decrepitude is wisdom; young
We loved each other and were ignorant.

WILLIAM BUTLER YEATS, 'After Long Silence'

A free person thinks least of all of death,
and his wisdom is a meditation on life, not on death.

BARUCH SPINOZA, *Ethics*, iv.67

Already in antiquity, age was understood to confer wisdom. Of course, the inevitable decline of both physical and mental powers was recognized. However, in Cicero's *De senectute* (44 BCE), a dialogue between the aged Cato the Elder and two younger men, a variety of strengths of old age are commended: memories and experience as assets for civic leadership; release from foolish passions and acceptance of limitations; a maturity of soul about life and death.[1] For the most part, in ancient art signs associated with age, such as baldness or beards in men, do not necessarily denote advanced years but merely maturity. Facial wrinkles or sagging flesh are only likely to appear in Hellenistic or, especially, Roman art, where portrait likenesses represent individual features. After a norm of standardized and softened generic images of age on grave steles, from the fourth century BCE memorials begin to distinguish deceased family members as older, sometimes with a walking stick or stooped posture. (Of course, modern life expectancy has expanded the number of years used to define old age).

What has been described as 'verism' – explicitness of distinguishing features, especially of older individuals – flourished during the Roman Republic near the turn of the Common Era. Ancestor portraits, often fashioned in wax,[2] preserved the memory of venerated family individuals. Whether on funerary altars and reliefs or as free-standing bust likenesses within a domestic context, these marble works resembled their sources' wax death masks. They stressed family continuity across generations and celebrated current family prominence. According to Pliny the Elder, they were carried in funeral processions or public family sacrifices, 'and thus, when anyone died, the entire roll of his ancestors, all who ever existed, was present.'[3] Their cumulative excellence on display provided admirable, virtuous models for the living while confirming their family status. A prime example (first century CE; illus. 12) shows a member of an upper-class family who stands at life-size in the toga of a citizen while he holds the busts of two ancestors, marked by their baldness as aged and venerable. Ironically, the head of the man in a toga is not original to the ensemble, but the group still conveys powerfully specific portrait features and the importance of the display bust figures as individuals.

Ancient carvers also celebrated culturally eminent figures in bust portraits, usually conveying the cumulative achievements of old age. Famous writers, including blind Homer but also

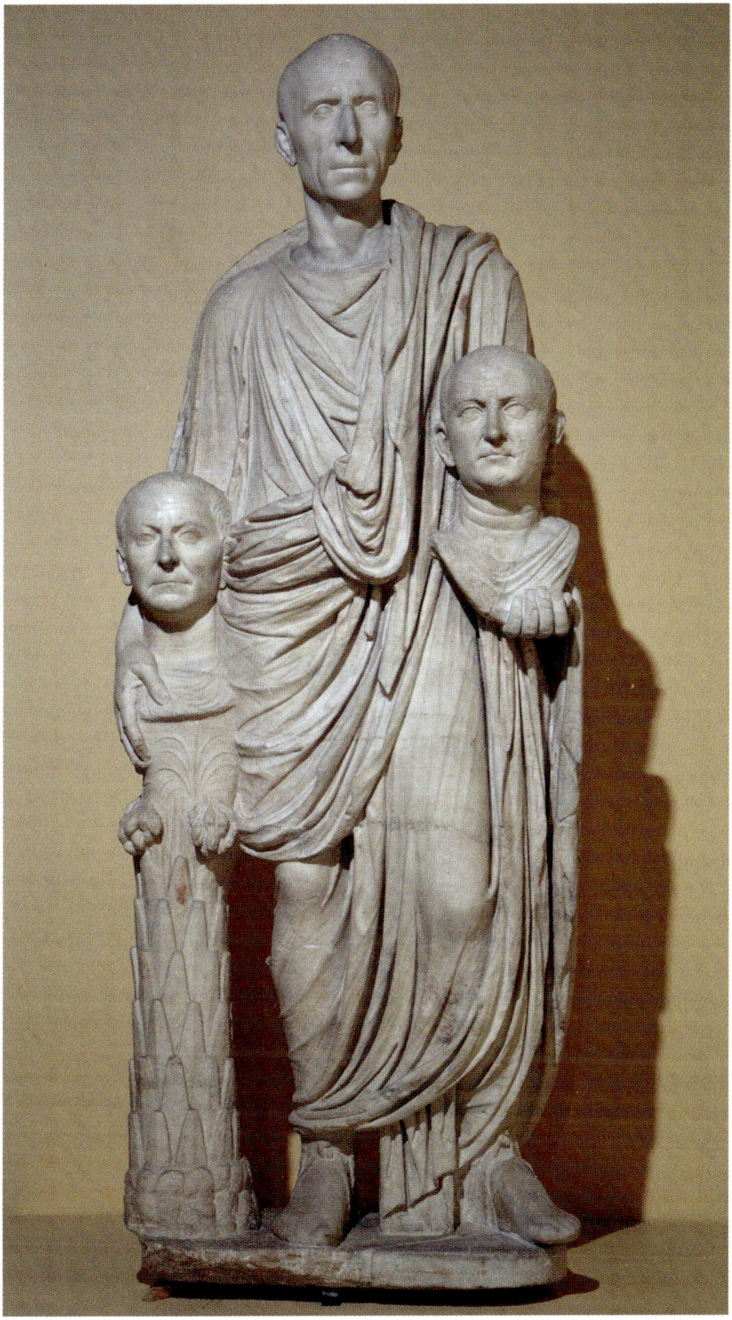

12 Patrician carrying portrait busts of two ancestors (*Togatus Barberini*), 1st century BCE, marble.

philosophers from Socrates (mid-fourth century BCE) to Seneca (first century CE), were celebrated in repeated portrait types, copied in Roman marbles after Greek bronze prototypes.[4] Prominent Republican political elders embodied the ideals laid out in Cicero's treatise. Later they informed the numerous replicated likenesses of successive emperors themselves for public

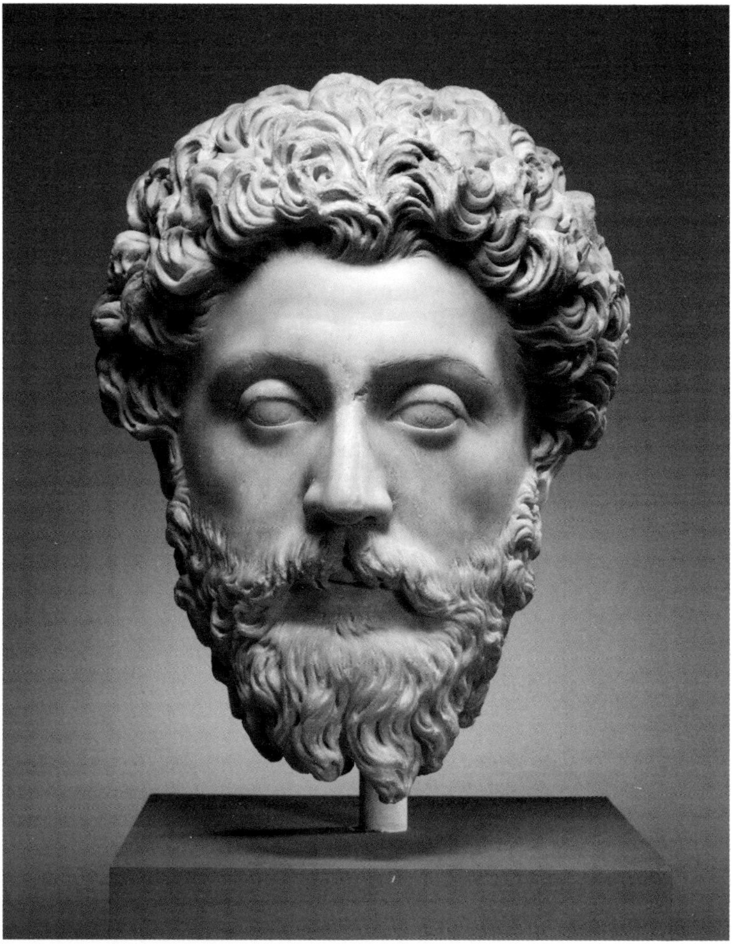

13 *Emperor Marcus Aurelius*, late 2nd century CE, marble.

portraits distributed across the empire (akin to modern photographs of leaders in national embassies).[5] While some youthful images of emperors celebrated their ageless, heroic status, especially portraits of the first emperor, Augustus, many later rulers presented their features and signs of age frankly, akin to their descriptions in contemporary biographies, such as Suetonius' *Lives of the Twelve Caesars* (second century CE).

Many of these trends converge in the bust image of Emperor Marcus Aurelius (r. 161–80 CE; illus. 13). Not only as absolute ruler, praised as the last of the so-called 'Five Good Emperors', but as philosophical author (in Greek) of Stoic *Meditations*, Marcus Aurelius shows maturity with his full beard and steady gaze. However, he also displays a full head of hair and frontal, symmetrical features, softened and idealized without sagging flesh or wrinkle. He does not appear wizened; instead he displays the calm self-control and moral strength of his writings. In addition, a rare surviving bronze equestrian statue on Capitoline Hill in Rome shows Marcus Aurelius' military command at over life-sized scale, and reliefs from his massive column (*c.* 176–80 CE) show him older, in major public roles as both *pontifex maximus* (chief priest) and triumphant general after campaigns in Germania. This carved image is personalized yet frozen in time, conveying an ideal of mature leadership.

Medieval representations of old age largely situated the stage of life in relative terms against concepts of greater youth, or in relation to framing clusters, such as planets or temperaments. Venerated individuals, however, were represented on church portals. Exemplifying the wisdom and spiritual distinction of biblical figures, whether Old Testament patriarchs or New Testament apostles and saints, one finds carved figures standing like literal pillars of faith on cathedral facades, such as Reims (*c.* 1241–5; illus. 14). This trio of apostles resembles the toga-clad elders of Republican Rome in their heavy draperies and signs of ageing, with thick beards akin to likenesses of emperors.[6] Thus many connotations of sound leadership, here spiritual leadership, especially by St Peter, the first pope, deliberately borrow from ancient models.

However, in the later Middle Ages depictions of individuals, usually for their carved likenesses on tombs, refined the standard image types of leaders with newly recognizable personal features. A good example is the donor statue of King Charles v of France (r. 1364–80; illus. 15).[7] The king is represented at full length, crowned and bearing his royal sceptre (restored, but possibly originally the French *main de justice*). He is complemented by a full-length representation of his queen, Jeanne of Bourbon. Those trappings of identity, like the attributes held by saints to identify them in medieval depictions, remain paramount indicators of royal status, dominant over the portrait aspects of the facial features of these two individuals (although these images could also be placed as late medieval examples of portraits; see Chapter Four). In addition, while the specific origin of these detached donor figures remains unknown, the king holds a miniature church structure in his left hand in tribute to his piety as patron of its original location, so his role is stressed as much as his identity. Significantly, both his features and his hair are repeated in other images, such as his tomb effigy, carved by a documented sculptor, André Beauneveu (1364), as well as in manuscript images or paintings where he again appears as pious donor. Thus this statue of King Charles v offers a mixture, like ancient Roman likenesses, of both the status of an individual,

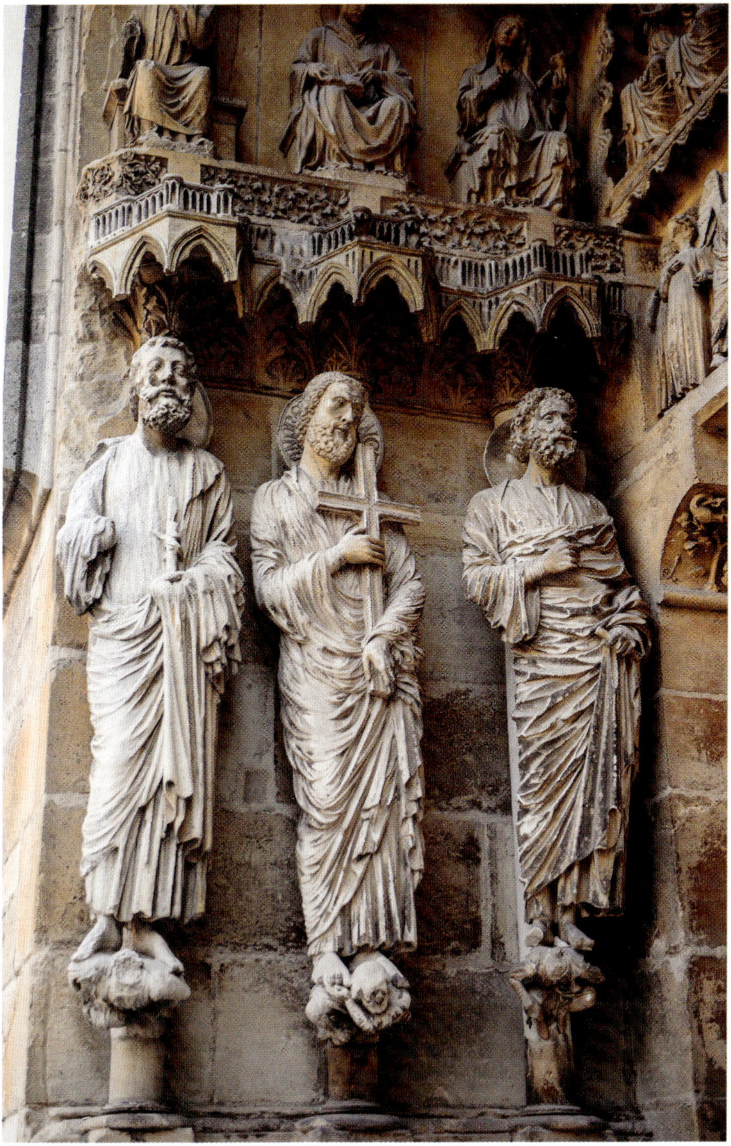

14 Jamb figures of Apostles Bartholomew, Andrew and Peter, from the left side of the Last Judgement Portal, North Transept, Reims Cathedral, 1230.

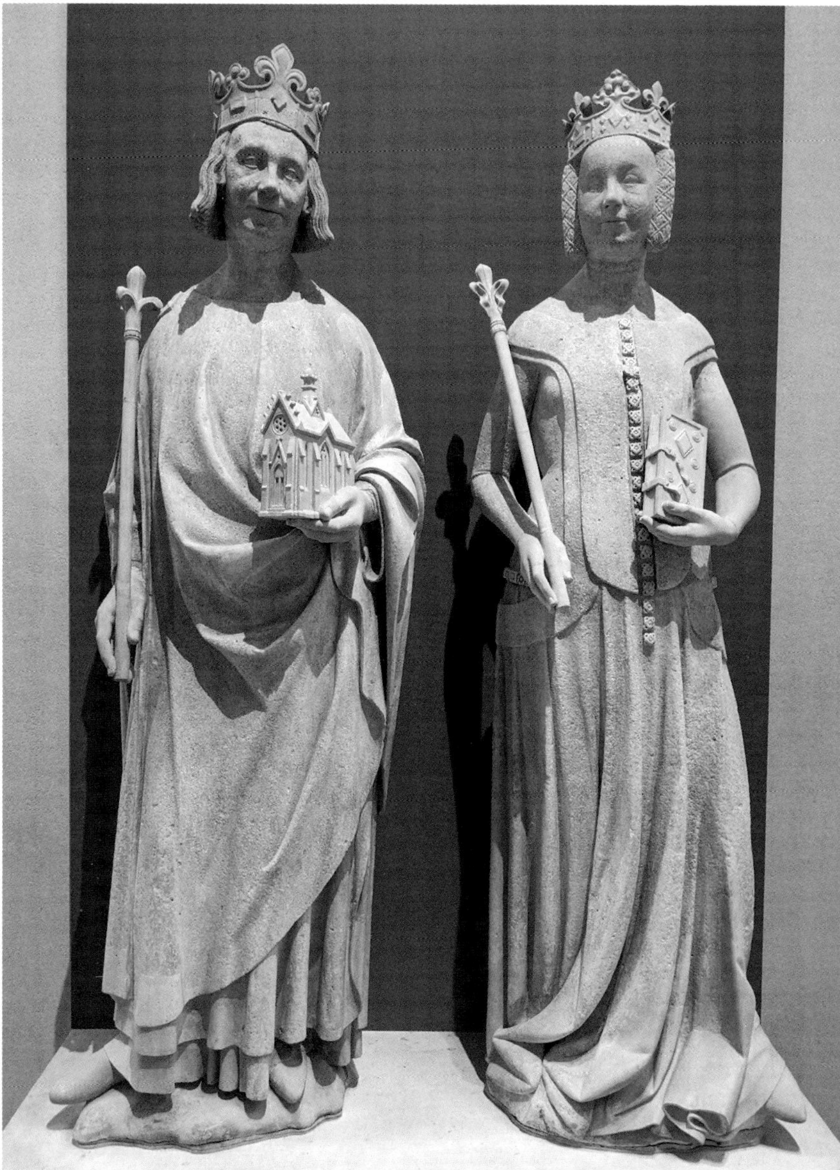

15 *King Charles V* and *Jeanne of Bourbon*, *c.* 1365–70, limestone.

such as an emperor or philosopher, and a recognizable differentiation of an individual through salient features, designed specifically to single out his social contribution. Moreover, beginning in this late fourteenth-century environment, another aspect of ageing, corpse decay after death, a form known as the *transi tomb*, appeared as a complement to the effigy of important individuals in repose or in prayer, to serve as a poignant spiritual lesson for viewers of mortality and the need for faith rather than worldly pride.[8] Wisdom indeed.

More than any other aged figure in art, God the Father as a white-bearded elder commands universal Christian recognition and response. Ironically, most medieval art depicted the Holy Trinity with figures of God the Father and Christ that are identical (with the dove of the Holy Spirit joining them from above in scenes of heaven, such as the Coronation of the Virgin). Yet with greater emphasis on the suffering of Jesus in the late Middle Ages, the need to distinguish between the Father and the limp body of the Son required visual redefinition of these separate divinities of the Trinity in the theme known as the Throne of Grace, or *Not Gottes*.[9] Cementing this image of white-bearded God the Father, Michelangelo's Sistine Chapel ceiling (1508–12) represents him in scenes of Creation, as well as the famous Creation of Adam. After this early sixteenth-century Sistine Chapel fountainhead, the figure of God the Father as a greybeard was fully canonical.

Moreover, Michelangelo adds the venerability of age to his representations of enthroned male prophets and female sibyls, the oldest of whom are quite wizened, such as stooped Jeremiah, a figure type repeated in the same artist's monumental marble *Moses* (*c.* 1515) for the tomb of Pope Julius II. In addition, Michelangelo emphasized the age of his depicted Cumaean

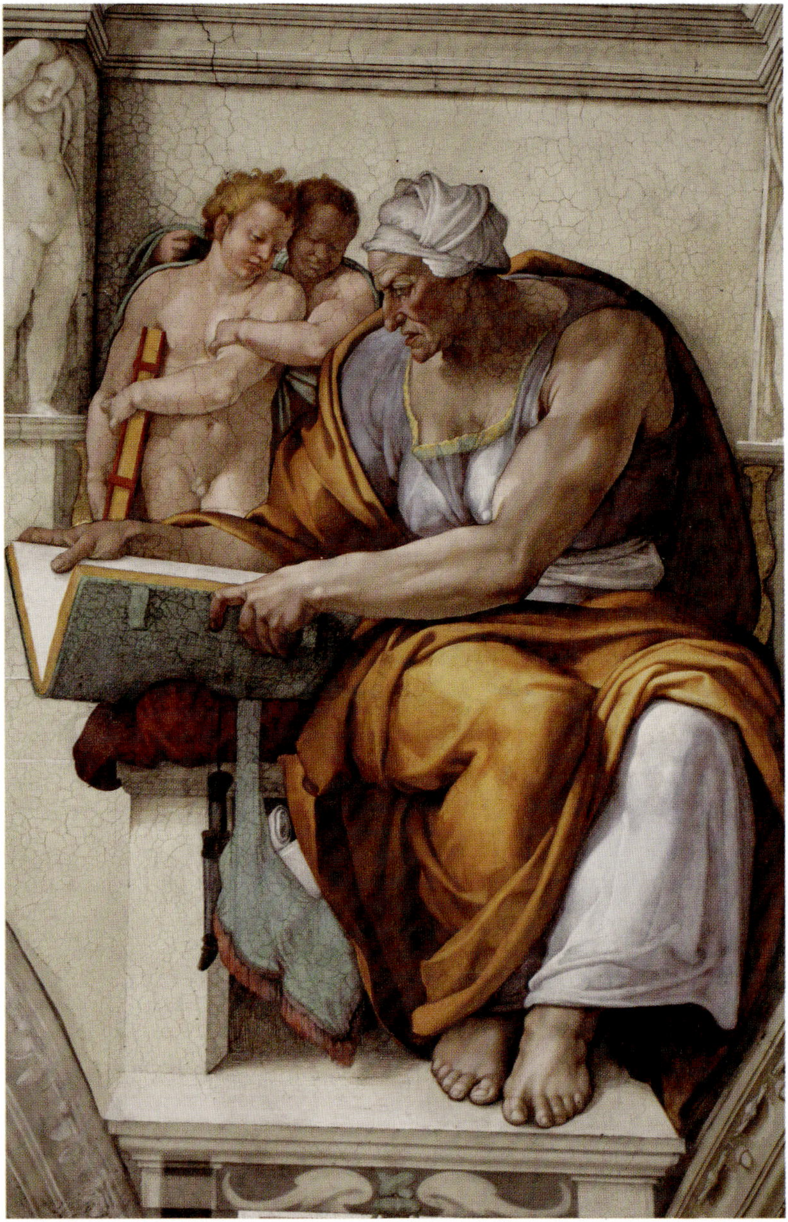

16 Michelangelo, *Cumaean Sibyl*, *c.* 1508–12, fresco, Sistine Chapel, Vatican City.

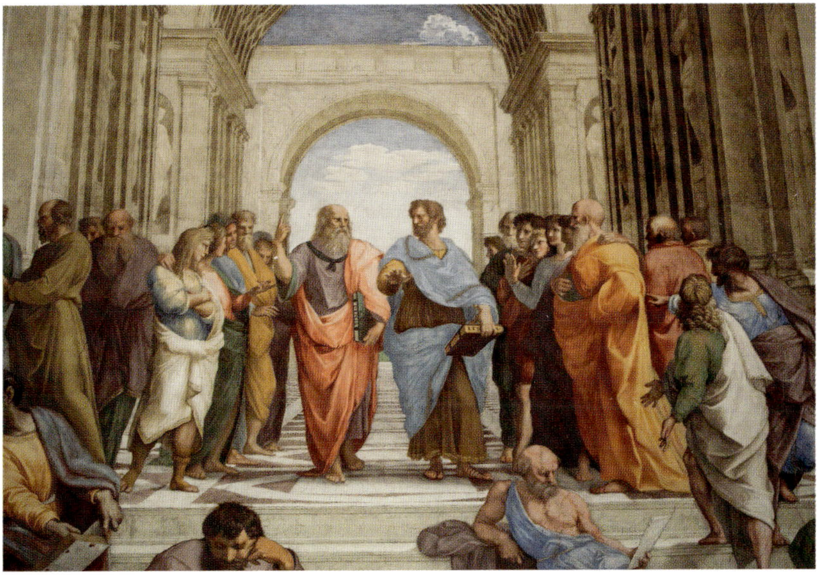

17 Raphael, *School of Athens*, detail, *c.* 1509–11, fresco, Room of the Segnatura, Vatican City.

Sibyl (illus. 16), the wise priestess and prophet of Apollo who prophesied the future for Aeneas.[10]

In another of the greatest Renaissance paintings, Raphael (1483–1520) frescoed the papal library in the Vatican with a collection of classical wisdom in all forms through a collection of celebrated individuals, assembled together in his so-called *School of Athens* (1509–11; illus. 17). On adjacent walls he also painted complementary tributes to ancient poets around the figure of Apollo with his lyre; appropriately for a papal library, he gathered leading Church theologians in learned discussion ('Disputa') about the mystery of the Trinity.[11] Together they visualize the major areas of learning: philosophy, poetry and theology. In the *School of Athens* the central figures in discussion, identifiable by the titles of their books, are white-bearded Plato, the idealist pointing heavenwards, and a mature – if younger – Aristotle, who extends his hand earthward in his systematic investigation of nature and society. Arranged atop the steps to either side of these two central figures are ancient thinkers whose works align with their opposing principles of idealism (Plato) and empiricism (Aristotle). Each individual across the fresco can be recognized by his activities, but most show their age with beards and baldness as they engage in teaching young acolytes. Moreover, as representatives of traditions from a distant past, they had acquired an additional patina of venerability. Among prominent thinkers, the geographer Ptolemy holds a globe at right, and the Persian prophet Zoroaster lifts a celestial globe. Below them Euclid stoops to demonstrate practical geometrical principles. At left Pythagoras writes in a large book to show abstract relations between mathematical ratios and such effects as musical tones and planetary motion. He is observed in turn by the turbaned medieval Arabic philosopher and astronomer Averroes.

Moreover, on an adjacent wall of the Stanza library, theology is personified in Raphael's *Disputà del Sacramento*. Accumulated Christian thinkers who dealt with the mystery of the Mass across history appear together around a central altar with the Eucharist in a gilded monstrance. Directly above the altar an axis of revelation presents God the Father, Christ and the dove of the Holy Spirit, who appear from a gilded heaven with angels and a flanking semicircle of saints on clouds. The gathering of theologians who approach the altar from both sides feature the four Church Fathers (Pope Gregory and saints Jerome, Augustine and Ambrose), seated and identified by books at their feet. Others (Thomas Aquinas and Bonaventure) bear inscribed haloes, while others still, including popes and other Church prelates, press inwards in animated discussion. Once more Raphael fuses history with the experience of age to celebrate accomplishments of civilization and faith.

As if in a close-up of one of the Raphael theologians, Albrecht Dürer (1471–1528) painted a single figure of St Jerome

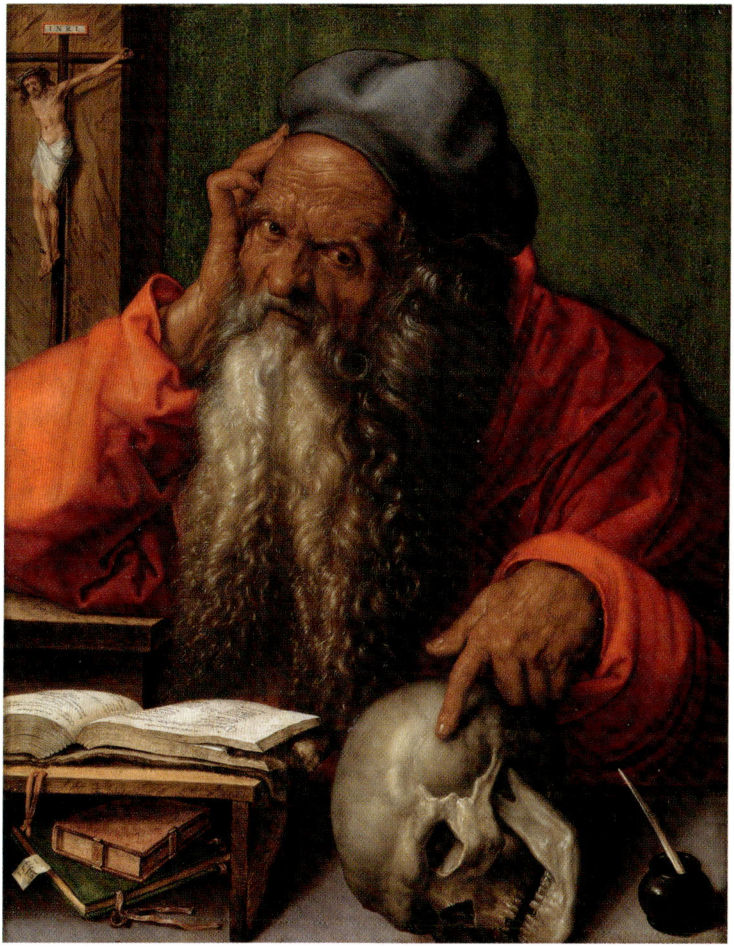

18 Albrecht Dürer, *St Jerome*, 1521, oil on panel.

at half-length (illus. 18).[12] For this image, Dürer made a careful study in a similar pose of someone he labelled on the drawing as a '93-year-old man and healthy and of good spirits'. In the eventual painting, seen behind his desk at bust length with only the meditational aids of open prayerbook, crucifix and skull, the wrinkled saint with a flowing white beard stares directly out at the viewer, his right hand at the side of his head in melancholy contemplation. With his left hand he points down at the skull, to impart a lesson, a reminder about the inevitability of death and the pressing need for faith. This sainted scholar, the Church Father who translated the Vulgate Bible into Latin, has put aside his studies and his inkwell to focus on ultimate spiritual concerns from the perspective of his own advanced age.

Medieval concepts of old age often included the older husband of the Virgin Mary, St Joseph. In the early modern period, the cult of Joseph flourished, portraying the foster father of Jesus as the family guardian and a model craftsman in his profession as carpenter.[13] For example, working at the Cathedral of Toledo in the wake of the Council of Trent and the Catholic Reformation, the Spanish painter El Greco (Domenikos Theotokopoulos, 1541–1614) painted an image (*c.* 1597–9) of a tall, standing Joseph with a staff, protectively guiding the young Jesus on the road before a dark, dramatic sky and the skyline of the city of Bethlehem, as angels hover above.[14] Artists who showed Joseph at the Nativity almost always took pains to show him as much older than the Virgin Mary, as if to stress the likelihood that he was physically unable to engender the Baby Jesus, so that Church doctrine could underscore the virginity of Mary and the divine origins of the Incarnation. In some respects this aspect of his greater age than his wife could be taken as an endorsement of marital chastity and the admirable qualities of spousal support, so the cult of Joseph flourished in the early modern period.

In a painting of the expanded Holy Family El Greco also explored aged figures of its three generations (*c.* 1595–1600; illus. 19).[15] White-haired, bearded St Joseph keeps apart from his wife; confined to the right edge, he is relegated to looking over her shoulder. In addition, here another admirable elderly saint appears, St Anne, the mother of the Virgin (and recipient of the Immaculate Conception, a medieval doctrine that only became Church dogma at a much later date, 1854). She tenderly covers the sleeping Christ Child with a veil (anticipating his death and burial shroud) as he rests on Mary's lap. Further generational contrast emerges from the foreground infant John the Baptist, who lifts his finger to his lips to compel silence during that nap (and reverence from the viewer). The entire picture generates reverence for the Holy Family, but it also reserves respect for its pair of aged members.

Certainly the Renaissance revival of admiration for classical culture and thought, exemplified collectively in Raphael's *School of Athens* (see illus. 17), continued to inspire later artists. Peter Paul Rubens (1577–1640) in particular spent the better part of a decade at the outset of his career in Italy (1600–1608), where he studied ancient statuary carefully, including surviving ancient carvings. Because of his special fascination with the Stoic writings of the Roman author Seneca, he made a drawing study (*c.* 1617/18; illus. 20) of a bust of an older man, believed to be that author.[16] In fact, Rubens owned such a bust, now known as 'Pseudo-Seneca', which he probably placed as an adornment in his personal library. Additionally, the artist incorporated his

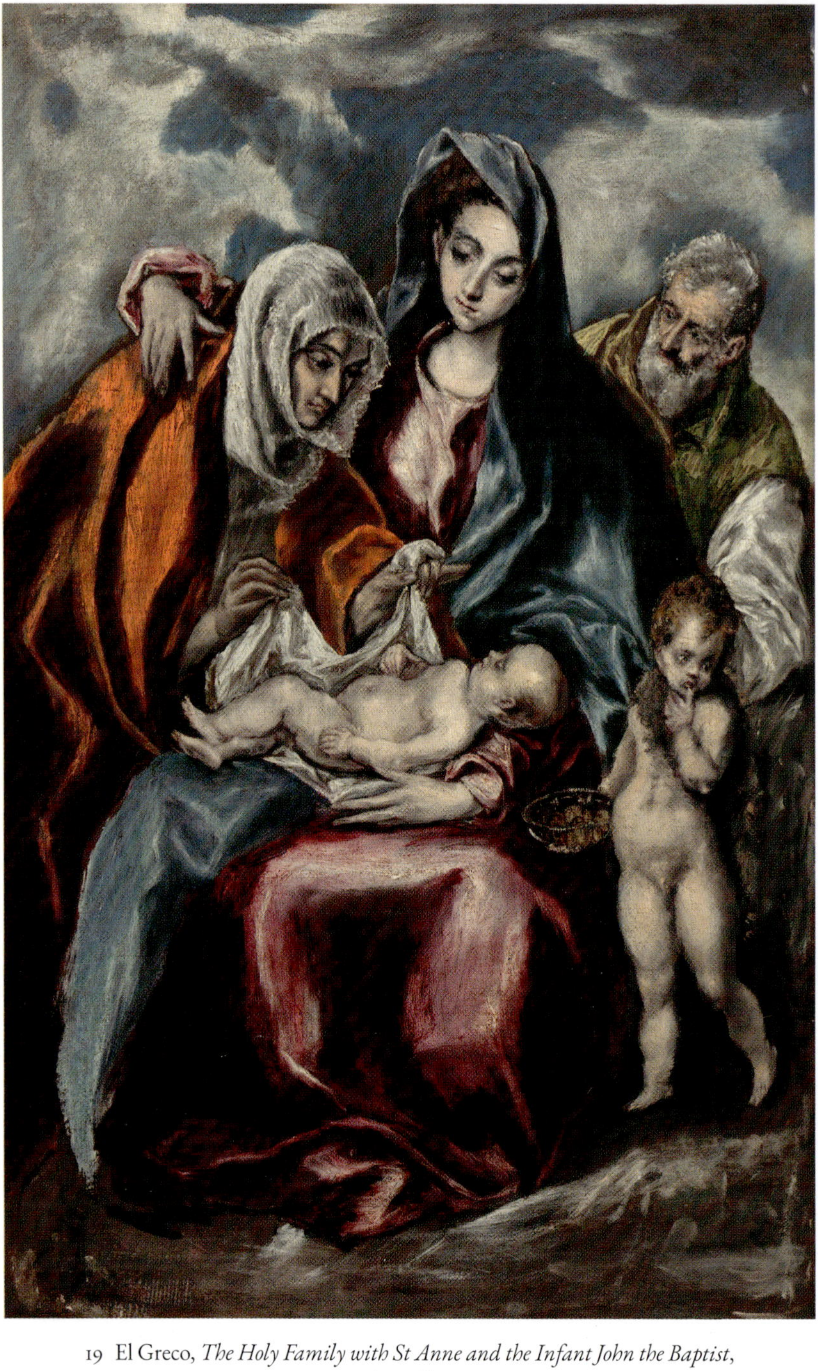

19 El Greco, *The Holy Family with St Anne and the Infant John the Baptist*, *c.* 1595–1600, oil on canvas.

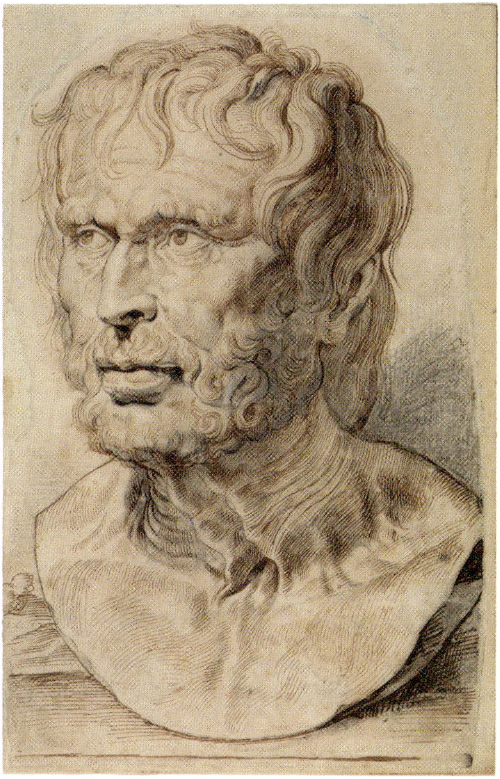

20 Peter Paul Rubens, *Bust of Pseudo-Seneca*, 1600–1626, pen and brown ink over black chalk heightened with white, with brush and grey ink.

supposed Seneca bust into a group portrait known as *The Four Philosophers* (*c.* 1611–12), where he had made the bust a kind of presiding genius over the portraits of his mentor, the philosopher Justus Lipsius, as well as Rubens's brother Philip, the artist himself and a friend. Rubens reused the bust as a model for the title page image of Seneca for the 1615 Antwerp printing of Lipsius's edition of Seneca's writings. Near the end of his career Rubens also used this drawing to prepare for its replication among a set of a dozen engravings by his printmaker associates of ancient Graeco-Roman thinkers, leaders and generals (1638–9; Lucas Vorsterman engraved the *Seneca*).

Rubens's engagement with Seneca also led him to make chalk studies in Rome of front and rear views of an antique black marble, falsely associated with the dying Seneca, depicting a stooped old man with sagging flesh, a bald head and a furrowed brow. Rubens would convert his drawing into the painting *Dying Seneca* (*c*. 1612–13), standing in the same posture while surrounded by soldiers and witnesses.[17] That ancient story provided an inspirational model of Stoic suicide by the philosopher, demonstrated by his calm yet heroic opening of his veins on the command of the emperor Nero for a falsely alleged conspiracy. To hasten his own demise, Seneca even stood in warm water.

Veneration of the wisdom attained in old-age maturity was not confined to the ancient world and its philosophers and writers. Medieval behaviour could also prove inspirational to later centuries. One event from the 1347 English siege of Calais during the Hundred Years War provided another instance of old-age heroism. According to the chronicler Jean Froissart, the city's mayor, Eustache de Saint-Pierre, agreed to deliver himself and five fellow citizens to sacrifice themselves in order to save their city. In 1884 the city of Calais decided to commemorate that deed, so it commissioned leading sculptor Auguste Rodin (1840–1917) to produce a bronze monument, *The Burghers of Calais* (1885–95; illus. 21). Following Froissart, he depicted these figures barefoot and in sackcloth with ropes around their necks as they emerge from the city citadel to present the keys to Calais. Instead of showing a single heroic leader on an elevated pedestal, as was customary, Rodin presented all six men unsparingly. Each one is self-absorbed, contemplating imminent death in a variety of poses and gestures suggesting despair, fear or resignation. These men are gaunt, bald, bearded and humbled, with

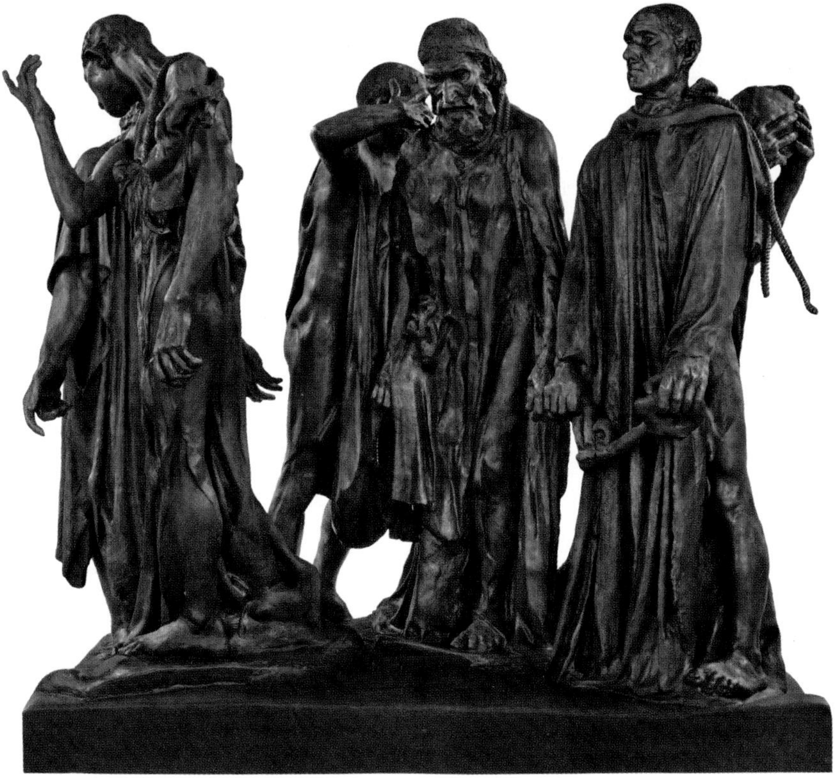

21 Auguste Rodin, *The Burghers of Calais*, 1885–95 (cast 1919–21), bronze.

oversized hands and lengthened arms, based on careful individual preparatory studies. None of them is singled out, and they stand on a most minimal platform, to be viewed individually in turn as an observer circulates around the entire monument. This quotidian, unconventional figure group was initially criticized by locals for its version of Calais history, but eventually Rodin's vivid recreation of history and the heroism in a moment of crisis by these seemingly ordinary old men prevailed.

Folly and Sin

Of course, the inverse side of ageing is bodily decline, most obvious from the tell-tale external signs of wrinkles, balding and loss of youthful vigour and beauty. Often the visual depiction of old people can become exaggerated into a form of ugliness. Inasmuch as the intellectual and moral dimensions of a personality are often construed to calibrate with physical appearance, an unattractive old person could also be viewed as misbehaving or acting foolishly: a dotard. A Dutch proverb asserts, 'the older the more foolish' (*hoe ouder, hoe sotter*), and artworks often equate a lack of personal control with physical deterioration.

Ancient sculptural depictions of old age during the Hellenistic and subsequent Roman periods often exaggerate wrinkled features, strikingly so in imagery of women. The most striking of these, *Old Drunkard*, based on a lost third-century BCE original, survives in a good copy with well-preserved details (illus. 22).[18] It emphasizes the ravages not only of the ageing process but of alcohol abuse. The woman's flesh sags around her mouth and neck while clinging tightly to the bone structure of her cheeks and shoulder. Yet she revels in her drunkenness, lifting her head in an open-mouthed grin as she clutches her large drinking vessel with both hands. She has sunk to the earth, just as the flowing folds of her chiton have slipped indiscreetly down her bony torso. No cup has informed her drinking, as she has indecorously given herself up to the large jug filled with the wine of Dionysus, whether in ecstatic rites or individual indulgence. Some scholars have seen her dress and ornaments as respectable, suggesting that she has fallen in status at society's margins, like a *hetaira*, an old concubine or brothel owner. Pliny the Elder describes a 'drunken old woman' at Smyrna in modern Turkey (*Natural History* 36.32), and drunken old women also appear in Greek comedy as a familiar stereotype.

These same exaggerated features also correspond to a sculpture known as *Old Market Woman*: the figure's garment slips from her stooped posture to reveal her sagging breasts as she carries a basket. Ivy wreaths around her cap suggest another link to Dionysus, so she might be bringing an offering to the god's shrine. She too displays wrinkles, sunken eyes and an open

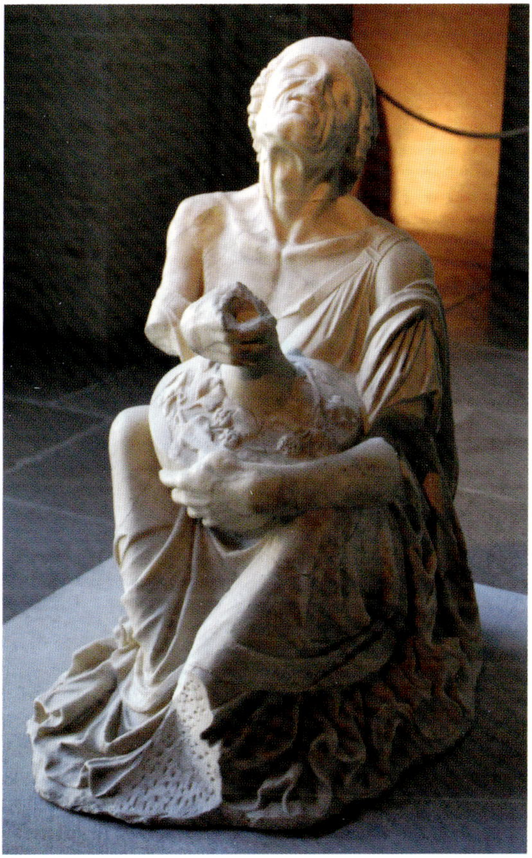

22 *Old Drunkard*, Roman copy after a Greek original, 2nd century BCE, marble.

mouth with a degree of detail akin to the veristic portraits of Republican Roman ancestors (see illus. 12) but used now in a generic fashion, seemingly in satirical parody of age.

In medieval literature, while often held up as a figure of respect, St Joseph also frequently formed the butt of jokes. Seen as isolated from proximity to the Virgin and Child, he was often portrayed as old and tired.[19] Early theologians, eager to define the marriage of Mary and Joseph as both chaste and true, sometimes surmised that he might even have suspected his wife of adultery (and 'put her away secretly'), until the explanation for her pregnant condition was explained to him by an angel in a dream (Matthew 1:19–20).

In a charming late medieval painting, *The Doubt of St Joseph* (illus. 23), his uncertainty is fully explicit. Not only is he isolated by a column into a narrow passageway of their shared bourgeois chamber (which still contains his tools, as well as her virtuous spinning and study of holy scriptures), but Joseph is expressly depicted as white-haired and bearded, hobbled with a walking stick. He also utterly lacks the halo attribute of Mary. While Joseph raises his hand sceptically, he is being visited by an angel who floats down from the ceiling (though not in his dream), bearing a scroll of communicated explanation to assuage his doubt.

Joseph is also frequently shown in narrative images of the Holy Family in the role of a servant.[20] For example, in *The Adoration of the Magi* by Hieronymus Bosch (active *c.* 1485–1516), he appears on the left wing, in complete isolation from the Virgin and Child in the centre panel, and he is assigned the undignified task of cleaning nappies for the Infant. In images of the Rest on the Flight into Egypt, Joseph is often depicted in humble activities, such as fetching water or fruit for the sustenance of Mary and Jesus.

Caricature, the exaggeration of features for comic effect, is frequently fastened onto old people. One of the most pervasive early practitioners of emphasizing the grotesque aspects of old age was Leonardo da Vinci (1452–1519), particularly in the form of sketches, possibly made for amusement during his stay at the

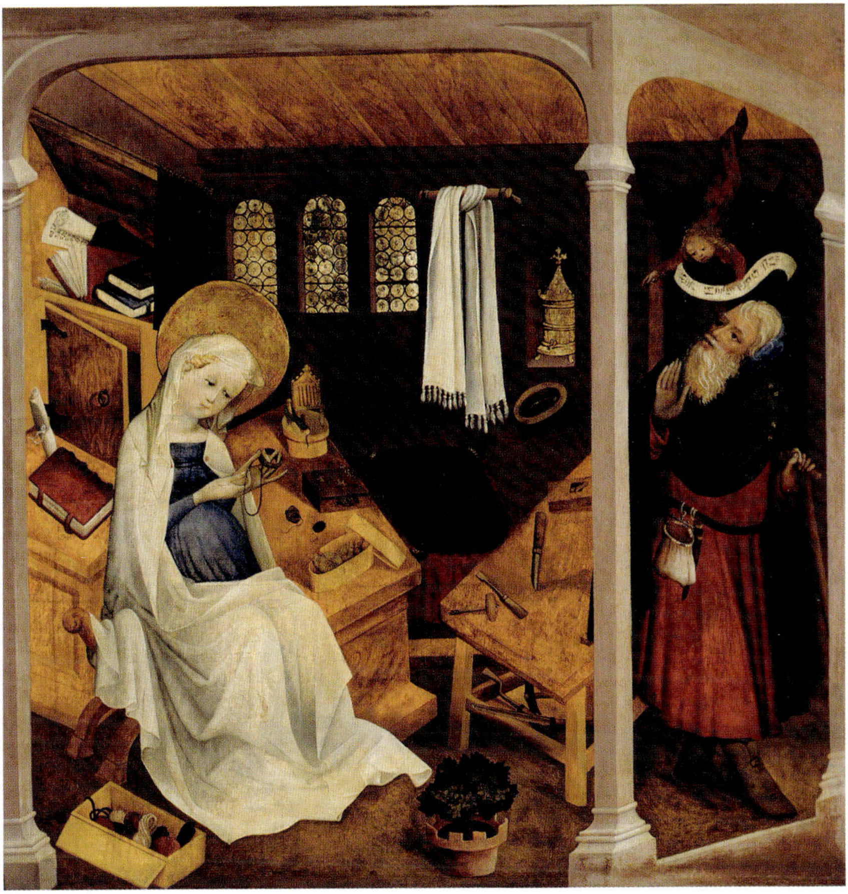

23 Upper Rhenish Master, *The Doubt of St Joseph*, *c.* 1410–19, oil on panel.

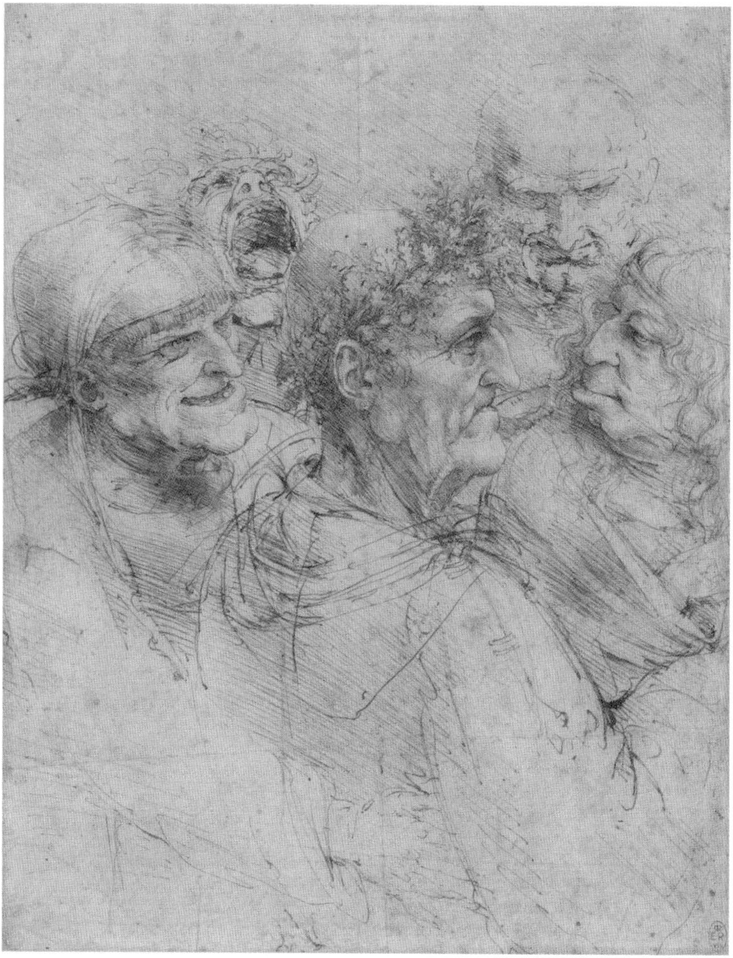

24 Leonardo da Vinci, *Study of Five Grotesque Heads,* or *A Man Tricked by Gypsies*, *c.* 1493, pen and ink.

Sforza court of Milan during the 1490s.[21] Most often, Leonardo featured profiles of toothless old men with nutcracker jaws and bald heads, but he also made fun of outlandish costumes with outdated fashions, such as the high-peaked headwear of women from earlier in the fifteenth century. One of Leonardo's most finished clusters of old men is usually called the *Study of Five Grotesque Heads* (*c.* 1493; illus. 24). Some narrative event might lie behind these interactive figures. One scenario has proposed that the central man in profile with a laurel crown – a distant descendant of the veristic Roman portraits of ancestors and emperors discussed earlier – is extending his hand to the thick-lipped figure at right, wearing a headband and toga-like drapery, who might be a Roma fortune-teller. Three remaining observers, all grotesques, offer varying responses to this interaction. At left, the toothy, grinning figure with a headscarf, possibly a crone, echoes many other Leonardo caricatures, especially a lost drawing, known from copies, of an old woman with moneybags who is wooed by an avaricious young gigolo. The remaining frontal pair of faces behind these main figures of the drawing

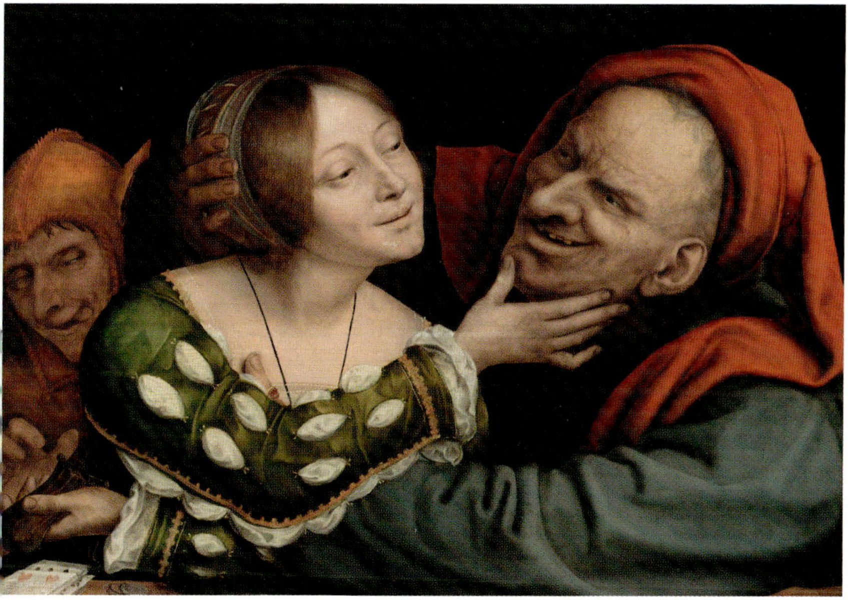

25 Quinten Massys, *Ill-Matched Lovers*, *c.* 1520–25, oil on panel.

ridicule the basic situation, one with an open-mouthed jeer, the other with a tight-lipped scowl.

Copies of these Leonardo drawings clearly circulated widely. One Antwerp painter who used them as models for foolish old men as well as evil tormentors of Christian saints was Quinten Massys (1465/6–1530). His *Ill-Matched Lovers* (*c.* 1520–25; illus. 25) unmistakably borrows its grinning old man, reversed, from the figure with a scarf in Leonardo's *Five Grotesque Heads*.[22] Here the interaction is explicit. This is a lustful old man who embraces the breast of an encouraging but avaricious young harlot; each person here is foolish and tempted into sin. Massys also plays a visual trick on the viewer by seemingly showing an extension of the man's arm as a devious sleight of hand by the woman, who has pickpocketed the man's purse and is passing it on to her confederate. Dressed in bright orange and showing the crossed eyes of a simpleton, the confederate wears the standard costume of a fool or jester, ass's ears and a cockscomb. Thus all three characters in this visual drama are fools, caught together in a web of sin and deceit. Their misbehaviour is reinforced by the corner still-life, which shows gambling with coins and cards, whose uppermost suit is hearts.

An easy target of old age, already exploited by Leonardo and his imitators, is loss of beauty. The ravaging effects of time are the express subject of a canvas by Giorgione, *The Old Woman* (*c.* 1506–7; illus. 26).[23] What might have begun as a portrait from a sitting model was transformed by the artist into a moral lesson about time's passing. Giorgione added a small inscription, 'Col Tempo' (With Time), reinforcing the gesture of the old woman, who points to herself as the physical exhibit of old age. A foreground balustrade adds still more significance, suggesting the

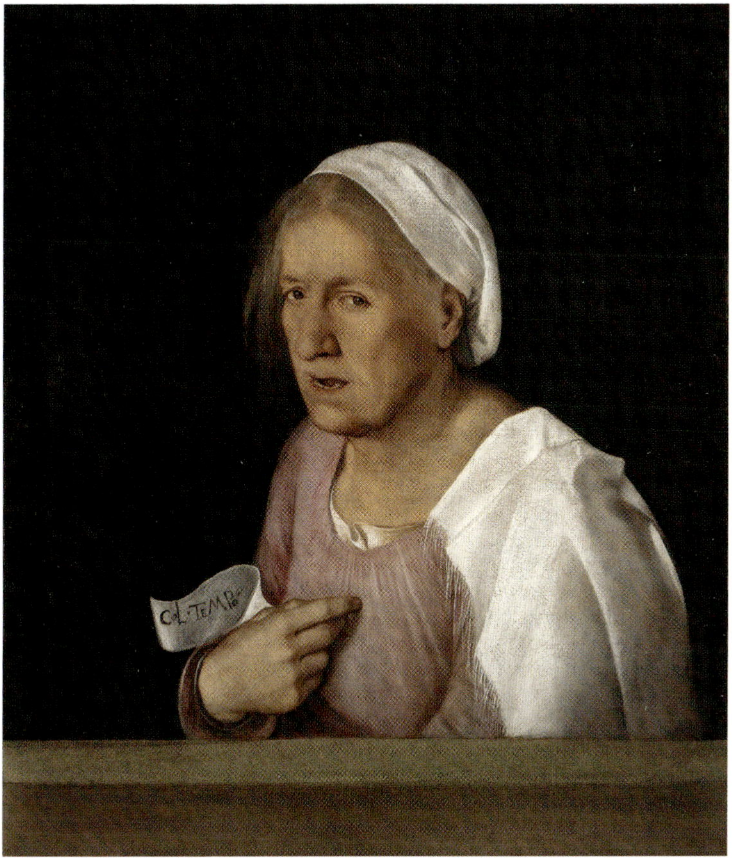

26 Giorgione, *The Old Woman* (*La vecchia*), *c.* 1506–7, oil on canvas.

presentation of ancient Roman memorial busts that usually evoke the wisdom and examples conveyed by venerated ancestors.[24] Unlike Massys's old man in his *Ill-Matched Pair*, or the Leonardo grotesques that inspired his image, this old woman is not a comical figure, but an instruction. She looks outwards in direct address, confronting the viewer with a basic fact of the human condition. Giorgione goes beyond the lifelike qualities of portraiture to provide a cautionary reminder, an allegory of time's passing.

Art about folly and misbehaviour has come to be known as 'genre' imagery: that is, art about ordinary, unnamed people in everyday situations, sometimes in unsavoury places, especially taverns or brothels (which sometimes amounted to the same thing), and often with a comic purpose that also carries a moral with it. Genre prints and paintings became staples of Netherlandish art as early as the turn of the sixteenth century. A pioneering example is a dismembered, non-religious triptych by Hieronymus Bosch (*c.* 1585–90), the painted wings of which included excesses of old people: avarice (*Death of the Miser*; illus. 27) and gluttonous indulgence (*Ship of Fools*). On the exterior of that same work, Bosch painted an old, ragged peddler who passes a dilapidated tavern-brothel, a place where he could squander his meagre custom in ephemeral pleasures.[25]

In the *Death of the Miser*, even with skeletal Death at the door, a bald, toothless old man on his deathbed still reaches for a bag of money proffered by a demon (the old man also once held a goblet in his other hand; although painted out, its drawn outlines are still visible). In vain does an angel at his shoulder point upwards to the ray of light that comes past a crucifix in the window, because demons still roam within this chamber of accumulation, filled with official documents, the armour of aristocratic assertion and still more moneybags. For misers like this one, not even death at the threshold can erase the endless temptation of avarice. Greed and love of possessions were traits commonly associated with old age.

Deadly sin forms the basis of another staple of old-age imagery: the witch. As the early modern witchcraft craze spread across Europe and to colonies in America, the chief accusation was that old women, the stereotypical image of witches, derived

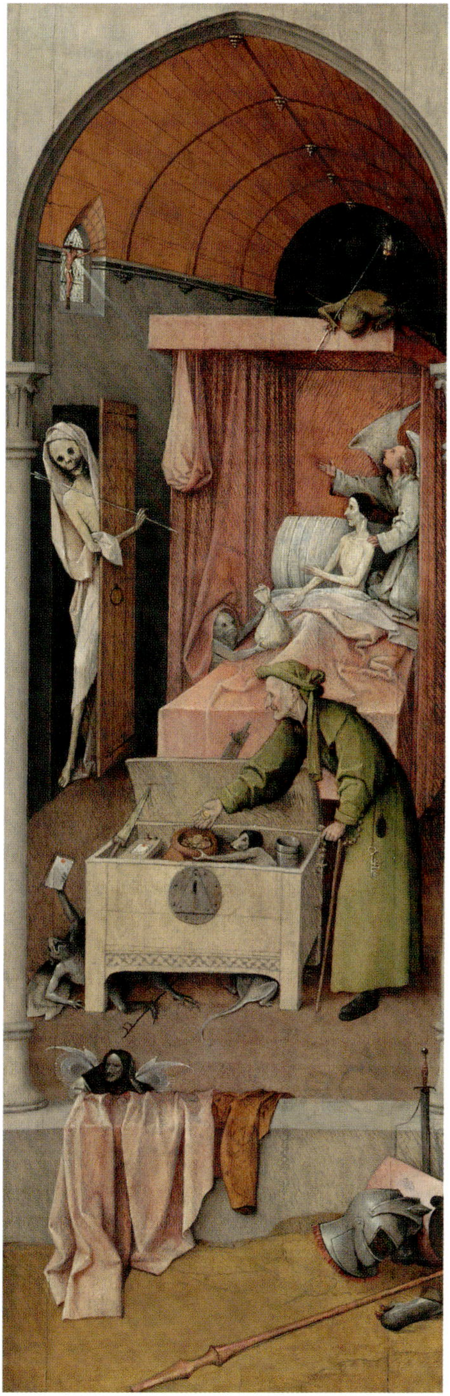

27 Hieronymus Bosch, *Death and the Miser*, *c.* 1485–90, oil on panel.

their powers to perform black magic from consorting with the Devil himself. A dramatic nocturnal witches' Sabbath gathering was printed as a large engraving (illus. 28) on two sheets by the early seventeenth-century Dutch artist Jacques de Gheyn II (1565–1629).[26] A trio of old women occupies the centre foreground, naked except for one, perhaps a Sabbath newcomer, still clothed. One obese figure, seen from behind, holds a thighbone in a pot between her legs and props an open book beside her on a skull. Fumes rise again from a pot opened by a topless crone behind a bare tree at the right edge. Bones, cats and a large lizard at left fill the space. Moreover, demons appear distinctly, especially at the lower left, where a bird-headed figure with bat wings supports a winged cherub on its back. Demons also fill the skies. At the top right a flying hag rises on fumes and rides a broomstick to encounter hovering demons, one of whom brandishes a cluster of snakes. At upper left, in the clouds, more naked women

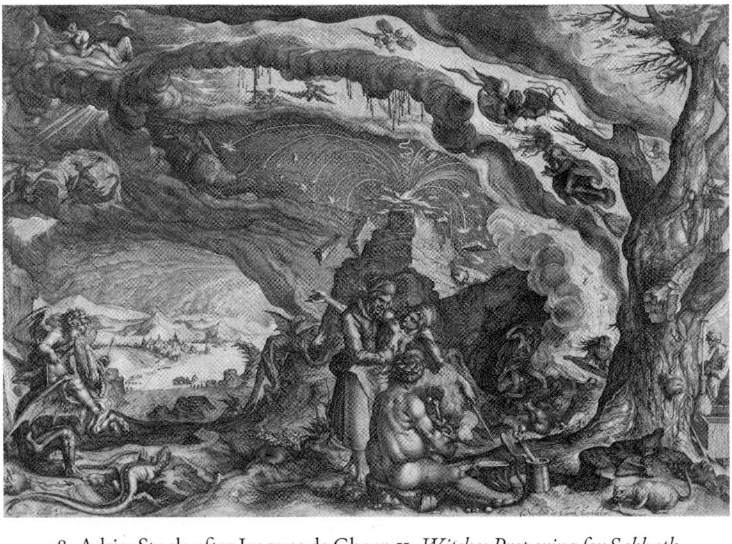

28 Adries Stock, after Jacques de Gheyn II, *Witches Preparing for Sabbath*, *c*. 1610, engraving.

ride dragon-like demons in a mock-joust, while in the top centre a nude woman reaches ecstasy on the back of a goat, underscoring both the gendered and the eroticized context of female witches, accused of intercourse with Satan. In addition, witches are associated with causing bad weather through sorcery. Here a lightning bolt strikes sparks on a central crag above the main trio. The very fact that this infernal gathering is isolated atop a hill shows its imagined distance from towns or villages, but also from the eponymous flat terrain of the Netherlands. Whether or not his image is based on his own belief in actual witches, De Gheyn still exercises his artistic power to create a vivid scenic illusion. In doing so the artist also raises another basic issue associated specifically with witchcraft – and with the Devil's deceptive illusions: the general unreliability of the senses. Importantly in witchcraft imagery, illusion was connected to delusion.

De Gheyn also produced several disturbing drawings of witches around 1600. They are populated entirely by women, both old witches and their young apprentices. One drawing, *Witches' Kitchen* (1604), revolves around a central smoking cauldron surrounded by witches and demons. One old hag sits spinning, and another woman rises on a broomstick as three women enter, one carrying a candle and a platter with a severed head. Finally, a basement gap shows demons around a reclining body, accompanied by demons, serpents and cats. De Gheyn's interior, gendered completely female, remains ominous, claustrophobic and unremittingly evil.

Later Dutch genre paintings of old women were often more benign, imparting lessons for good living through gentle satire. A good example is Nicolaes Maes's *An Old Woman Dozing over a Book* (*c.* 1655; illus. 29). Resting her head on her hand, this old

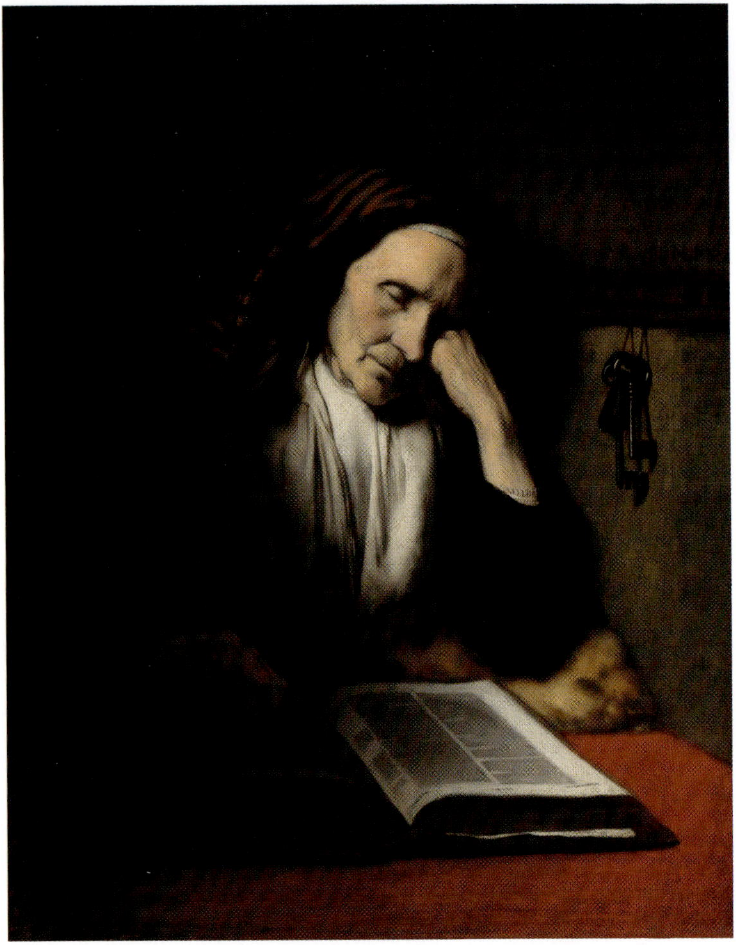

29 Nicolaes Maes, *An Old Woman Dozing over a Book*, *c.* 1655, oil on canvas.

woman has fallen asleep in the midst of reading. Her book stands open, and her shadowy right hand still rests on the last passage that she studied. The spotlight that shines on her features also illuminates a set of unused keys hanging on the wall. A viewer can infer that the book is the Bible, consulted but now neglected, and that the keys, used for practical daily efforts, signal a neglect of her household duties. In a related Maes painting, *Old Woman Dozing* (*c.* 1656), the task neglected by another sleeping woman is the virtuous activity, always gendered as female, of lacemaking. In yet another picture (*c.* 1656), an old woman wearing spectacles has dozed over her account books with her quill pen still in hand – more neglect of household management. It would probably be going too far to ascribe to any of these women the deadly sin of Sloth, but their pose of head in hand was a staple of medieval representations of both that sin and the related ill of melancholy. Maes also painted the positive side of pious domestic practice in another picture, *Old Woman Praying* (*c.* 1655) – featuring

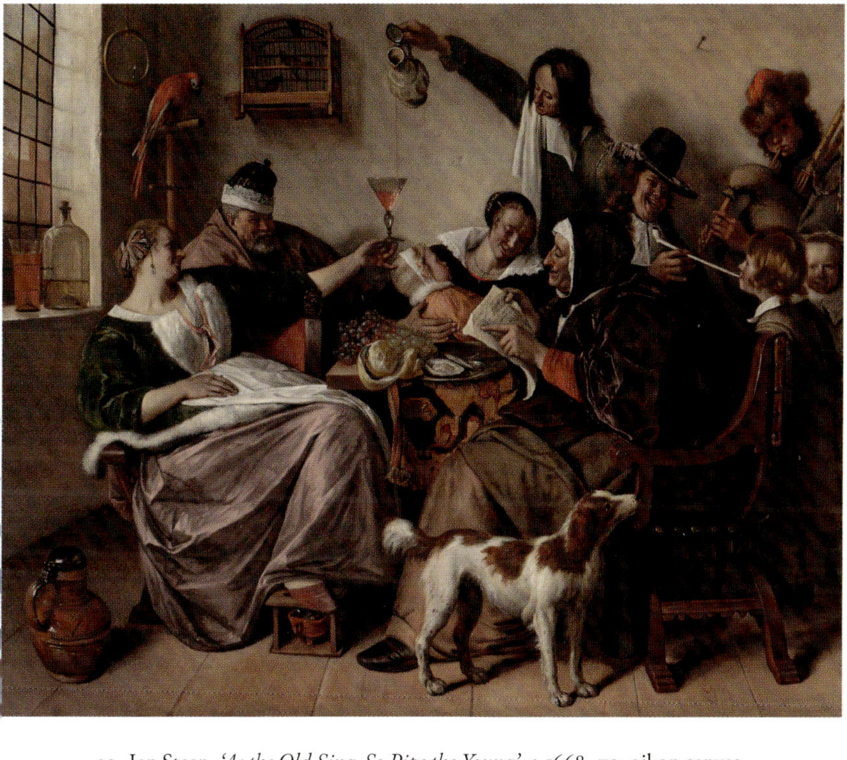

30 Jan Steen, *'As the Old Sing, So Pipe the Young'*, *c.* 1668–70, oil on canvas.

the same old woman, presumably based on a model – who is praying at a table with a skull, hourglass and candle, the same props of mortality already pictured in Dürer's *St Jerome* (see illus. 18). A similar Maes painting, *Old Woman Saying Grace* (*c.* 1656), shows this familiar old figure blessing her simple meal; her eyes are closed in reverence, but her keys still hang on the wall beneath an hourglass and a Bible.

Dutch and Flemish painters of the same mid-seventeenth-century moment also painted pictures both comical and critical that literally enact a familiar proverb, 'as the old sing, so the young pipe,' a negative commentary on poor child-rearing. Jan Steen (1625/6–79) and Jacob Jordaens (1593–1678) both placed family groups of three generations, secular versions of El Greco's *Holy Family*, around a table, where both parents and children self-indulgently partake of food and drink without a care.[27] The slovenly behaviour of the elders spoils their descendants. So much chaos emerges in Steen's interiors, such as his *Dissolute Household* (1660–65), that his paintings have generated their own verbal characterization: a 'Jan Steen household'.

In Jan Steen's canvas of the intergenerational theme, *'As the Old Sing, So Pipe the Young'* (1668; illus. 30), domestic dysfunction begins with the old man at the head of the table; he holds up a wine glass and sings heartily with a violin perched at his shoulder. His wife and their daughter also sing along from sheet music, accompanied by a blaring bagpiper, presumably the family's father. Meanwhile, the numerous children are unsupervised. In the window at left one youth holds a trumpet as he smokes a clay pipe, misbehaviour that his sister imitates before the fire on the opposite side. Above her on the mantel hangs the title proverb itself. Sprawled on a stool, an older son plays the flute, adding to the overall music. In the foreground an older sister offers a drink pot to her younger sibling, but both are clearly underage. The floor is littered, in contrast to the usually spotless Dutch household: frying pans, eggshell, an empty pewter plate, a spoon, an empty bottle and a wine jug. Even the dog beside the table seems to join the festivities with (and because of) the misbehaving old grandfather.

If Steen's figures display a cartoon-like comic quality, the images of age by Francisco de Goya (1746–1828) use caricature to deliver a greater social sting. In his etchings series *Los Caprichos*, published in 1799, old women in particular come in for sardonic representation. One of the images (no. 17), captioned 'It's Pulled Tight', shows a young woman pulling up her stocking while being observed by a seated old woman rendered as a grotesque worthy of Leonardo. In fact, the ugliness is also a moral ugliness, for the old woman is a procuress, overseeing the dress of her young protégée, a prostitute. Other images of prostitutes, led by old women, appear in *Los Caprichos*. In 'All Will Fall' (no. 19) human-headed bird imagery shows an officer, a monk and a gallant fluttering around a handsome female wearing a low-cut bodice in a treetop, while down below another old bawd and a pair of prostitutes are sitting, having captured, plucked and spitted one of them as a victim. Here the sexual allure of women is seen as the downfall of men, and the following image, 'They've Been Fleeced' (no. 20), completes the sad tale as a trio of plucked man-birds is swept away by two old crones and two young prostitutes wielding brooms.

But Goya's imagery of women can turn darker still. In several images of *Los Caprichos* old women are also portrayed as witches, the embodiment of general evil in society. 'Pretty Teacher!' (no. 68; illus. 31), a nocturne with an ominous owl

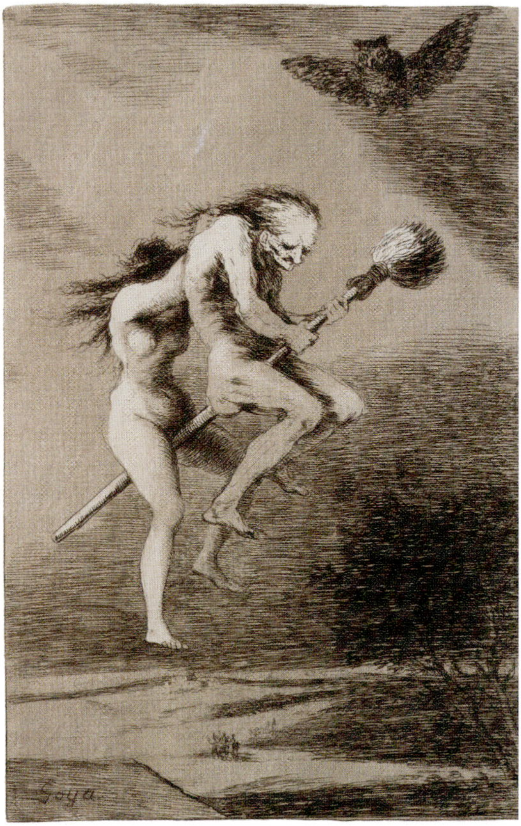

31 Francisco Goya, 'Pretty Teacher!', plate 68 from the series *Los Caprichos*, 1797–8, etching and aquatint.

above, shows a pair of naked women riding a backward-facing broomstick; the young, nubile one rides behind, holding the shoulder of a slumping, ugly old hag. In a subsequent image (no. 71) the assembled, naked old witches, who meet at night in the shadowy silhouette of a demon's wings, are almost unrecognizable as humans, as they declare, 'When Day Breaks We Will Be Off.' Goya also painted a number of images of witches, such as *Witches' Sabbath* (1798), in which a circle of old witches brings sacrifices as they surround a central devil in a form of a large black goat under a crescent moon.[28]

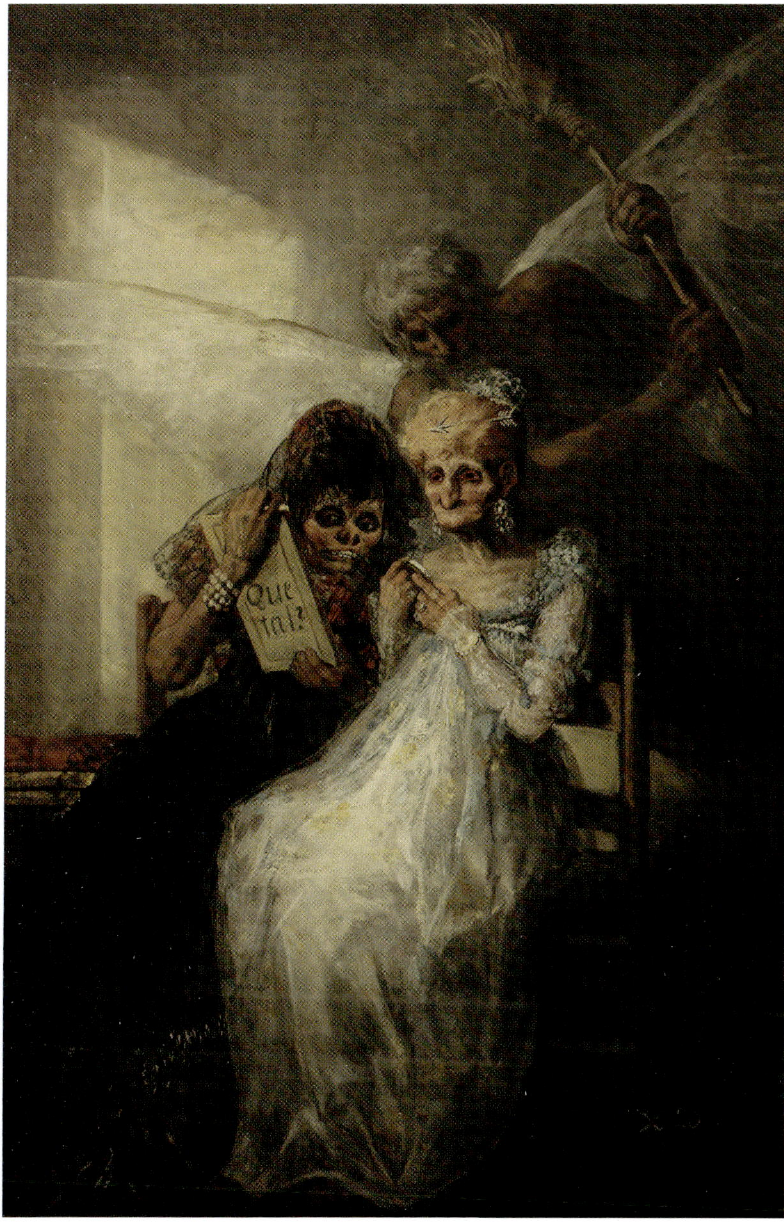

32 Francisco Goya, *Time and the Old Women*, *c*. 1810, oil on canvas.

Later still in his long career, Goya painted an image with his characteristic brio that is equally misogynist but simply portrays old women as steeped in absurd vanity. His *Time and the Old Women* (*c.* 1810; illus. 32) depicts two fashionably dressed women with hideous faces inspecting what seems to be a mirror (whose reverse Spanish phrase, ironically, enquires, 'How is it going?'). The toothless woman at right with a Leonardesque nutcracker nose and jaw combination has dyed blonde hair and seems to be holding a small compact in her hand, fully decorated with jewelled rings. Her haggard features contrast totally with the flowing fashion of her white muslin dress. Her skull-like companion with dark-rimmed eyes and dark dress and mantilla holds the mirror for them both to look. Unseen behind them, however, is the white-haired, winged figure of Father Time, wielding a broom with which to shortly sweep them away. 'Vanity of vanities . . . All is vanity . . . And there is nothing new under the sun' (Ecclesiastes 1:2, 9).

Three

Old-Age Stories

Let's talk of graves, of worms, and epitaphs . . .
For God's sake let us sit upon the ground
And tell sad stories of the death of kings.

SHAKESPEARE, *Richard II*, III.2

Pictures that tell stories from the Bible, myths or ancient events are usually called 'histories'. They enjoyed the greatest prestige within formal training in academies because they demonstrated learning, as well as mastery of how to depict the noble figures of those histories. We have already seen the reverence accorded to figures of patriarchs and apostles on church facades such as Reims (see illus. 14), and the prestige closely associated with ancient figures of philosophers, authors and political leaders. Thus prestigious narratives associated with such estimable characters and their actions fulfilled major ambitions of artists across centuries. Many examples could be supplied.

To begin at the beginning – at least in the initial book of Genesis in the Bible – the patriarch Abraham occupies a founder's position. Throughout the Genesis story great emphasis is placed on Abraham's advanced age. Only at age 99 did the patriarch and his wife Sarah learn of the miraculous birth of their only son.

That notice arrived only through the explicit intervention of a trio of angelic messengers (Genesis 17:1–19; 18:1–15; 21:1–7; illus. 34). Like the New Testament miracle of Mary's virgin birth, underscored by her husband Joseph's much greater age and thus his unlikely role in Jesus's parenthood (emphasized visually in numerous images, such as illus. 19 and 23), Sarah's own advanced age confirms that the birth of Isaac was divinely ordained. The covenant between Abraham as the father of an entire people stems directly from this fulfilment in the form of the birth of Isaac, an heir, who will be the first of the ongoing line of the Children of Israel through this divinely mandated miraculous birth.

Rembrandt emphasizes Abraham's principal role in this etching, where the nonagenarian plays humble host to the three strangers (illus. 33). He emphasizes the old man's hospitality by placing him, bearded, balding and stooped, in an inferior position at the lower right. Abraham is serving his guests both bread and wine, already evoking the components of the Christian Eucharist. Aged Sarah eavesdrops within a darkened open doorway, while Abraham's older son, Ishmael, distracts himself with bow and arrow. The three strangers will turn out to be angels who announce that God will bless aged, childless Sarah with a son of her own. The attentive viewer will note the wings of two of those visitors, while their bearded, older leader conforms to biblical commentary that assigned that lead role to God himself. Thus the Lord directly favoured Abraham and Sarah for their humble faith. Rembrandt's condensed narrative deftly suggests the initial unfolding of

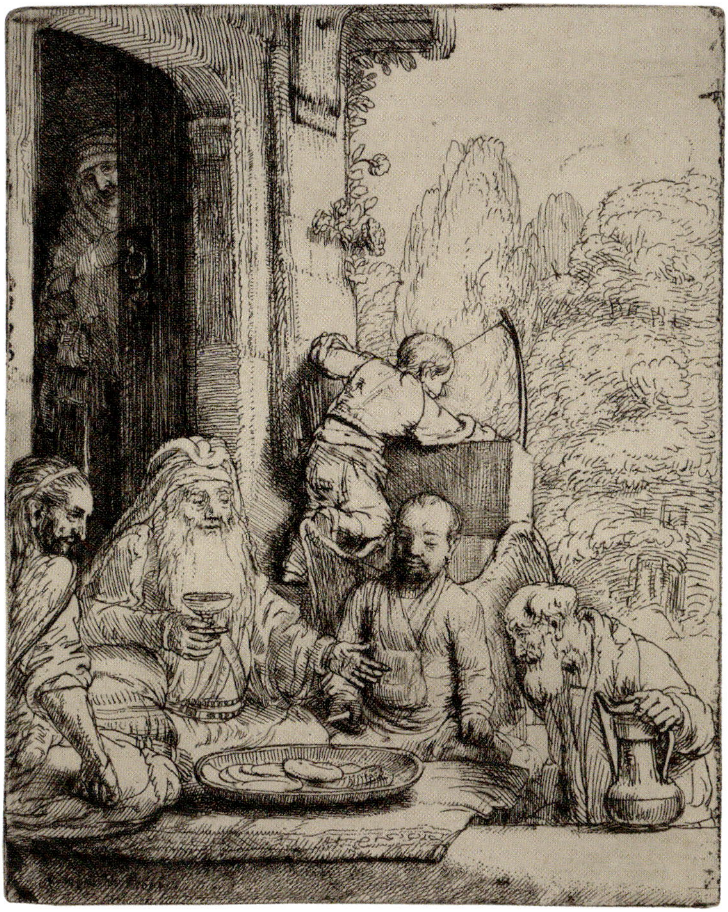

33 Rembrandt, *Abraham Entertaining the Angels*, 1656, etching.

the divine plan through God's favour to his aged servant, Abraham.

One of the most moving events that challenged the abiding faith of the first monotheist was his agonizing test, the moment when God summoned the patriarch to sacrifice his son, Isaac, like a lamb. That tragic outcome was averted at the last second when an angelic messenger arrived to stay Abraham's hand

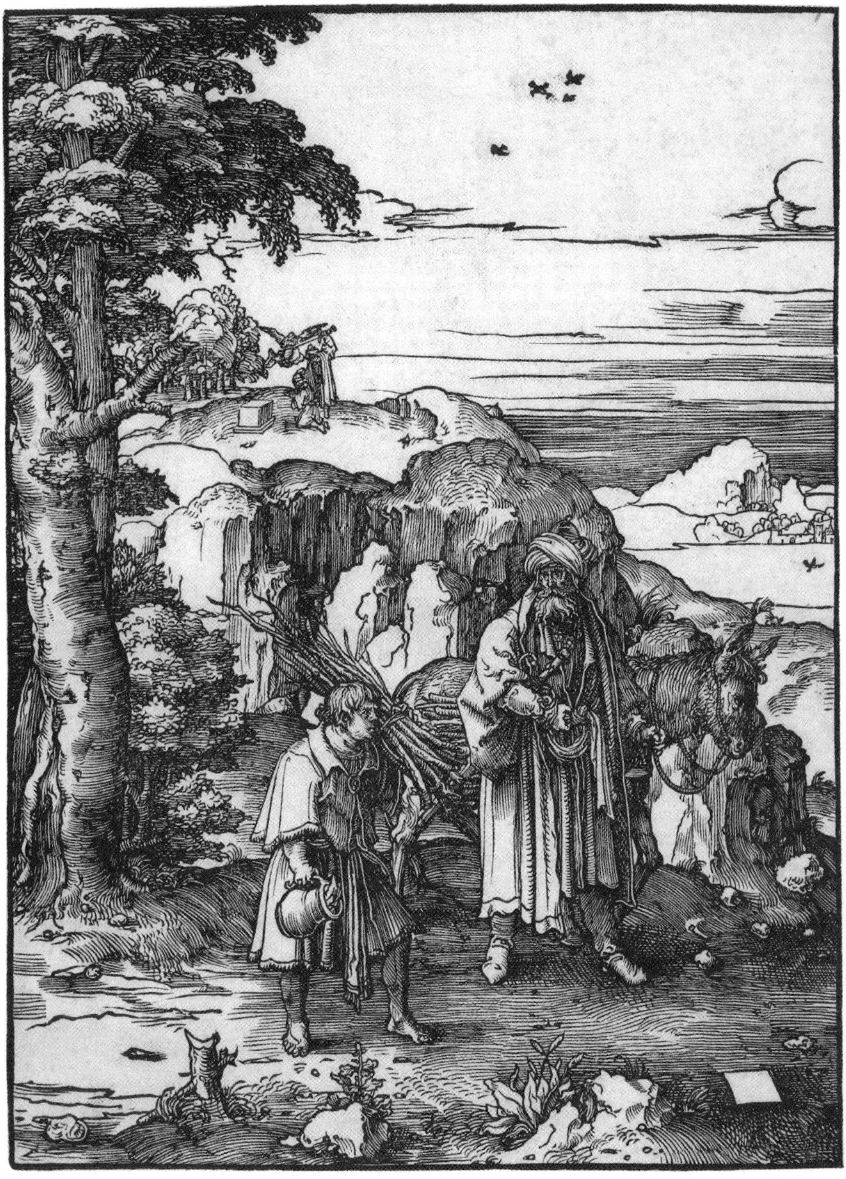

34 Lucas van Leyden, *Sacrifice of Isaac*, 1517–19, woodcut.

(Genesis 22:1–14). This challenge, an event that seems to indicate a sadistic or perverse divinity, occupies a special place in Jewish liturgy within the New Year (Rosh Hashanah) service, where it poses a question about divine providence and issues of life and death for the coming year. In a prayer that serves as a reaffirmation of Abraham's covenant with God, the prayer beseeches: 'May God account to His people the sacrifice of Isaac according to Your oath, and reverse Your decree from stern judgement to mercy.' The subject of the Sacrifice of Isaac also held special significance for Christians of the Middle Ages, because it formed an Old Testament typological prefiguration for the New Testament sacrifice on the cross of Jesus as the Son of God.[1]

Rembrandt particularly liked to depict this subject, especially its climactic moment of the angel's intervention, in both paintings and prints made across his career, and he chose Abraham as his most frequent protagonist from the Old Testament.[2] But an earlier Dutch image focuses on the prelude to that climax, the journey to Mount Moriah. A woodcut (*c.* 1517; illus. 34) by the Dutch artist Lucas van Leyden (*c.* 1494–1533) shows a diminutive Isaac carrying the wood for his own sacrifice while following behind his aged father across the foreground.[3] A bearded Abraham wears a turban and kaftan of the region. In Lucas's version, the crucial intervention later by the angel occurs in the distant background hilltop. This scene is the final biblical confirmation of the pact or covenant between Abraham, as founder of a great people, and God, who speaks directly to him on numerous occasions, including this call to bring forth Isaac for sacrifice.

Old age can also give way to folly. The Bible provides its own equivalent of the lascivious oldster of Quinten Massys's

Ill-Matched Pair (see illus. 25) in the form of two conniving old men who conspire to spy upon innocent Susannah while she is bathing. They then attempt to coerce her into sex with them (Daniel 13, apocryphal). In the text the men are identified as 'elders' and judges, well respected by the people; however, both were overcome by lust when confronted with Susannah's nakedness and beauty. Unlike the easy virtue of Massys's greedy, unnamed young woman, Susannah refuses to sin with them, so they falsely accuse her of seeing a young man for sex, for which the penalty is death. Fortunately, Daniel wisely separates the two elders, so he is able to catch them in lying contradictions between their competing accounts; Susannah is exonerated, and the elders are executed.

Many artists used this encounter between Susannah and the Elders as an opportunity to show a luscious female nude in stark contrast with two grotesquely aged men, in a biblical version of the *Ill-Matched Pair* theme. But as a demonstration of virtue

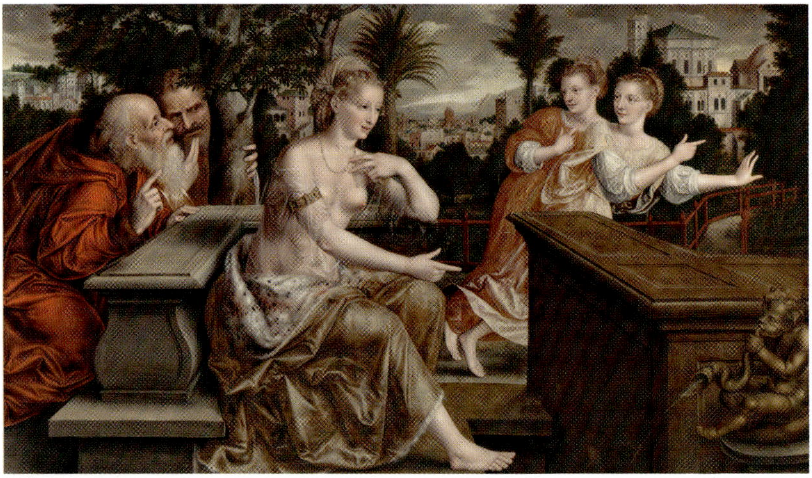

35 Jan Massys, *Susannah and the Elders*, 1564, oil on panel.

rewarded, the Daniel text presents a contrast between her virtue and their vice, her youth and their old age. A typical example, *Susannah and the Elders* (1564; illus. 35) by Jan Massys, draws on the models for the ugly faces of his father Quinten for the elders, who are gesturing in conspiratorial speech at left. At centre poses a topless young Susannah, placed tantalizingly before the viewer. Her married status is conveyed by her bound hair; the extensive garden and pair of maidservants display both her wealth and social status. But her back is turned to the two elders, so she remains unsuspecting of their plot, even though her servants seem to be departing. Filling her pool at right, an ornate fountain relief shows the mythic god Cupid blowing a horn, thus inserting an erotic tone of temptation into this biblical subject.

To a modern eye this situation smacks of sexual harassment, redolent of the #MeToo moment of our current century. Indeed, several artists also depicted the subject of Susannah and the Elders in order to emphasize the vulnerability of a defenceless woman. Notably the seventeenth-century female painter Artemisia Gentileschi (1593–1653), but also Rembrandt himself, painted this scene. Artemisia's early work (1610; illus. 36) takes pains to emphasize both the discomfort and vulnerability of her naked young woman. Her more ordinary body and defensive gesture remove her from the more conventional display of female beauty for male delectation as well as the (presumed male) viewer's own gaze. Artemisia shows Susannah cringing before her conspiratorial assailants, turning away from them and raising her hands in protest to preserve her modesty.[4] Most artists, however, followed the same pattern as Jan Massys, using this scene to display ideal female beauty and to tempt a male viewer visually, just as fully as Susannah's nakedness tempts the voyeuristic elders.

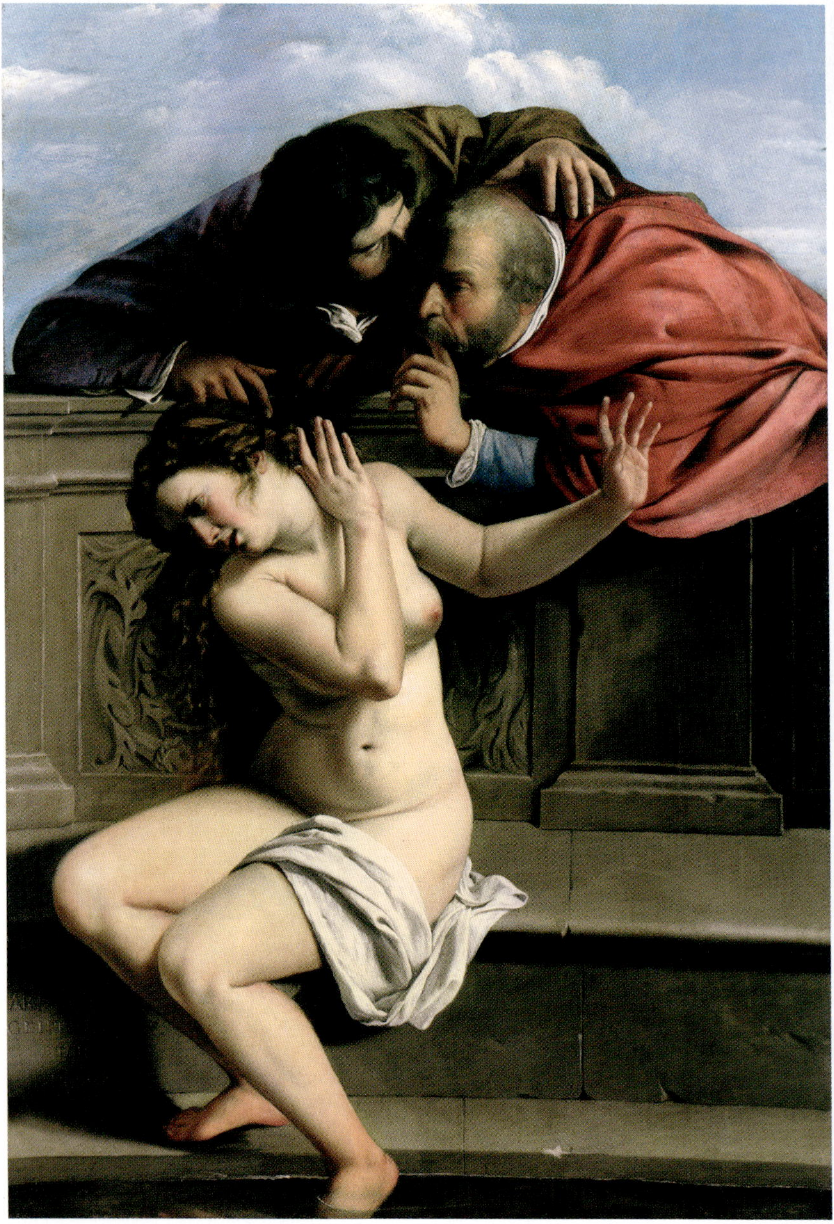

36 Artemisia Gentileschi, *Susannah and the Elders*, 1610, oil on canvas.

Like the sculpted medieval church facades (illus. 14), painted New Testament narrative figures often emphasize venerable, aged prophets. In particular, the chief disciple, St Peter, appears conventionally represented as a bald greybeard – in contrast to the youngest disciple, John, who is shown as beardless with a full head of hair. But even disciples can have their human failings and complex moments of indecision. Rembrandt's *The Denial of St Peter* (1660; illus. 37) shows the disciple at the centre in a moment of crisis. He wraps himself in a Jewish ritual prayer shawl and stands in deep shadow broken by the glare of a hidden

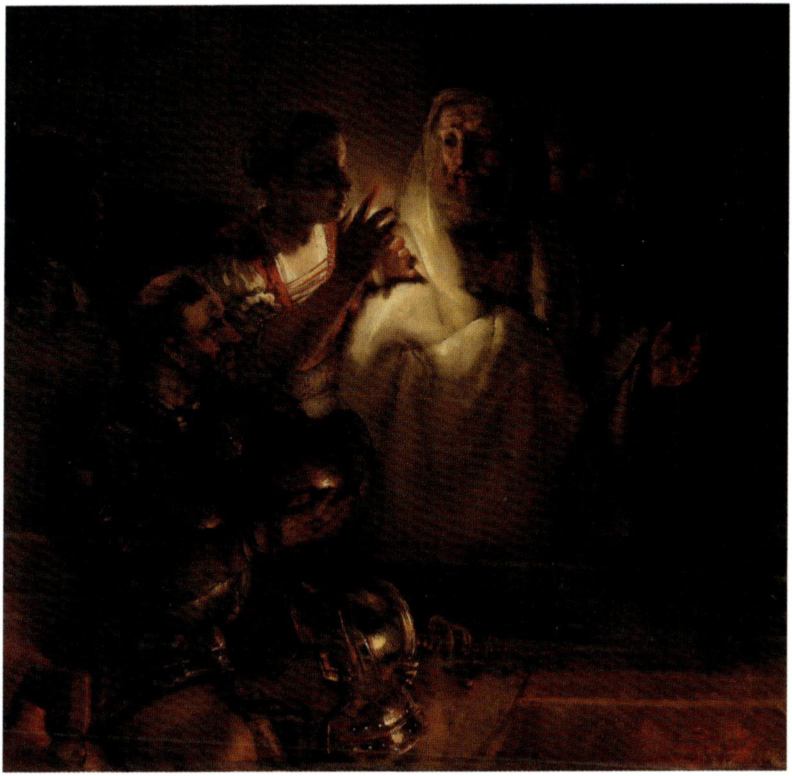

37 Rembrandt, *The Denial of St Peter*, 1660, oil on canvas.

candle, which reaches his face enough to show his internal stress. This pictured moment (Luke 22:54–62) happens when Peter is interrupted by a servant who recognizes him while he is still following behind Jesus, already under arrest by Roman soldiers. As Peter turns back towards both the servant and an inquisitive Roman soldier in shining armour, he decides to save his own life by pretending not to know the prisoner. Reluctantly, Peter must halt, while Jesus departs further from him into the upper right distance of the composition. Dramatic lighting, a Rembrandt hallmark, is complemented here by bold paint application of the artist's late style. But this chosen subject, which complicates the steadfast adherence of the chief disciple in a threatening moment, shows how his otherwise steadfast faith (already rewarded with leadership of the apostles; John 21:15–17) could still be challenged. Rembrandt thus poses a dilemma for pious viewers to consider their own spiritual commitment.

One of the most compelling figures from the outset of the Gospel story is the aged prophet Simeon (Luke 2:25–35), who can be viewed as the bridge between the Old and New testaments.[5] While holding the baby Jesus in his arms in the Temple, Simeon is visited by the Holy Spirit, so he suddenly recognizes that this moment begins the fulfilment of earlier biblical prophecy of the coming Messiah. Realizing that his own mission is complete, Simeon utters the memorable forecast:

> Lord, now you are letting your servant depart in peace, according to your word;/ For my eyes have seen your salvation/ Which you have prepared before the face of all peoples,/ A light to bring revelation to the Gentiles and the glory of your people Israel.

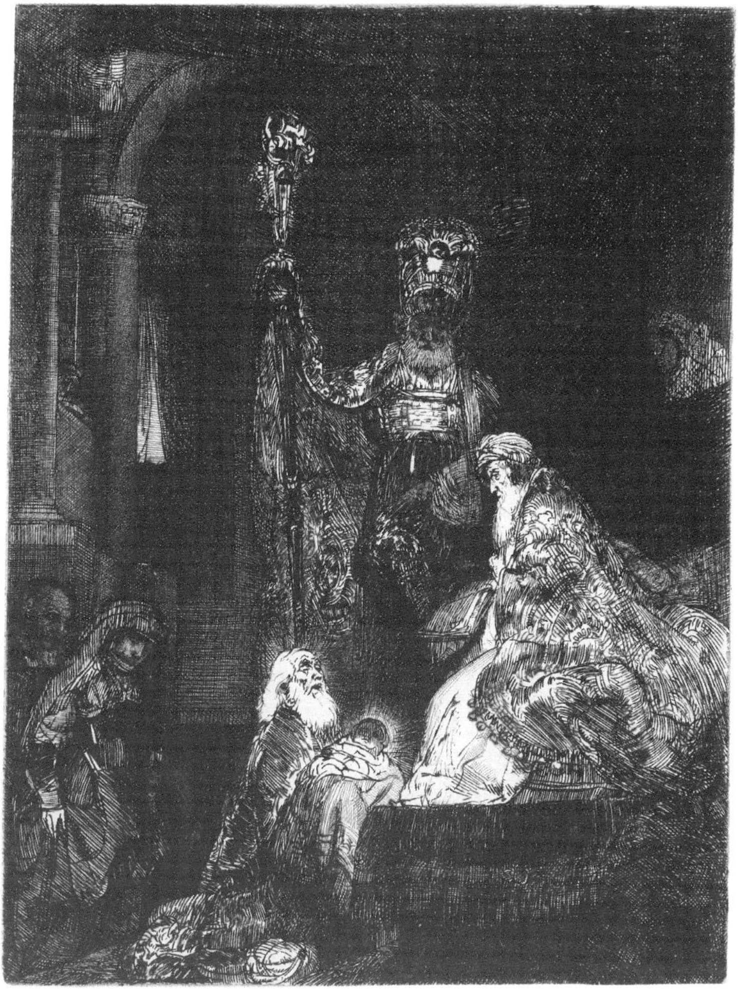

38 Rembrandt, *The Presentation in the Temple in the Dark Manner*, *c.* 1654, etching.

Like Abraham, Simeon and the scene of the Presentation of the Christ Child in the Temple was another of Rembrandt's favourite subjects in paintings and, especially, in his prints. In this etched *The Presentation in the Temple in the Dark Manner* (*c.* 1654; illus. 38) Rembrandt fashioned one of his most poignant

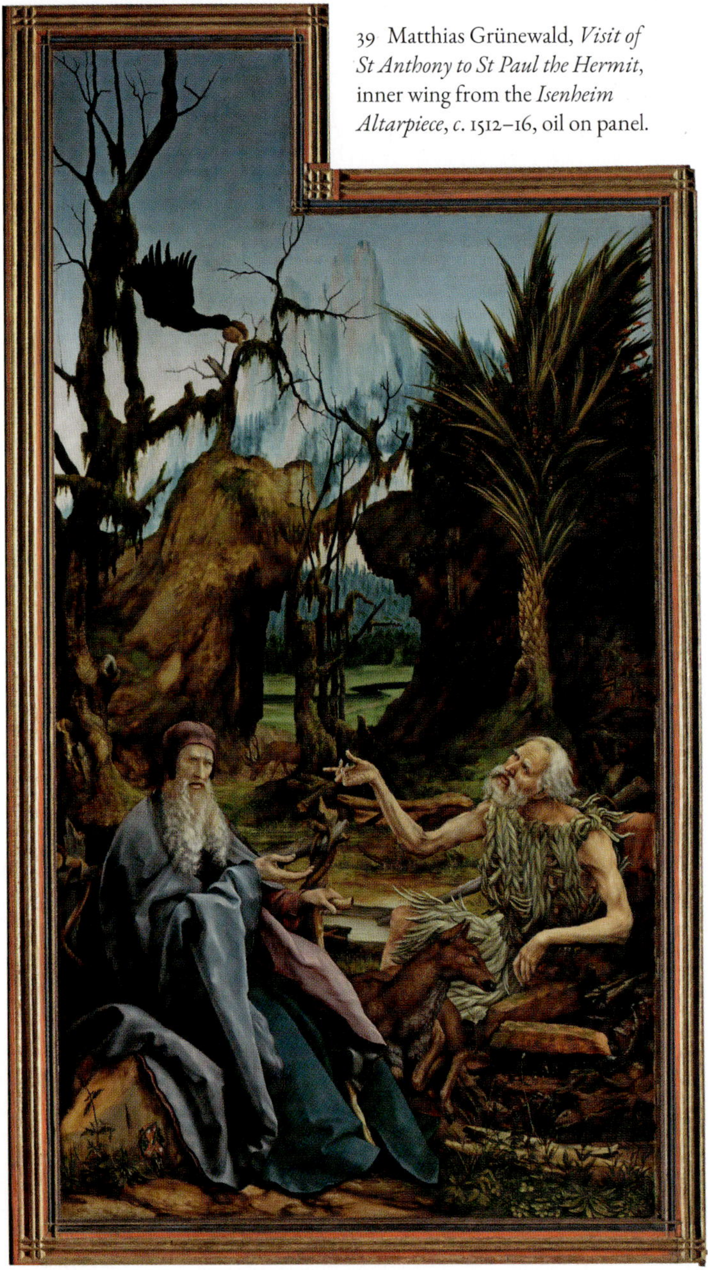

39 Matthias Grünewald, *Visit of St Anthony to St Paul the Hermit*, inner wing from the *Isenheim Altarpiece*, *c.* 1512–16, oil on panel.

versions of the moment. He uses a spotlight effect to single out the white-bearded prophet with baby Jesus in his arms. Even though Mary and Joseph are present behind Simeon, they remain in shadow. The print emphasizes his own crucial role in the scene in the centre foreground, juxtaposed with the enthroned high priest of the Temple, elevated before him. A looming secondary priest (*sagan*) emerges from the darkness, standing upright and frontal above Simeon in the centre of the composition. Here the narrative's formal presentation also underscores its prophetic significance, where Christ will supplant the Temple priesthood as the leader of the true religion. Light physically symbolizes the personal enlightenment encapsulated in Simeon's prophetic biblical speech.

Depictions of the legends of later saints in Christian art also reinforced the visible correlation between wise old age and committed faith. A good example is one of the wings from Matthias Grünewald's *Isenheim Altarpiece* (*c.* 1512–16; illus. 39), which recounts an event in the life of St Anthony, the name saint of the Antonite monastery that housed this retable.[6] Though a hermit himself, Anthony receives a vision to seek out a much older hermit, St Paul, so that the two holy men could exchange thoughts. By a miracle, the raven who ordinarily brings a single daily ration of bread to nourish Paul arrives on this day with two loaves instead. The isolated wilderness setting of Paul's hermitage is a verdant river valley with tame deer that convey an utterly peaceful stillness. Paul's garment in retreat has been woven from leaves as an emblem of his own spiritual renunciation. While Paul is white-haired, Anthony's longer beard conveys his identity as a model of monastic piety (his striking likeness has been read as based on a portrait in tribute to the monastery's abbot,

Guido Guersi, whose coat of arms appear in the lower left corner). In Grünewald's other *Isenheim Altarpiece* shutter, Anthony's faith is put to an extreme test when he is attacked and abused by demonic monsters of all kinds, causing him to cry out in despair and doubt (through words taken from his hagiography and written on a sheet in the lower right corner): 'Where were you good Jesus? Why did you not come to heal my wounds?'[7]

Classical mythology also has stories that hold old age in high regard. In one tale, Baucis and Philemon (Ovid, *Metamorphoses*, 8:611–724), a humble elderly couple, were visited by Jupiter and Mercury disguised as mortals. After being denied hospitality at 'thousands' of houses, the gods were generously received by the two old people in their cottage, despite their poverty. As a reward, the gods converted the dwelling into a temple and granted the couple a wish. Their simple desire was to grow old together as priests of that temple and to die together. When they expired, they became two intertwined trees, oak and linden. Their example indicates that the gods look after good people, but for Christians there is also a biblical resonance conveyed in a Gospel event. In a post-Resurrection scene, Christ (in disguise) joins two of his disciples on a country journey to Emmaus. At an inn there he breaks bread with the disciples, the Supper at Emmaus (Luke 24:30–31), at which point they finally recognize him, only to have him disappear. Like Jupiter and Mercury, Christ reveals himself only after sharing a meal with his followers.

Rendering the rarely illustrated tale of Baucis and Philemon at a small scale, the German painter in Rome Adam Elsheimer (1578–1610) shows the two gods bringing brightness through

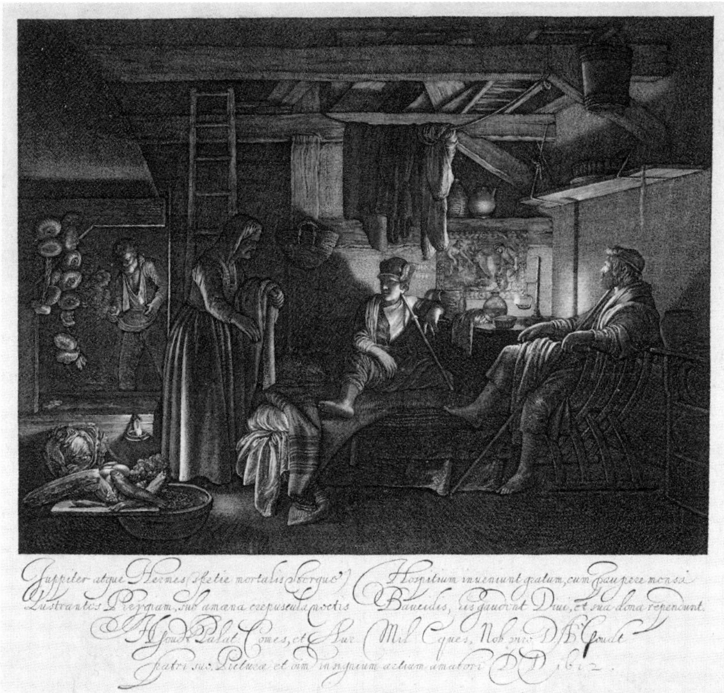

40 Hendrick Goudt, after Adam Elsheimer, *Jupiter and Mercury in the House of Philemon and Baucis*, 1612, engraving.

their own radiance to the dim light of the windowless cottage; meanwhile, Baucis and Philemon attend them in shadow, which is broken only by the dim light of candles beside each of the old couple.[8] Easier to read than the painting (and a virtuoso display of both printmaking and calligraphy in its own right) is the richly dark engraving made after it by a Dutch artist, Hendrick Goudt (1573–1648), who lived with Elsheimer in Rome and made numerous prints after his pictures, including the 1612 *Jupiter and Mercury in the House of Philemon and Baucis* (illus. 40). The gods, relaxing while the two old people are waiting on them, are not given preternatural scale or obvious identifying attributes, though

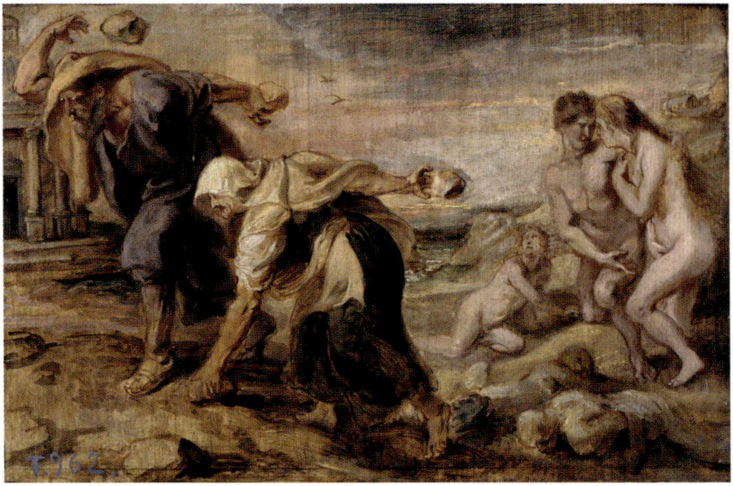

41 Peter Paul Rubens, *Deucalion and Pyrrha*, 1636–7, oil on panel.

Mercury's winged cap reveals his identity to the perceptive viewer. Jupiter is characteristically older and bearded, though neither his eagle mount nor his thunderbolt appear to give him away.

Another related subject of pious old people appears in Ovid (1:313–415). After a massive flood, sent in anger by Jupiter to wipe out humankind because of its evil nature, only one mortal couple remains: Deucalion, son of Prometheus, and his wife Pyrrha. When they despairingly plead for a repopulation of the world so that they won't remain utterly alone, they receive counsel from a divine oracle to throw the 'bones' (rocks) of Mother Earth behind them. From this act, a miracle occurs, and men spring up behind Deucalion, women behind Pyrrha, so human life returns to the world.

Peter Paul Rubens included this subject among the many Ovidian subjects that he produced for the Torre de la Parada hunting lodge of King Philip IV of Spain, and his oil sketch survives (1636–7, illus. 41).[9] The couple are veiled and face forward,

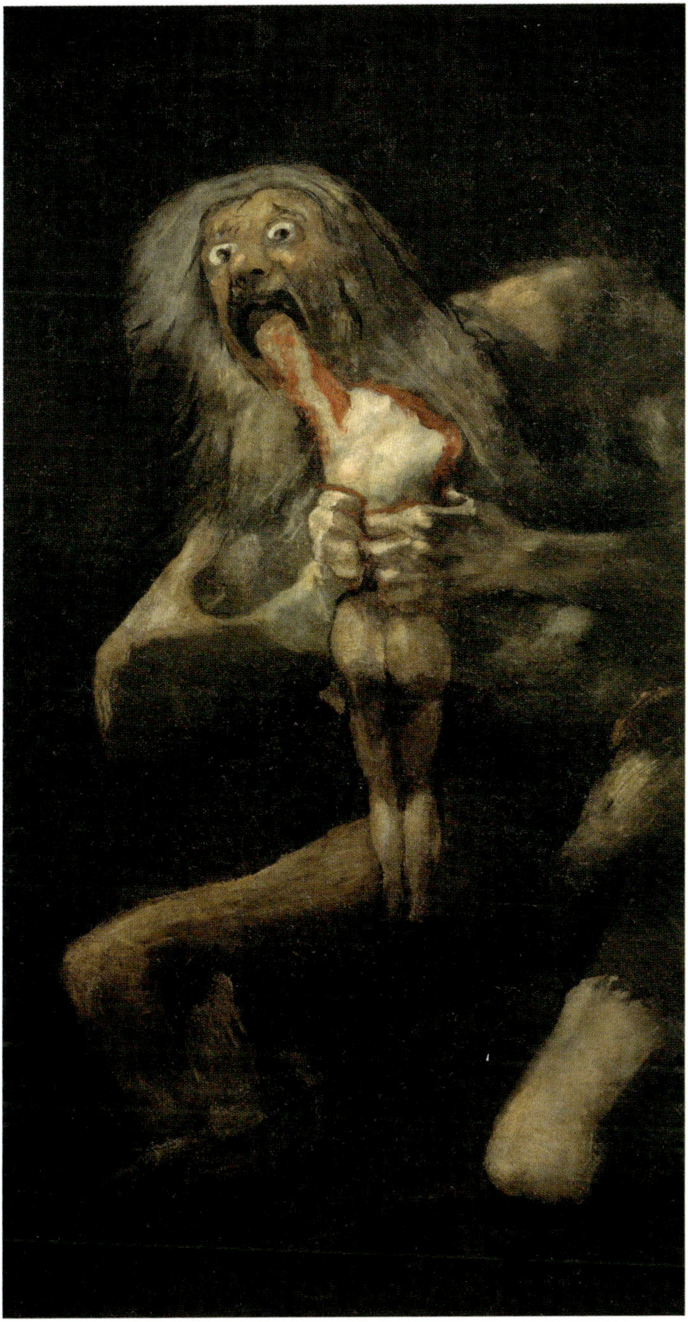

42 Francisco Goya, *Saturn Devouring His Child*, *c.* 1820–23, oil on mural (transferred to canvas).

not looking where the rocks that they pick up are landing. Behind them, nude youthful figures of men and women emerge from the earth. Their collective image resembles the resurrected souls in Last Judgement scenes, and this mythic repopulation also echoes the world after the biblical flood that purged sinful humankind (Genesis 6–9; additionally, a boat, recalling Noah's ark, is visible in the upper right, resting atop a hillside). Ultimately, this subject remains one of sin, redeemed through the saving remnant of the pious. Also visible in the upper left of the composition is a small temple building, presumably the site of the healing oracle.

For the same mythic cycle at the Torre de la Parada Rubens dramatized a different scene, one of horror: the god Saturn devouring his own children to hold on to his power as ruler.[10] Even more disturbing than Rubens's image, however, is Francisco Goya's emulation of it among the *Black Paintings* for his own home in Madrid (*c.* 1820–23; illus. 42).[11] Here the god's age and seniority result in unspeakable cruelty; indeed Goya replaces the chubby infant of Rubens with a gory, partially dismembered adult body fragment. Saturn, as discussed in Chapter One, is the planet already associated with old age and with the passage of time in his guise as Chronos, or Father Time. He also presides over the combined cold/wet mentality of melancholy. Goya's grey-haired figure is wide-eyed and crazed, gigantic and naked. He is surrounded in other paintings of the same *Black Paintings* mural series by such subjects as groups of witches and the Three Fates. Madness and ferocity unite this image with Goya's habitual profound pessimism about bestiality and cruelty, the essential nature of this aged, cannibalistic miscreant (see Chapter Five).

As a concluding section about old age in ancient myth and story, two examples of filial piety – devotion and assistance by a child before an aged parent – stand out. First, Virgil's *Aeneid* tells the story of the hero and founder of Rome, Aeneas, at a moment of greatest distress (Book Two, ll. 634–754). Fleeing from the ruins of Troy during its capture and sack by Greek forces, the young man from Troy's royal family manages to escape with his family. Not only does he bring out his young son Ascanius on foot, but he literally carries his resisting, elderly father, Anchises, out of the city. The grandfather, in turn, follows good Roman fashion by bearing out the ashes of his own ancestors, whose veneration along with the household gods, or *penates*, formed a Roman devotion. A particularly vivid and moving realization of this narrative moment is the marble carving (*c.* 1618–19; Rome, Galleria Borghese) by a youthful Gian Lorenzo Bernini, where the three figures are tightly bunched in a vertical composition.

Another powerful ancient story, tinged with equivocal erotic overtones, is the tale of Cimon and Pero, or Roman Charity. An exemplary story, 'on piety in parents', derived from Roman author Valerius Maximus's *Factorum ac dictorum memorabilium* (Memorable Deeds and Proverbs, IX, chapter four; first century CE), it features an old man, Cimon, who is starving in prison. Thanks to the generosity of a guard, his daughter Pero can visit him daily, where she sustains his life by breastfeeding her own father. This story, the very epitome of filial love, here between daughter and father, became a favourite for painters influenced by early seventeenth-century Roman models. Among others: Peter Paul Rubens (*c.* 1612; St Petersburg, Hermitage Museum; *c.* 1635, Amsterdam, Rijksmuseum); Utrecht painter Dirck van Baburen (*c.* 1623; York Art Gallery); and the female painter Artemisia Gentileschi (*c.* 1644–5; private collection) in a reversal of her lustful imagery in *Susannah and the Elders* (illus. 36).

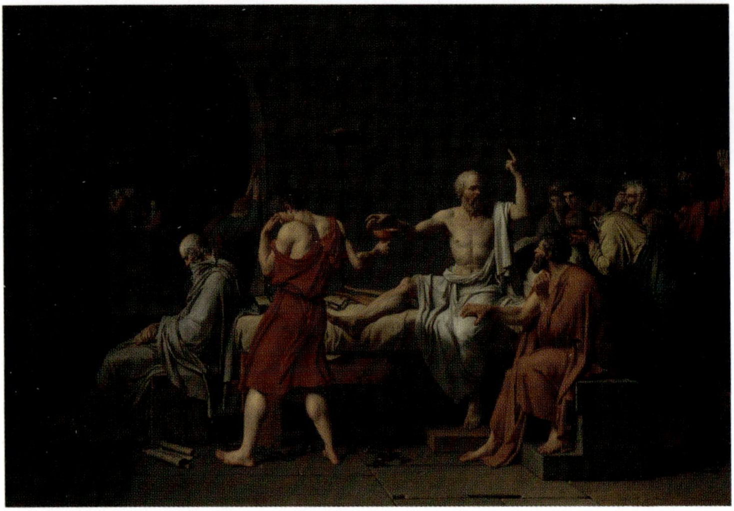

43 Jacques-Louis David, *The Death of Socrates*, 1787, oil on canvas.

Along with the likenesses of classical philosophers and authors to represent their ideas (see Chapter Two), a number of paintings also celebrated their deeds, notably their suicides. As noted, Rubens expanded on his supposed bust of Seneca to create *The Death of Seneca* (*c.* 1615).[12] Following the account of Tacitus' *Annals*, Rubens represents a frontal, full-length view of the philosopher and adviser of Nero, who followed the command to die issued by the emperor himself in 65 CE. In the process he urged his friends to follow his model of Stoic virtue and self-control, and he even sped up the process by opening his veins and standing in a warm water basin to increase the blood flow from his aged body. Rubens shows the central sage surrounded by Roman soldiers, and a doctor attending to Seneca's arm as well as a young scribe taking down his last words.

On the eve of the French Revolution in 1787, Jacques-Louis David (1748–1825) painted another suicide of a philosopher, *The*

Death of Socrates (illus. 43). That event from 399 BCE is based on Plato's account in the *Phaedo*.[13] As with Seneca, the death of Socrates by hemlock was imposed by civic authorities in Athens as punishment for his alleged corruption of the minds of young Athenian men. Like Rubens, David based his philosopher's features on a supposed ancient bust. David's several years as a young artist in Rome led him to embrace the austerity and authenticity of neoclassical visual vocabulary, which is very much on view in this picture. Socrates sits at the edge of his bed near the centre of this large, multi-figured composition. He actively raises one hand skyward (echoing Raphael's figure of Plato in his *School of Athens*, see illus. 17), as if to display his confidence and steadfast commitment to his principles; that gesture also evokes his discussion in Plato's dialogue about death and the soul. With his other hand he reaches out for the fatal cup of poison. His muscular

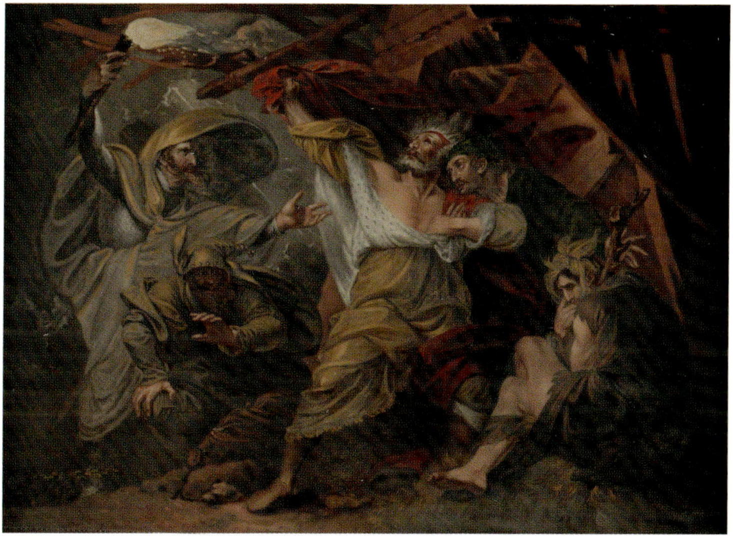

44 William Sharp after Benjamin West, *King Lear on the Heath*, from Shakespeare's *King Lear*, Act III, Scene 4, *c*. 1789, oil on panel.

torso (an idealized image belying his true age) is exposed and vulnerable. Presumably he is lecturing about the soul and immortality in accord with the words of Plato's dialogue. The young man in red before Socrates extends the cup back to him, but he looks away and shades his eyes from witnessing the death of an esteemed mentor. Emotions among his ten followers are generally restrained, but more overt and demonstrative among the youths at the far right. At the foot of Socrates' bed another old man slumps with hands clasped and eyes closed in despair. Other figures depart in the left background; one of them, a woman, is presumably Socrates's wife Xanthippe, who turns and gestures her farewell with an upraised hand. The prison location, a gloomy, windowless space constructed from large grey stones, reinforces the seriousness of the event even as it foregrounds all the figures. On the floor beneath Socrates are his shackles and a scroll with inkwell to show that his ideas would survive through Plato's recording of his probing questions in the *Dialogues*. Ultimately this image conveys the aged philosopher's unrepentant pursuit of rational enquiry despite his suppression by political authority, although he still accepts the legitimate verdict of that same authority. David would go on to participate actively in the French Revolution, organizing festivities and paintings of principal figures, such as *The Death of Marat* (1793).

Contemporary with David's use of classical antiquity, both national historical events and scenes from English canonical literature formed subjects for British painters. In 1786 one entrepreneur, the engraver and publisher Alderman John Boydell, established a commercial Shakespeare Gallery, calling for artists to represent subjects devoted to the literary works of Shakespeare and Milton, especially *Paradise Lost*.[14] For lively actions, Boydell attracted such painters as Henry Fuseli (1741–1825) from Switzerland and Benjamin West (1738–1820), artist to King George III, from the American colonies. He then issued prints after their paintings for wider distribution and aspired to compile them together into an illustrated edition of Shakespeare. Both Fuseli and West turned often to Shakespeare, including the play most concerned with the pride and folly of old age: *King Lear*. Fuseli chose the dramatic banishment of Cordelia by an angry, enthroned Lear (Act 1, scene 1). West, in turn, depicted the climactic turning point of Lear's madness during the tempest on the heath (Act 3, scene 4). This 1788 painting was engraved by the professional printmaker William Sharp (illus. 44). It shows the king's fool cowering in his ass-eared costume alongside faithful Kent, who holds a torch aloft. They all enter a hovel and encounter exiled Edgar, huddling while disguised as a madman, Poor Tom. West shows Lear at the centre, dishevelled with hair blowing in the wind while he tries to hold a cloak over his head against the elements. The print made after the painting also carries a line from its chosen scene, 'Off, off you lendings – come unbutton here!' In the case of the fictional Lear, tragedy ensues when the aged king's reluctant withdrawal from actual power gets confused with family love and loyalty. His foolish, vain misjudgements about true character in his inner circle result in catastrophic consequences.

In a further narrative, drawn from contemporary legend regarding its subject, *Benjamin Franklin Drawing Electricity from the Sky* (*c.* 1816; illus. 45), West paid a final, posthumous tribute to the scientific genius of his fellow Philadelphian Benjamin Franklin. While his narrative is based on Franklin's fundamental 1752 scientific discovery about lightning, West based his portrait image not on Franklin's younger likeness at the time of the event, but rather on the more familiar face of the aged Franklin, as carved in France by Jean-Antoine Houdon in 1779.[15] In his pictorial reformulation of the experiment, West has raised his image into an allegory of inspired experimentation. Franklin himself

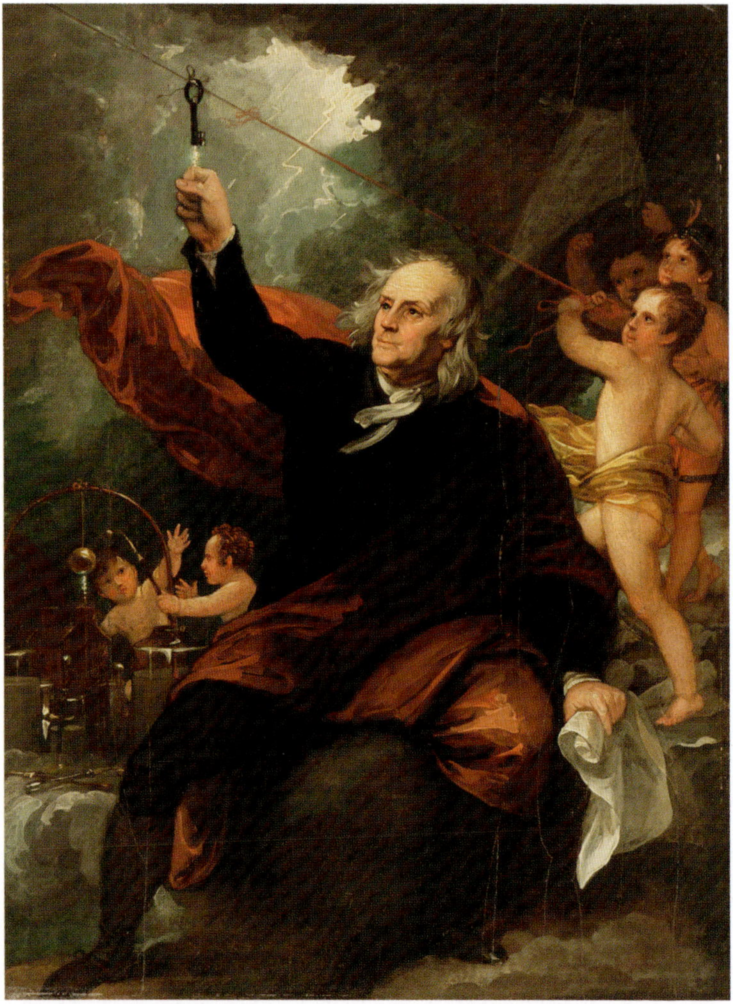

45 Benjamin West, *Benjamin Franklin Drawing Electricity from the Sky*, *c.* 1816, oil on slate.

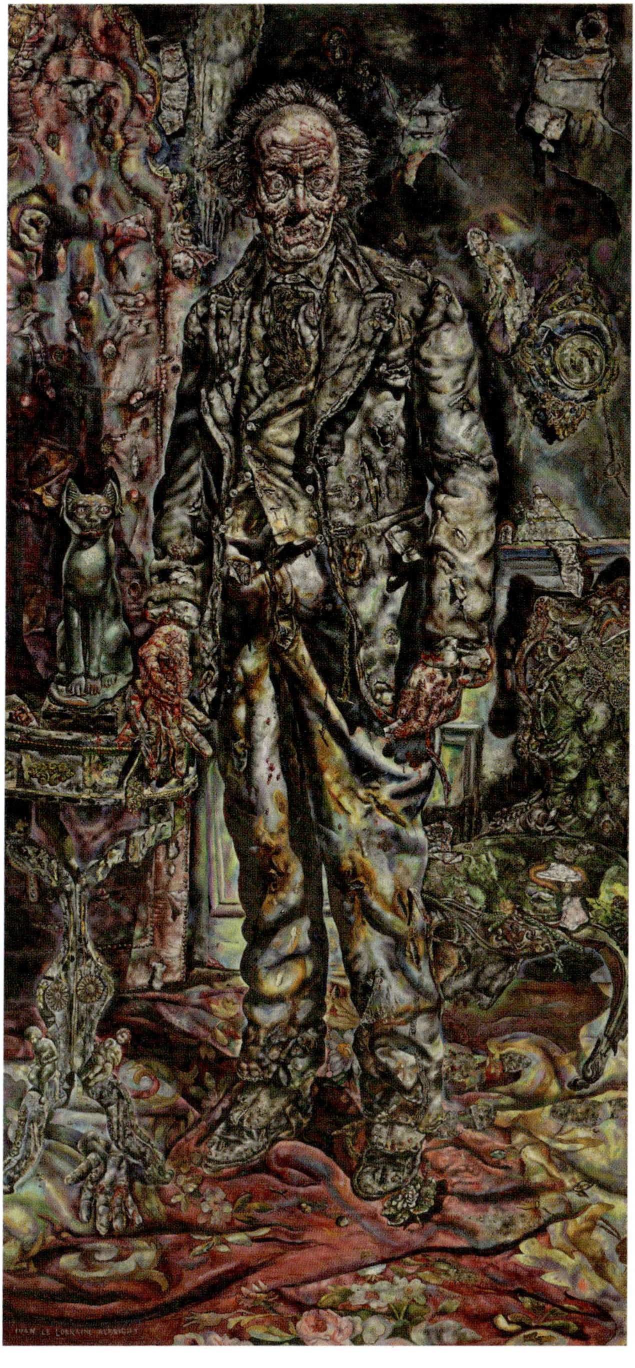

46 Ivan Albright, *Picture of Dorian Gray*, 1943–4, oil on canvas.

is perched on clouds, and he is surrounded by angelic assistants who both fly his kite and monitor the transfer of electricity, which flows from the key at his fingertip to the nearby Leyden jars for storage. In this formulation Benjamin West follows the leading contemporary English painter Joshua Reynolds (1723–1792) in raising portraiture to the so-called 'grand manner' (compare such Reynolds portraits as *Mrs Siddons as Tragic Muse*, or *David Garrick between Tragedy and Comedy*).[16]

A twentieth-century image about old age also derives from English literature, but it emphasizes the grotesque ugliness brought on by dissipation and evil as much as by the passage of years. Basing his image on Oscar Wilde's 1891 novel *The Picture of Dorian Gray* (made for the occasion of its adaptation as a 1945 movie), the Chicago artist Ivan Albright (1897–1983) produced a horrific fictive portrait of the protagonist (1945; illus. 46). The book follows its decadent, eponymous dandy as he commits every manner of self-indulgence, extending even to crime, yet he never seems to age or change at all. Its premise is that Gray's youthful portrait, stored in secret, not only ages but grows more hideous as Gray's moral corruption deepens. That painted image thus revisits a traditional association in art between beauty and moral virtue, whether in portraiture or in life itself. In Wilde's concept the reverse can be equally true: moral turpitude can reveal itself in ugliness, especially over time and with ageing. Albright's revealing picture of the sinful Dorian Gray uses its literary premise to engage earlier mocking images of ugliness in conjunction with either foolish or sinful old age. But it also challenges the frequent equation of sitters with their painted representations in portraits.

Four

Portraits – Self and Others

And so from hour to hour we ripe and ripe,
And then from hour to hour we rot and rot,
And thereby hangs a tale.

SHAKESPEARE, *As You Like It*, II.7

Ars longa, vita brevis.

Ascribed to HIPPOCRATES, *Aphorisimi*

Images of aged individuals are certainly not unique to European visual traditions. As we have already seen in Chapter Two, venerated leaders such as Roman ancestors, emperors or Christian saints are the most likely to be portrayed from life, even – or especially – in old age. For example, in medieval Japan, instead of representing an imagined figure of the Buddha or of his disciples (*arhats*), akin to the apostles who symbolically support the portal of Rheims Cathedral (see illus. 14), the actual leader of the great Japanese imperial monastery Tōdai-ji, Shunjōbō Chōgen (*c.* 1206 CE; illus. 47), became the subject of a moving portrait. This image of the aged priest (d. 1206) in meditation with his prayer beads was used in memorial services held posthumously in his honour, not least for having supervised the restoration of his destroyed monastery. To make the likeness more convincing, painted flesh tones define his sunken cheeks, wrinkled flesh and bald head as well as his black monk's robes. Similar figures even include crystals for the eyes to add to the uncanny lifelike representation. While the artist remains unknown, like the veristic ancestors carved in ancient Rome (see illus. 12), Chōgen combines graphic realism with suggestions of individual character.

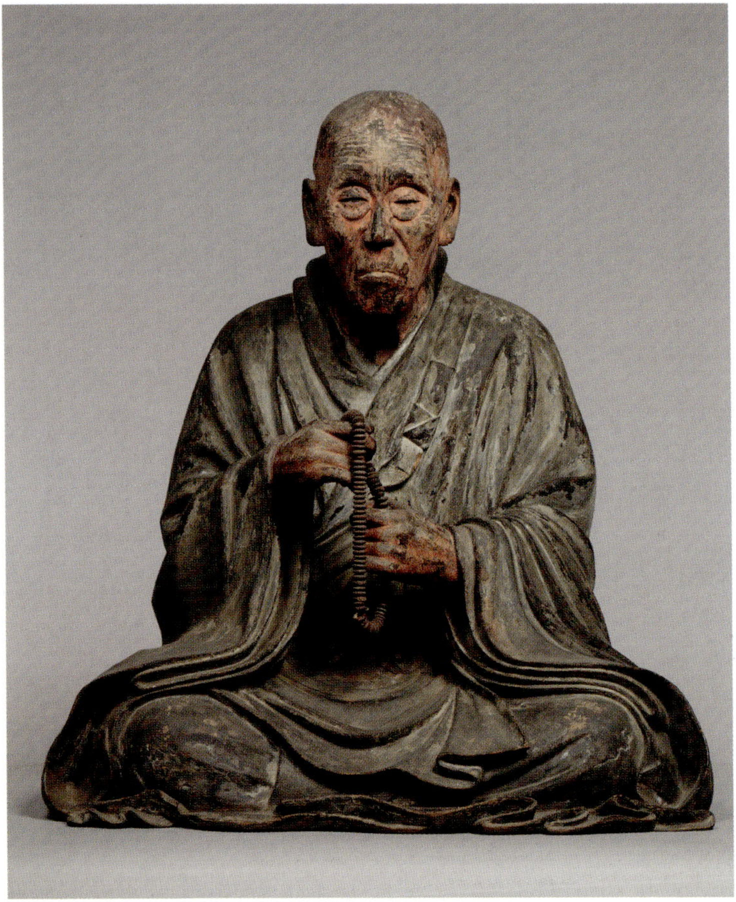

47 *Shunjōbō Chōgen*, *c.* 1206, wood with polychrome.

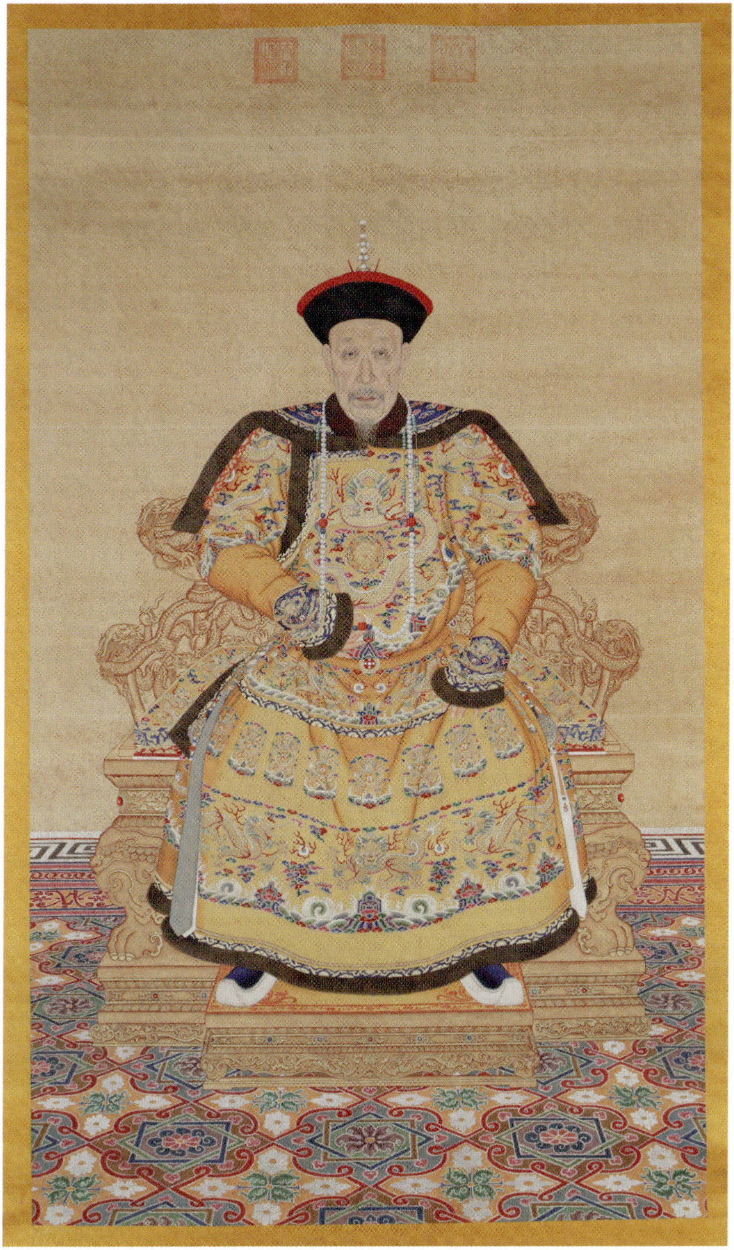

48 Miao Bingtai, *Emperor Qianlong in Court Dress at the Age of Eighty*, 1791, scroll, ink and colour on silk.

Old age has long been culturally valued in Japan, so much so that in 1966 a national 'Respect for the Aged Day' (*Keiro no Hi*) was established.

Akin to the Roman tradition of emperor portraits, one of China's longest reigning emperors, Qianlong (1711–1799), commissioned personal portraits of himself and his consort (as well as his prized horses) by his court artist, an Italian-trained Jesuit named Giuseppe Castiglione (1688–1766), or Lang Shining in Chinese, after his arrival in China in 1715.[1] Although he often worked with Chinese or Manchu collaborators, Castiglione mastered conventions of Chinese painting, which he combined with his meticulous training in oil painting to produce an unprecedented hybrid style where the importance of lifelike features combines nicely with the strictly ceremonial aspects of Chinese imperial court protocol. In a portrait painted near the end of the Qianlong Emperor's sixty-year reign (1791; illus. 48) he is seated on a dragon throne in absolute frontality and symmetry. He is garbed in silk imperial court robes (*chaofu*) whose yellow colour was reserved for the imperial family alone, and whose rich embroidery features dragons, waves and clouds as well as other symbols of authority. The emperor also wears a sable hat topped with pearls mounted on gilt bronze, and his long sleeves are fur-trimmed. Perspectival space shows Castiglione's influence, as do the carefully delineated sagging, aged features of Qianlong's face (his age, eighty, is asserted in one of the three imperial stamps at the top of the painting). Other portraits of the Qianlong emperor, some of them by Castiglione, show him as a mounted warrior on a prized stallion, as a scholar and a traveller, and as a collector and connoisseur of art, as well as the head of his family. He also posed for portraits across his entire reign.

The English queen Elizabeth I (1533–1603) was often portrayed by artists, in media ranging from portrait miniatures by renowned artists such as Nicholas Hilliard and Isaac Oliver and full-scale panels (all anonymous) to a memorial engraving, which finally concedes her age (so often covered by white makeup in her later years).[2] Indeed, the intensified cult of an older Elizabeth I emphasized her divine status or roles as mythological goddesses (Diana/Cynthia, Astraea) while promoting her eternally youthful and virginal unmarried state. In 1596 an official proclamation ordered that 'unseemly' portraits of her, revealing her real appearance and age, be inspected by a serjeant painter and then destroyed. It should be noted that death masks of European rulers often went on display in royal funeral rites.[3] Wax effigies of past British monarchs are still preserved in Westminster Abbey; included among them is the figure of Elizabeth I, a copy of a waxwork that was paraded in the queen's funeral cortege in 1603.[4]

A posthumous memorial print of Elizabeth I was made by Flemish engraver Crispijn de Passe the Elder (*c.* 1603–4; illus. 49). Based on a drawing from life by Isaac Oliver around 1592, it does finally reveal the aged queen's likeness, albeit with a ceremonial stance and costume befitting a monarch. Her coat of arms adorns the upper right corner of the engraving with the motto of the Order of the Garter and the Latin inscription *semper eadem* (always the same), denying the effects of time, placed directly above the Order's own combination of the sword of Justice upon a Bible (*Verbum dei*). That juxtaposition together signifies Christian governance, following St Paul's armour of God (Ephesians 6:11–17). Depicted thus as the Woman of Faith, her role as the head of the Church of England, the queen

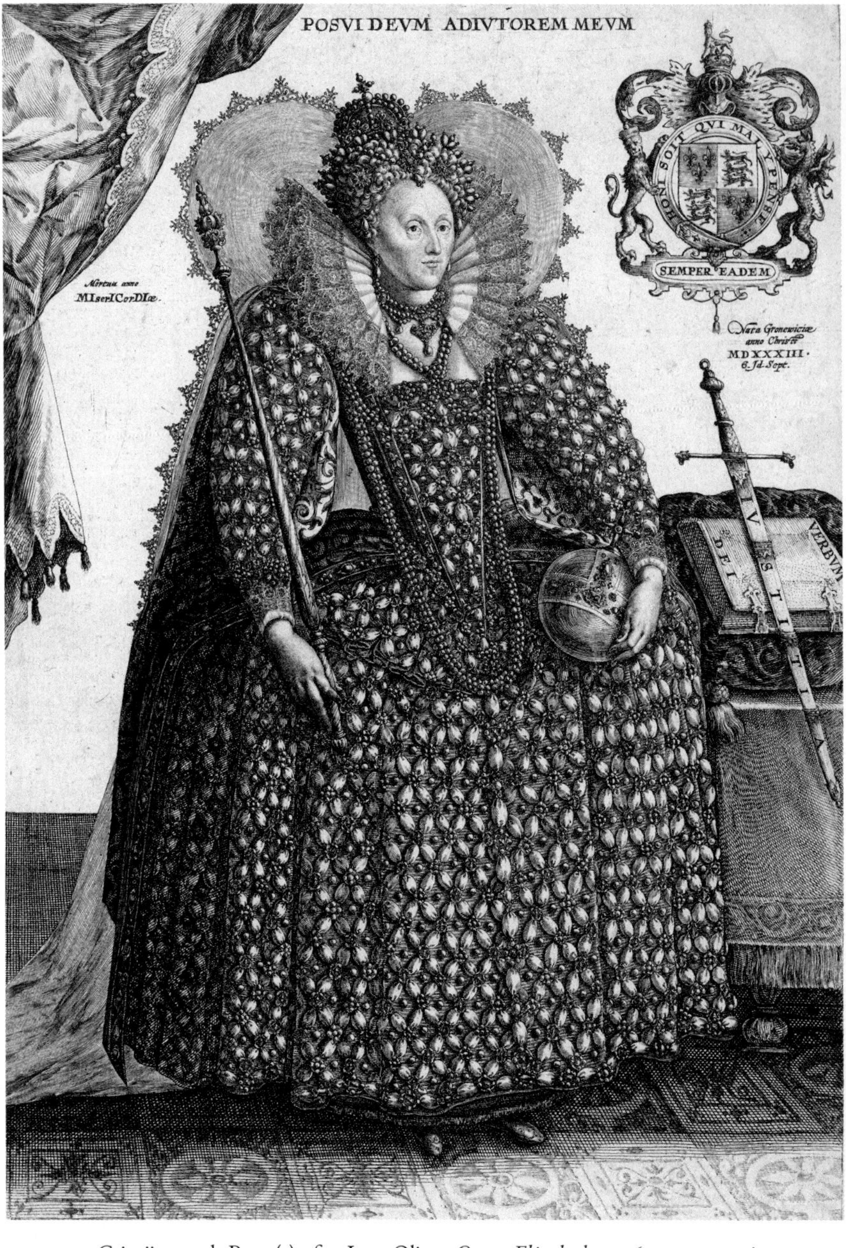

49 Crispijn van de Passe (I), after Isaac Oliver, *Queen Elizabeth I*, *c.* 1603–4, engraving.

is clad in rich ceremonial garments worthy of the Chinese court tradition. She holds an orb and sceptre while wearing a jewelled crown surmounted by a cross, together with jewelled necklaces and a choker. The Latin motto above her head, *Posvi devm adivtorem mevm* (I have made God my help), indicates that she has ruled with divine favour and authority. The queen's death is underscored in the inscription by her sceptre: *Mortua anno MIserICorDIae* (Died in the year of mercy, 1603). Opposite it, above the sword, is her birth date at Greenwich in 1533, claimed as the eve of the Nativity of the Virgin Mary herself.

Her namesake, the late Queen Elizabeth II (1926–2022), the longest ruling monarch in English history, was often portrayed in films and photographs, both formal and informal. At several points in her career deliberate revisions were made to update her profile portrait on British coins and banknotes with more mature likenesses. In her final year of rule she was photographed a mere two days before her death when appearing in her official role of greeting the new prime minister, Liz Truss, who was half a century younger. The contrast between their ages and postures is striking, akin to the presence in traditional history paintings of old maidservants who set off the youth and beauty of young protagonists, such as Danaë or Bathsheba (an inversion of the contrast between Susannah and the Elders). Of course, by the twenty-first century royal ceremony was much reduced, except on the most formal occasions; thus the queen shows a new informality in her kilt and spectacles (another sign of age), as well as in her cordial handshake and smile as she receives her prime minister. The site is one of the queen's palaces, within a political ritual about royal rule in the parliamentary traditions of the UK.

Another portrait of an aged Elizabeth II was painted by the contemporary artist Lucian Freud (1922–2011) in 2001 (Royal Art Collections). A small work, viewed at close-up from the neck up, it utilizes the painter's characteristic thick impasto surfaces, which delineate the folded surfaces of her facial features with visible, unblended shapes of colour. The queen's white hair, in particular, is laid down with thick swirls over a grey base, the tone of which echoes the shadow above the monarch's lips and on her chin. For good measure Freud fashioned the glitter of the royal crown and its multiple diamonds and pearls as the ultimate marker of Elizabeth's sovereignty. According to reports, the queen agreed to pose over a period of almost two years and imposed no stipulations on her artist, who was renowned for his unflattering depictions of the ravages of age. The picture was controversial and considered ugly by some viewers, but it displays the characteristic bold strokes and frank candour of Freud, well known for his painted images of nudes, including aged, fleshy, naked women.

Indeed, all Freud paintings are portraits, and many emphasize old age. He also painted eighteen portraits of his own aged mother, Lucie Freud, in London (1972–84), followed by a pair of candid older self-portraits: one startling full-length, large-scale self-portrait in the nude but with brush in hand at age seventy (*Painter Working, Reflection*, 1993), and a half-length at age eighty (2002). According to Martin Gayford, an art critic who also posed for a Freud portrait, 'Lucian was quite interested in the process of aging, and he certainly dwelled on signs of aging in himself, he welcomed them for their visual possibilities.'[5] In many ways Freud's fleshy, sagging realism in depicting old age was anticipated by Ivan Albright, whose *Dorian Gray* (see illus. 46) is a fiction, but whose close-up self-portrait with glasses from 1982, the year before his death, or rear view of an anonymous corpulent female, *Nude* (1931), and numerous other imagined craggy figures with decaying flesh (*Into the World There Came a Soul Called Ida*, 1929–30) come uncannily close to what Freud would later paint in London.[6]

Another portrait of the infirmity of old age is combined with a personal connection to the artist herself: *Last Sickness* (1953; illus. 50) by American painter Alice Neel (1900–1984). The subject is Neel's mother, Alice Concross Hartley Neel, in her last weeks of life. Neel is celebrated for the candour of her portraits, many of which show frankly naked sitters, whether males in a state of repose usually associated with traditional nude females, or women in late stages of pregnancy with swollen breasts and bellies. Here Neel's mother slumps in her chair, clad informally in a patterned bathrobe with sunken cheeks and stringy white hair astray. Her aged hands with prominent veins hang listlessly on the chair arm or on her lap. But she gazes through thin spectacles directly out at her painter-daughter, who memorializes her at this terminal moment.

As previously discussed, Albrecht Dürer (1471–1528) used the portrait of a 93-year-old man as the basis for his own 1521 image of a meditative *St Jerome* (see illus. 18). But closer to home, the Nuremberg artist also made moving portraits of the two people of whom he was most fond: his painting mentor, Michael Wolgemut, and his own aged mother.[7] *Wolgemut* (1516; illus. 51) is set close-up and bust-length against a monochrome green background, inscribed in gold letters: 'This [image] was portrayed [*abconterfet*; literally: 'counterfeited' or replicated from life] by Albrecht Dürer of his teacher [*Lehrmeister*] Michell

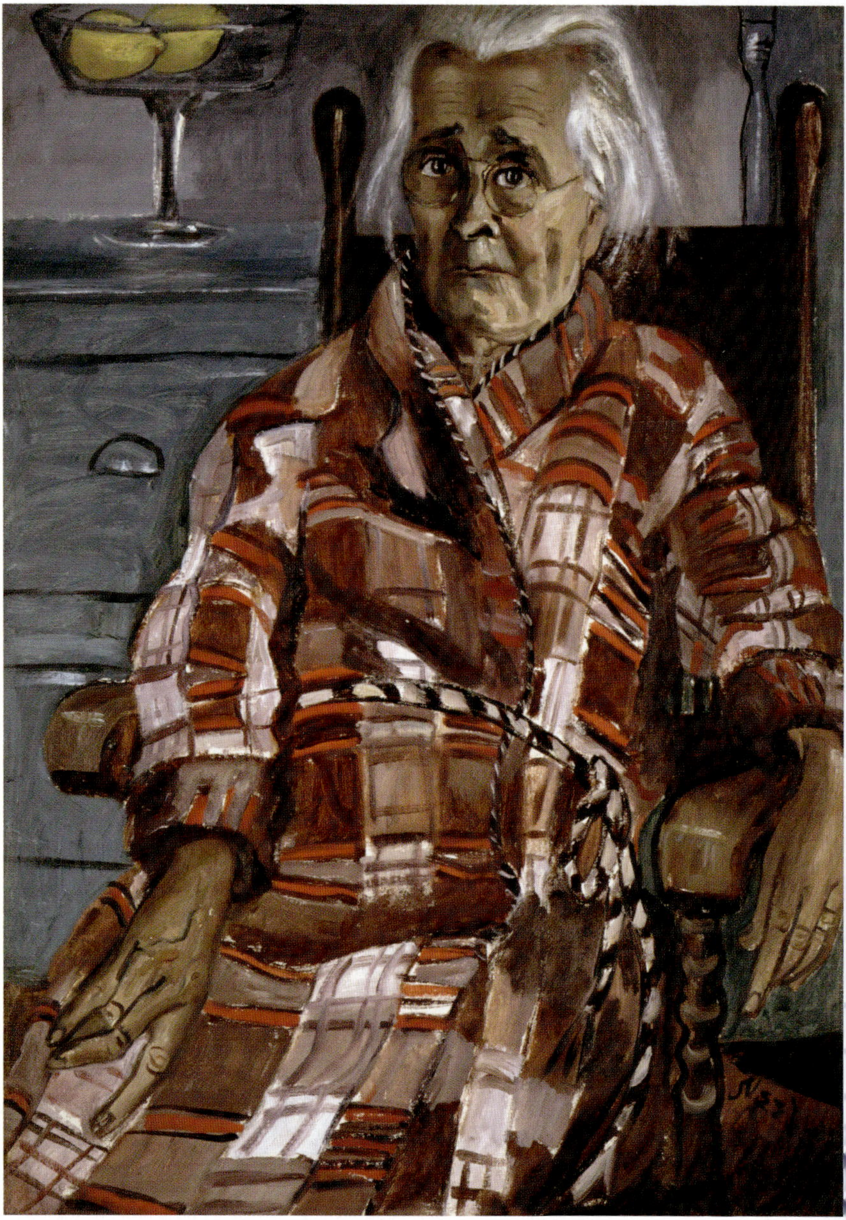

50 Alice Neel, *Last Sickness*, 1953, oil on canvas.

Wolgemut in the year 1516.' To that basic identification he later added a mournful coda, 'and he was 82 years and lived until 1519 and died on St Andrew's Day [30 November] before the sun went down'. Dürer had begun his three-year apprenticeship with the city's most successful painter in 1486, but clearly retained a fond, continuous relationship with his old teacher.[8] Wolgemut's features are rendered with Dürer's characteristic

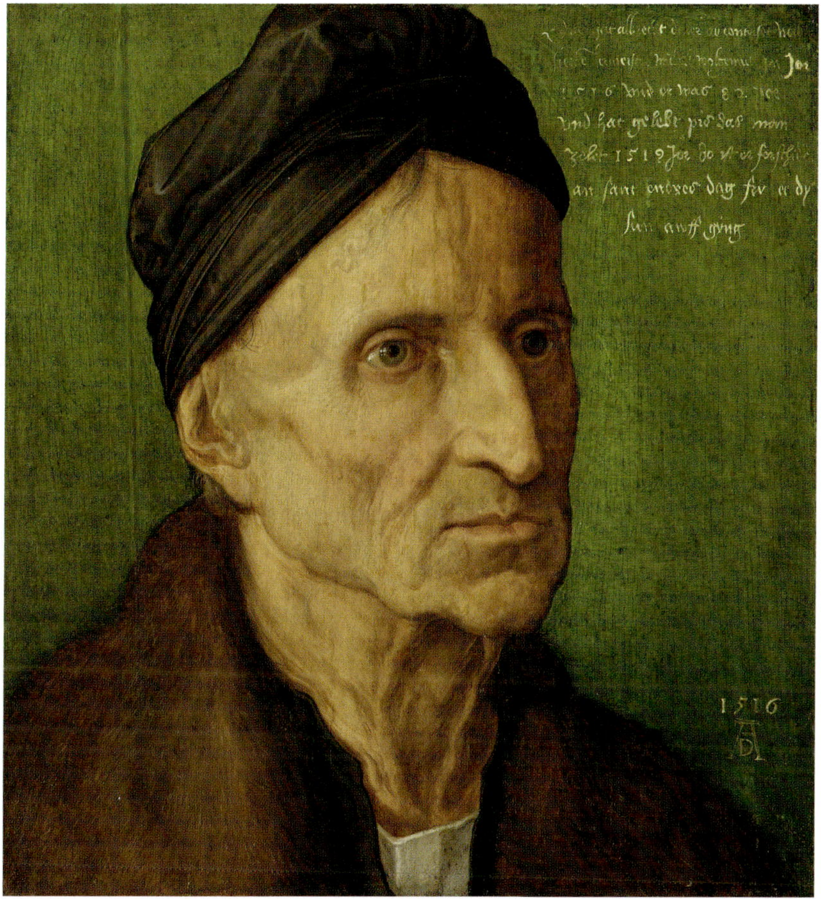

51 Albrecht Dürer, *Michael Wolgemut*, 1516, oil on panel.

meticulous details: the sunken cheeks and sagging neck skin; stray hairs and veins emerging on the sitter's brow from under his cap; and deep-set eyes with red rims and crow's feet wrinkles. Even the cruciform shape of a window is visible in Wolgemut's eyeball. So detailed is this rendering that the pupil of his right eye has been diagnosed with an iris inflammation called iridocyclitis. Since he was able to add a postscript with such specific detail, akin to the rendering itself, Dürer probably retained this affectionate, if unsparing, portrait as a personal memento of the aged painter.

Even more personal and emotionally moving is Dürer's charcoal drawing of his mother, with inscriptions in his own hand: one at the time of the drawing, the other added later in ink (1514; illus. 52). Here the inscriptions reveal: 'This is Albrecht Dürer's mother who was 63 years old; and [added in ink] she died in 1514 on Tuesday before Rogation week, 16 May, at 2 a.m.' The portrait was made two months before Barbara Dürer, née Holper, died, already anticipated as a memorial. Even more than in his *Wolgemut*, the artist has unflinchingly recorded his parent's failing health as well as all of the ravages of her aged body, most especially her bony cheek, rippling forehead wrinkles, protruding eyeballs and her neck's skin folds. Charcoal and chalk were Dürer's favourite mediums for taking a portrait quickly from life, and this drawing has both firm, sure delineation and shading from the hand of a master. Elsewhere, Dürer offers admiration for his mother's patience under numerous hardships: 'This my pious Mother bore and brought up eighteen children; she often had the plague and many other severe and strange illnesses, and she suffered great poverty, scorn, contempt, mocking words, terrors, and great adversities. Yet she bore no malice.'[9]

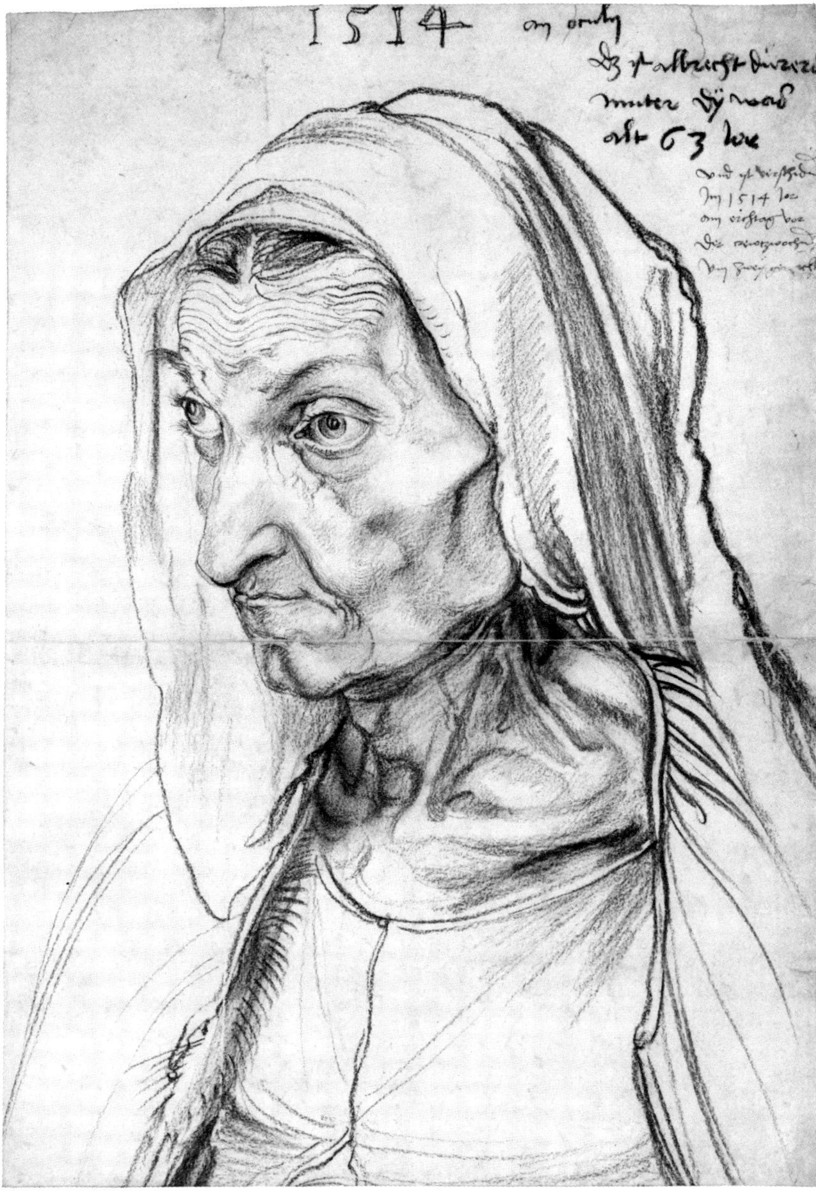

52 Albrecht Dürer, *Barbara Dürer, née Holper* (*The Artist's Mother*), 1514, charcoal on paper.

Surely the most famous portrait of a beloved aged person is the profile likeness of his own mother by James McNeill Whistler (1834–1903). Yet the proper title of the work betrays its experimental, formal ambitions: *Arrangement in Grey and Black, No. 1: Portrait of the Artist's Mother* (1871; illus. 53).[10] The subject is posed in an unmoving profile, facing left, but the left third of the painting is occupied by a black curtain that reaches nearly to the footstool on the floor, significantly accented with grey strokes in the same colour as the thinly painted background wall. Its verticality is complemented in the centre by a horizontal print, one of Whistler's own works, the etching *Black Lion Wharf* (1859), set within a black frame with a white border. Those tones set the range of a pictorial harmony that the painter considered 'threads', repeated across a picture: 'the same colour reappearing continually here and there like the same thread . . . the whole forming in this way a harmonious pattern.'[11] From these components, Whistler gave stronger white highlights to the bonnet and flesh tones of his black-clad, pious mother with sober expression and hands resigned to her lap. Her reverse L-shaped silhouette rounds out the painting at right along the strong black vertical of her chair back. Whistler then followed up this maternal portrait with another *Arrangement in Grey and Black, No. 2: Portrait of Thomas Carlyle* (1872–3; Glasgow), the famous historian and social critic. In that more nearly square image, the sitter again occupies a black chair and wears a black frock coat, balanced by a pair of prints stacked on the background wall, but in this image Carlyle turns his head slightly and is prominently backed by Whistler's personal trademark butterfly seal. Once more, however, the title reveals the basic goal of formal placement of shapes and colours against a neutral background and within a shallow space.

Whistler's formalism belies the personal connection with his mother and with the famous Carlyle, who sat for many painters and photographers (such as Julia Margaret Cameron; see below). But the works of Neel and Dürer reveal how much those personal affections between beloved sitters, whether public figures or not, and their portrayers find expression in these remarkable, personal portraits of old-age sitters.

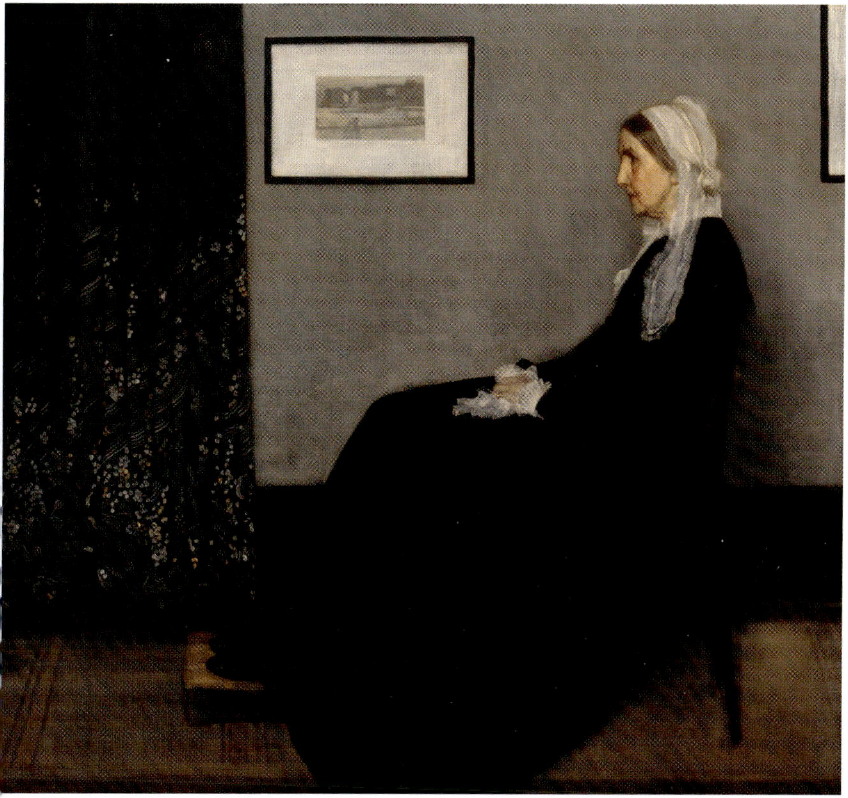

53 James McNeill Whistler, *Arrangement in Grey and Black No. 1: Portrait of the Artist's Mother*, 1871, oil on canvas.

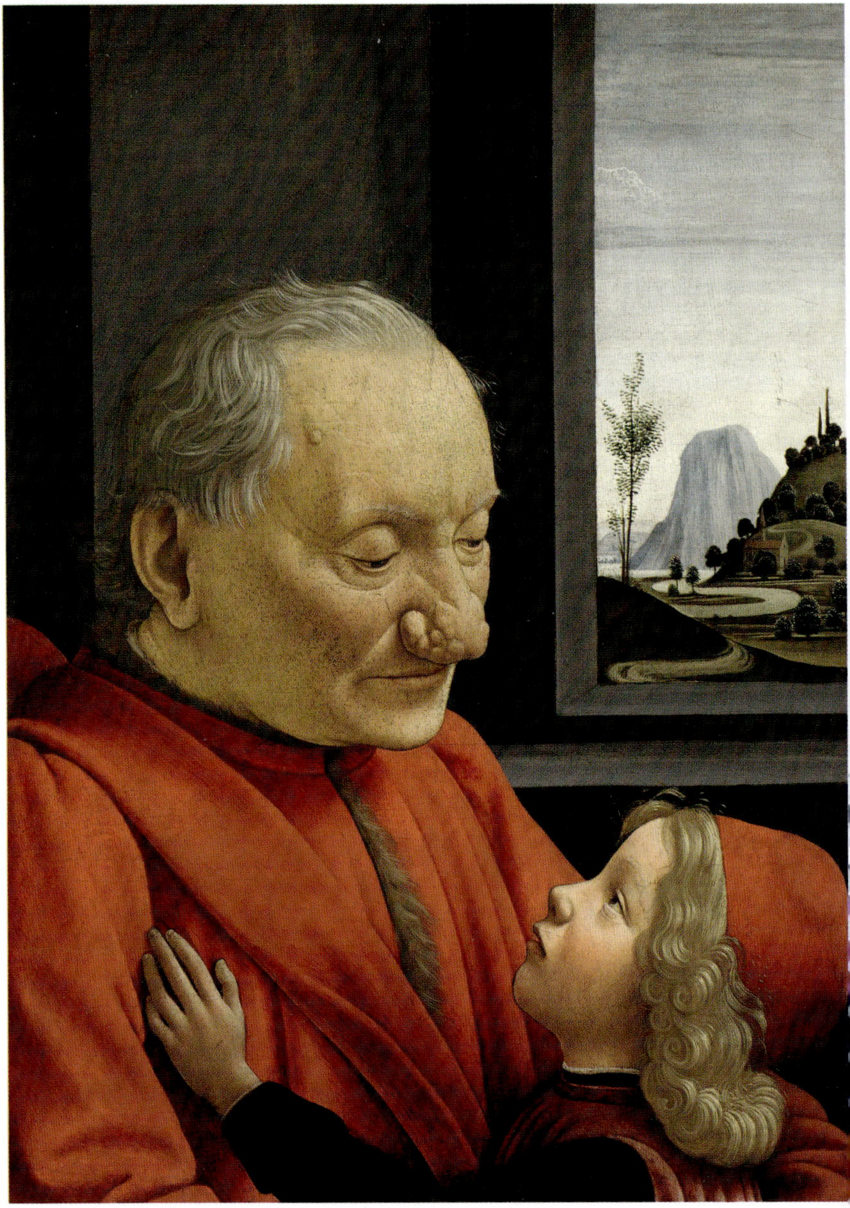

54 Domenico Ghirlandaio, *An Old Man and a Boy*, 1490, tempera on panel.

For more ordinary individuals the same kinds of counterpoint add poignancy to old age. A paradigmatic example comes from the fifteenth-century flowering of portraiture in Renaissance Florence. Domenico Ghirlandaio (1448/9–1494) painted an unknown old man with thinning grey hair tenderly embracing his young grandson (*c.* 1490; illus. 54).[12] The painting is noteworthy for its departure from the standard convention – derived from ancient coins and replicated on Renaissance medals as well as paintings – of static profile presentation. Instead it activates movement, showing the main sitter in three-quarter position, momentarily involved in a touching exchange with a young boy, who turns his head upward with an intense gaze. The old man here sits at an open window in the upper right corner, which adds a further note of place to that of time. Of course, the most striking feature of the old man is his disease of nasal tissue, rhinophyma, an affliction associated with old age. Despite that condition, however, a bond of affection clearly links these separate generations – a persuasive sentiment that is all the more surprising when one discovers that the old man was painted posthumously; a study drawing at bust length shows him on his deathbed. This portrait surely held familial significance rather than public display, and it exemplifies one of painting's celebrated purposes, expressed by art theorists from Alberti in Florence to Dürer in Nuremberg: to provide an image of the absent for their friends or families long after their death.

Bust portraits in terracotta, stemming from ancient Roman models (see illus. 12 and 13), also commemorated leading public figures in Renaissance Florence.[13] A good example by Benedetto da Maiano (1442–1497) is inscribed with the name of its sitter: *Pietro Mellini* (1474; illus. 55). Maiano's rich detail in his terracotta sketch model for the bust survives only in a close copy (a similar Maiano bust of leading Florentine merchant-banker Filippo Strozzi is in Berlin, Sculpture Collection).[14] A prominent merchant, Mellini was responsible for the donation of a large marble pulpit, also by Maiano, in the Franciscan Church of Santa Croce in Florence. Almost certainly this likeness was based on a life cast in wax or gesso of the sitter's features, stressing the uniqueness of the individual but also leaving a record to commemorate his contributions as a citizen. Such portrait images

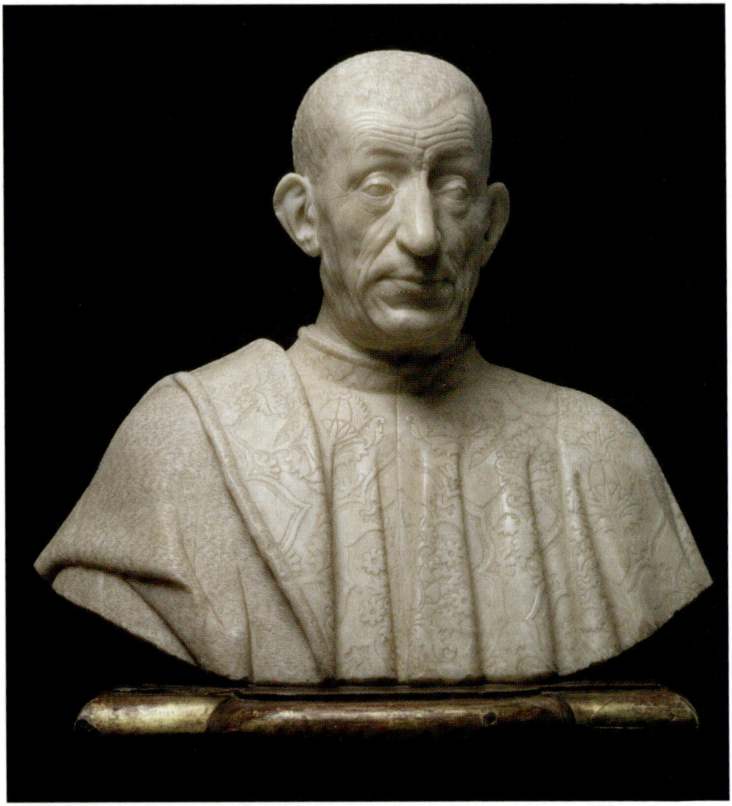

55 Benedetto da Maiano, *Pietro Mellini*, 1474, marble.

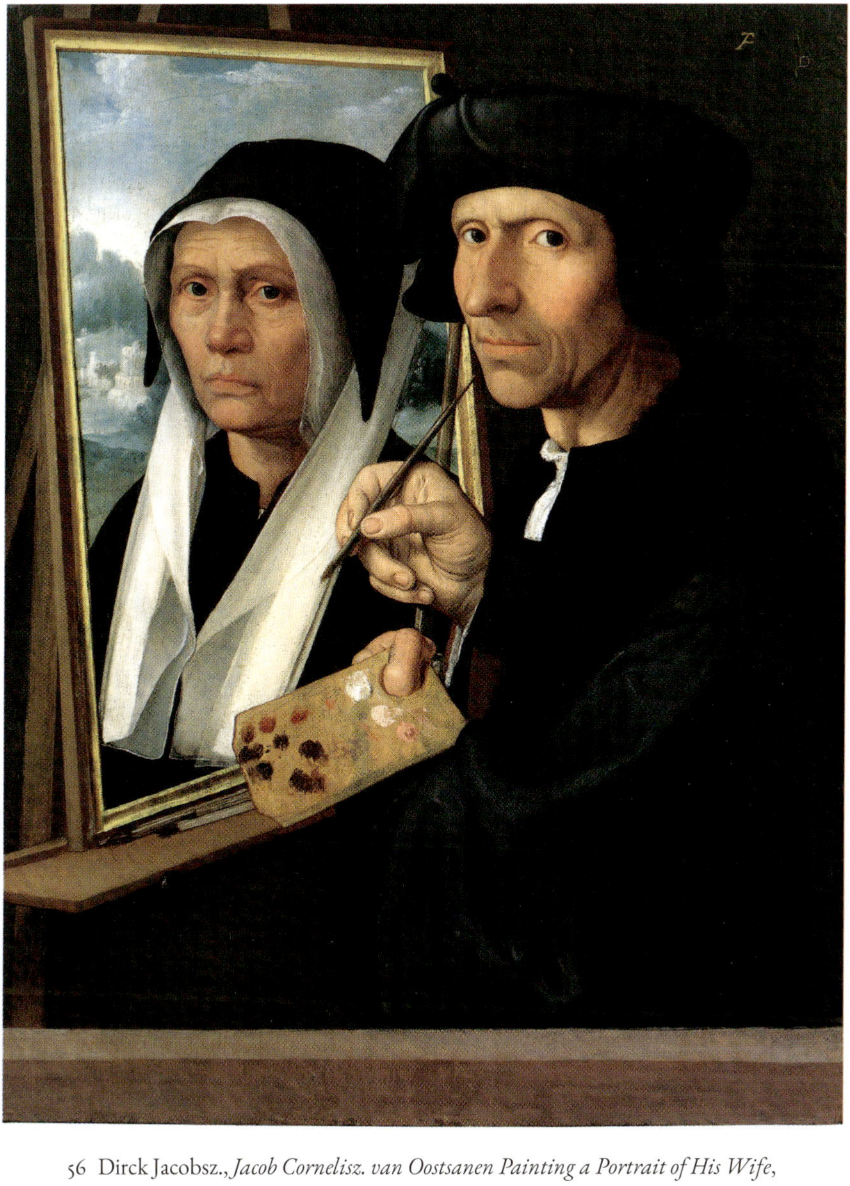

56 Dirck Jacobsz., *Jacob Cornelisz. van Oostsanen Painting a Portrait of His Wife*, *c.* 1550, oil on panel.

of pious donors, particularly as ex votos in gratitude for healing or miracles, appeared in both medieval and Renaissance churches.[15] A contemporary of Ghirlandaio, Maiano brought the same unsparing verisimilitude to his likeness's bald head and wrinkled brows or cheeks, again evoking the verism of ancient Roman bust portraiture. In the case of *Mellini*, Maiano devoted just as much attention to detail for the sitter's elaborate brocade costume.

A double portrait of an old couple that also served as a private family memorial was cleverly devised by the Dutch painter Dirck Jacobsz., son of an Amsterdam painter, Jacob Cornelisz. van Oostsanen (*c.* 1550; illus. 56).[16] Jacobsz.'s image shows his father busy at his easel, working on a portrait of his wife Anna. Thus the painter-son is able to portray his own father and also to pay tribute to both his parents by simulating her portrait being painted by her painter-husband. A self-portrait, signed by Jacob Cornelisz., survives (dated 1533; Amsterdam), which confirms the identity of the depicted artist in the picture; however, the hazy blue background landscape behind Anna is characteristic of Dirck's own pictures. So successfully has the son simulated a plausible work of his father that the picture was long regarded as the work of Jacob Cornelisz. himself. Like the nearly contemporary Dürer tribute to his mentor Wolgemut, here both faces are recorded with sympathy and respect by their adult, professional painter-son, but he also represents true, ageing likenesses of their faces and hands (Anna would have been around sixty as shown; Jacob died in 1533).

Already in the ancient world, bust portraits celebrated living thinkers, both philosophers and authors (cf. Rubens's drawing, illus. 20, after a so-called bust of Seneca, who was both

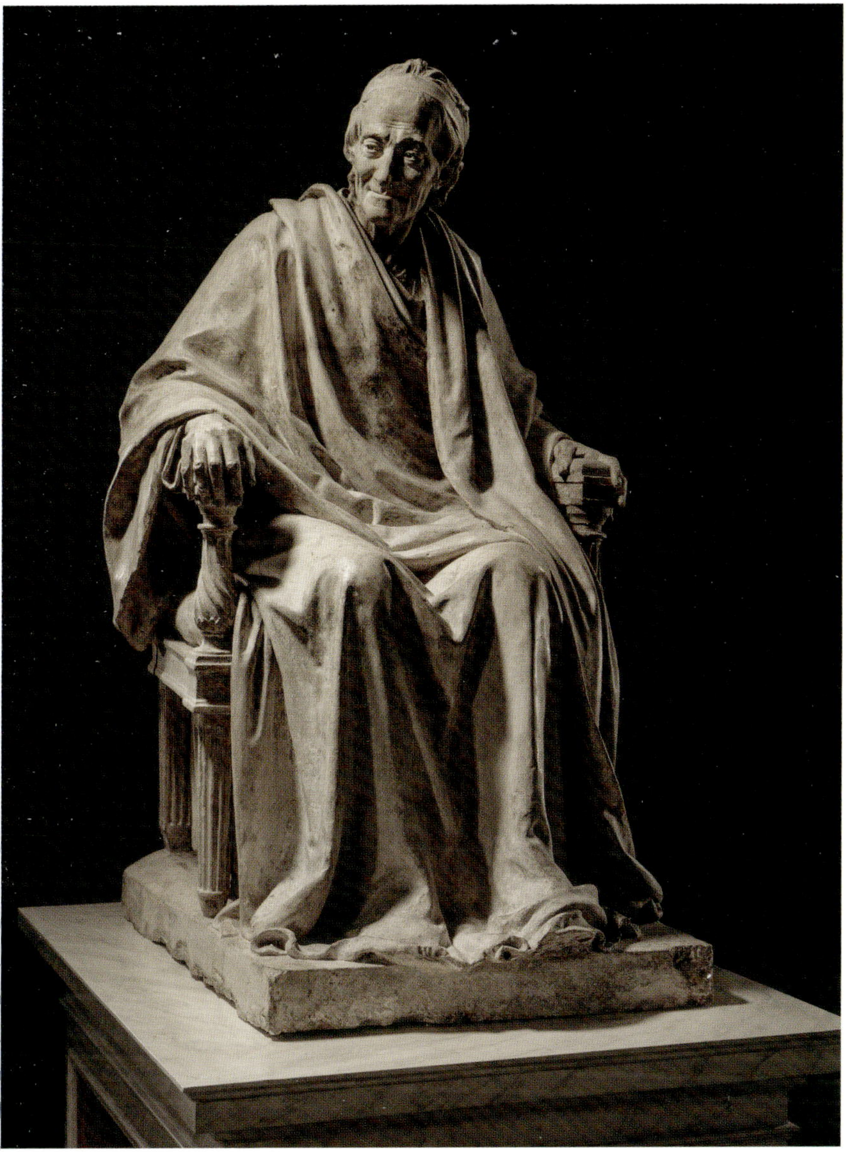

57 Jean-Antoine Houdon, *Seated Voltaire*, 1781, terracotta.

a dramatist and a Stoic philosopher).[17] Italian Renaissance medals and busts continued this tradition, such as the medal made of Leon Battista Alberti.[18] In the Enlightenment Europe of the later eighteenth century Jean-Antoine Houdon (1741–1828) led the way in carving likenesses both as busts and sometimes as full-length figures, not only of leading political leaders or inventors but of celebrated thinkers and authors (some from the previous century), or even performers.[19] Foremost among French thinkers was the philosopher, historian and author Voltaire (1694–1778), for whom Houdon made both busts and full-length marble carvings.[20]

The sculptor first made a sketch in clay, fired as terracotta, in 1778, as the old man sat in the studio. From that initial sketch Voltaire's niece commissioned a life-sized statue, completed in 1781, showing the philosopher seated and dressed in his dressing-gown, in echo of antique garb (1781; illus. 57). The antique bust and marble were commissioned and delivered to the avid Francophile Empress Catherine the Great of Russia (today in the Hermitage, St Petersburg). Another full-length marble version is in Paris at the Comédie-Française. Houdon began with a bust of Voltaire 'tête nu' – that is, without the periwig customarily worn by eighteenth-century men. The bald head, small eyes and sagging cheeks all point to the age of the sitter, then in his final year of life (he would die a mere two months later). This model remained the most frequently copied of all his Voltaire images (in marble, bronze, plaster and terracotta). Adding to the informality and candour of the bust image is the sitter's naked, undraped torso, which complements his wry, toothless smile. This affectionate image recalls the personal tributes, such as Dürer's, discussed above.

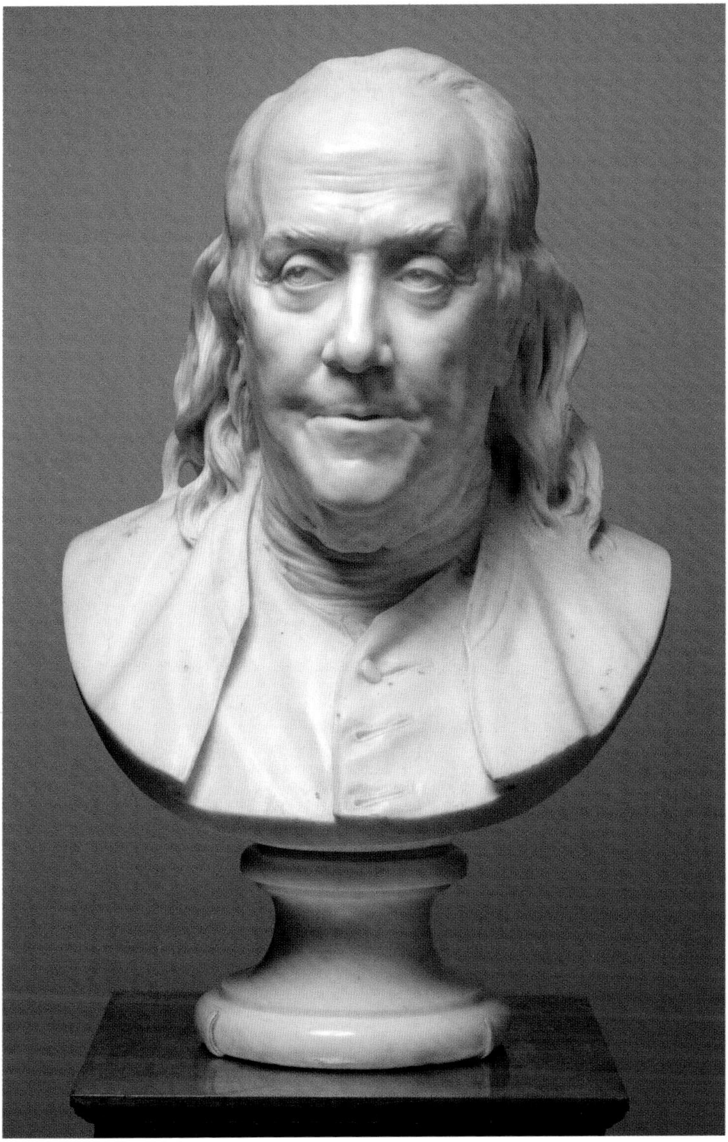

58 Jean-Antoine Houdon, *Benjamin Franklin*, 1779, marble.

Houdon then generated several other, more formal bust versions of Voltaire: one with wig and cloaked in contemporary costume ('à la française'); another ('à la antique') draping him in a toga to associate him most closely with ancient precedents. Houdon's full-length terracotta version shows Voltaire seated on his throne-like chair in his dressing-gown, head turned downward and to the right with a mild air of condescension emanating from his smile and deep-set eyes. Houdon's admiration emerges from this own description of the finished work: 'Marble statue of Voltaire, seated in antique chair, in the mantle of the philosopher, his head circled by the fillet of immortality.' This commemoration of the achievements of the great French *philosophe* more closely resembles the formal tributes of royal portraiture.

Another of Houdon's multiple bust images (1779, Philadelphia Museum of Art, illus. 58) was devoted to Benjamin Franklin (1706–1790), minister to France from the young United States from 1776 to 1785, but also renowned as a scientist and publisher.[21] Its lifelike quality stems from the slightly parted lips and careful modelling of the eyes (with projecting pupils in the manner of Gian Lorenzo Bernini), wrinkled brow and unwigged hair falling from a bald pate to his shoulders. Dressed in the simple tailoring of his Philadelphia home, Franklin conforms to an increasing contemporary emphasis on modernity, extending even to the depiction of current events in the grand manner of scenes from history, such as Benjamin West's *Benjamin Franklin Drawing Electricity from the Sky* (*c.* 1816, see illus. 45) or his painting *The Death of General Wolfe* (1770; Ottawa).[22]

The American patriot and painter Charles Willson Peale (1741–1827) developed a gallery of famous heroes of the American

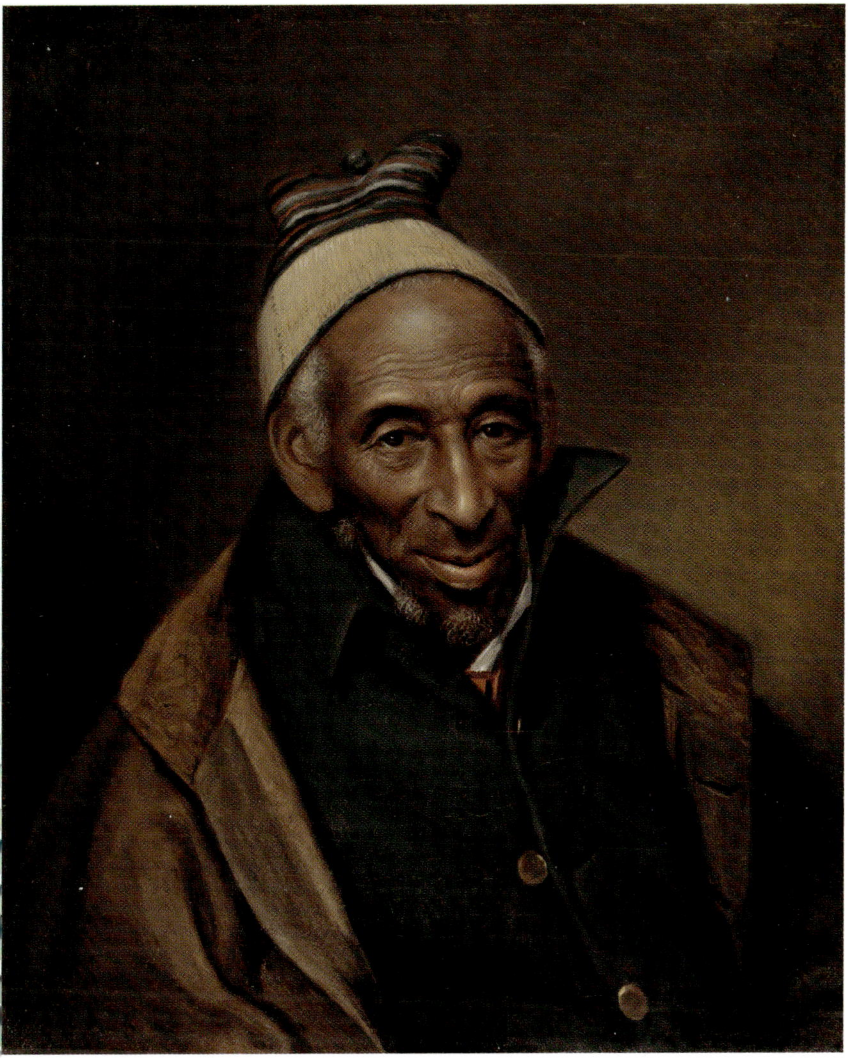

59 Charles Willson Peale, *Yarrow Mamout*, 1819, oil on canvas.

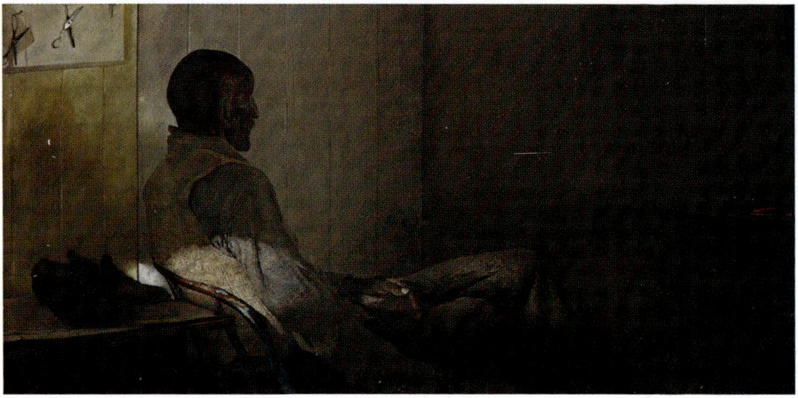

60 Andrew Wyeth, *That Gentleman*, 1960, tempera on panel.

Revolution as a kind of hall of fame in what he eventually developed as the first museum in the young country. Founded in 1784, it featured 'the Portraits of Illustrious Personages . . . Also a Collection of preserved Beasts . . . Fossils, Minerals . . . and other curious objects, natural and artificial'.[23] In this same eclectic spirit Peale (then in his seventies) made a portrait in 1819 of a freed slave, Yarrow Mamout (illus. 59), who claimed to have been captured in 1752 at age sixteen from his native Guinea and freed in 1796, making him 134 years old.[24] He was a homeowner and possessed stock. Remarkably, this portrait hung amid 'illustrious Personages' in the Peale Museum and was given their same dimensions, integrated into the total installation in Independence Hall. Mamout's portrait may have been intended to display the variety of human forms as well as an astonishing longevity, but there is also a sympathetic attention to the features of the old man, including his grizzled goatee and washboard forehead wrinkles. The focus of attention and modelling fixes firmly on his face, including light that reflects above his brow and, on his nose, light from his dark skin. A practising Muslim who still wrote in Arabic, Mamout (a variant on Muhammed) wears a wool cap akin to a Muslim *kufi* skullcap. Peale's work remains an isolated and sympathetic early portrait of an African American.

A century and a half later, Andrew Wyeth (1917–2009) painted *That Gentleman* (1960; illus. 60), depicting another African American, seen in an informal seated pose but from behind and in near profile. The room is dimly lit and composed in a limited palette of harmonious earth tones. The only bright spot lands on the rough jacket and the worn hand of the sitter. Wyeth explained that this aged man, without hair or teeth, was a neighbour and friend named Tom Clark. He characterized him with the respectful outlook of old-age praise: 'His voice is gentle, his wit is keen, and his wisdom enormous. He is not a character but a very dignified gentleman who might otherwise have gone uncorded.'[25] The setting is a humble wooden room, whose late afternoon atmosphere suggests quiet contemplation. According to Wyeth, the work's title came from Mr Clark himself, who referred even to inanimate objects or insects as 'that gentleman'. In its pictorial setting and informal pose from behind, the full environment of this sitter is revealed, along with the affection bestowed on him by his painter-neighbour.

Photography immediately expanded the capacity for portraits, especially once exposure time had been decreased across the nineteenth century. By the spring of 1840, less than a year after the invention of the daguerreotype, two commercial portrait studios had opened in New York and Philadelphia.[26] Their subtle tonal scale and focused detail made daguerreotypes the overwhelmingly favoured technology for early portraiture, although they required long posing sessions by sitters. Led by

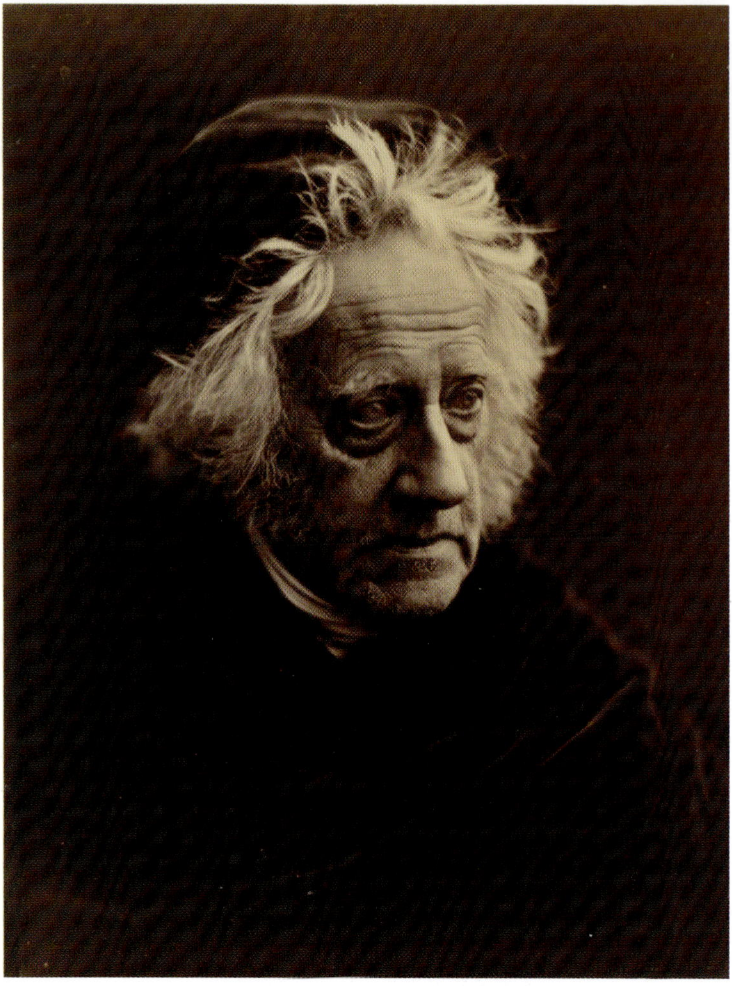

61 Julia Margaret Cameron, *Sir John Herschel*, 1867, albumen silver print.

President Abraham Lincoln and the abolitionist, writer and freed slave Frederick Douglass (the most photographed man of the entire nineteenth century, with more than 160 likenesses), prominent Americans became familiar faces through their widespread portraits. In Edinburgh, however, David Octavius Hill and Robert Adamson chose the calotype process for their collaboration on portraits (1843–7), because calotypes emphasized high contrast over sharp detail and suggested a more momentary capture.

In England Julia Margaret Cameron (1815–1879) took up photography in middle age in 1863, but she quickly aimed to make her images attain the status of artworks: 'My aspirations are to ennoble photography and to secure for it the character and uses of High Art by combining the real & Ideal and sacrificing nothing of Truth by all possible devotion to Poetry and beauty.'[27] By 1866 she was exhibiting in spaces such as the venerable Colnaghi gallery in London. Her evocative soft-focus images included religious and allegorical imagery as well as illustrations to an 1874 edition of Tennyson's *Idylls of the King*. Cameron's portraits, too, strove for ideal types, whether the Madonna or a patriarch, in an aesthetic resembling contemporary Pre-Raphaelite painting. Like modern patriarchs and wise men, Cameron particularly sought out major British intellectual figures such as Thomas Carlyle, Charles Darwin and Tennyson. For all of them she claimed to record the greatness of the inner man as well as their outer features. One favourite subject was her friend the famed astronomer and fellow experimenter with photography Sir John Herschel (1792–1871). She made a series of close-ups of his face in dramatic contrasts (1867; illus. 61), where oblique lighting brings out his age through beard stubble and the bags beneath his eyes. Herschel's shock of uncombed white hair frames his face within a dark cap and cloak, suggesting the active mind of the polymath, as does his fixed outward stare.

Imogen Cunningham (1883–1976) is best known for her geometric imagery, especially close-ups of female nudes and plants or flowers, much like contemporary art by fellow photographer Edward Weston and the painter Georgia O'Keeffe. But her later work, made during her own old age in the 1960s and '70s, focuses on images of older people, for example, in her series *After Ninety* (1976). In 1936 she made *My Father at Ninety*, a portrait that highlights her father's long white beard and walking stick as he sits on a pile of firewood. In a 1974 photograph by her associate Judy Dater (b. 1941), Imogen at age ninety appears as a subject in her own right, white-haired and with her camera around her neck, as she encounters a beautiful nude woman, Twinka Thiebaud, under a tree in Yosemite National Park. The photo juxtaposes age with youth, clothing with nudity, and it also poses fundamental issues about the camera as voyeur, even when wielded by a woman already well known for her own photos of female nudes.

In old age Cunningham sat for numerous other portraits. One of them, by Abe Frajndlich, shows her at 91 before a large bush, holding an open pair of pruning shears like a camera; as in all of her late self-portraits, she wears spectacles, and although her prominent white fringe and upraised wrinkled, spotted hands reveal her age, she is also wearing a Vietnam-era protest pendant, which aligns her with youthful politics. However, in one of the most striking self-portraits (1976), Cunningham lets her white hair go wild, like a stereotype of a witch, and stands open-mouthed as if shrieking. Here she presents another juxtaposition of youth with age, as she holds an old, undated photograph, a self-portrait from early in the century (*c.* 1910) of herself as a young woman, without glasses and wearing the pinafore dress of her past. The overall image is one that encapsulates time and the ageing process itself, while still asserting

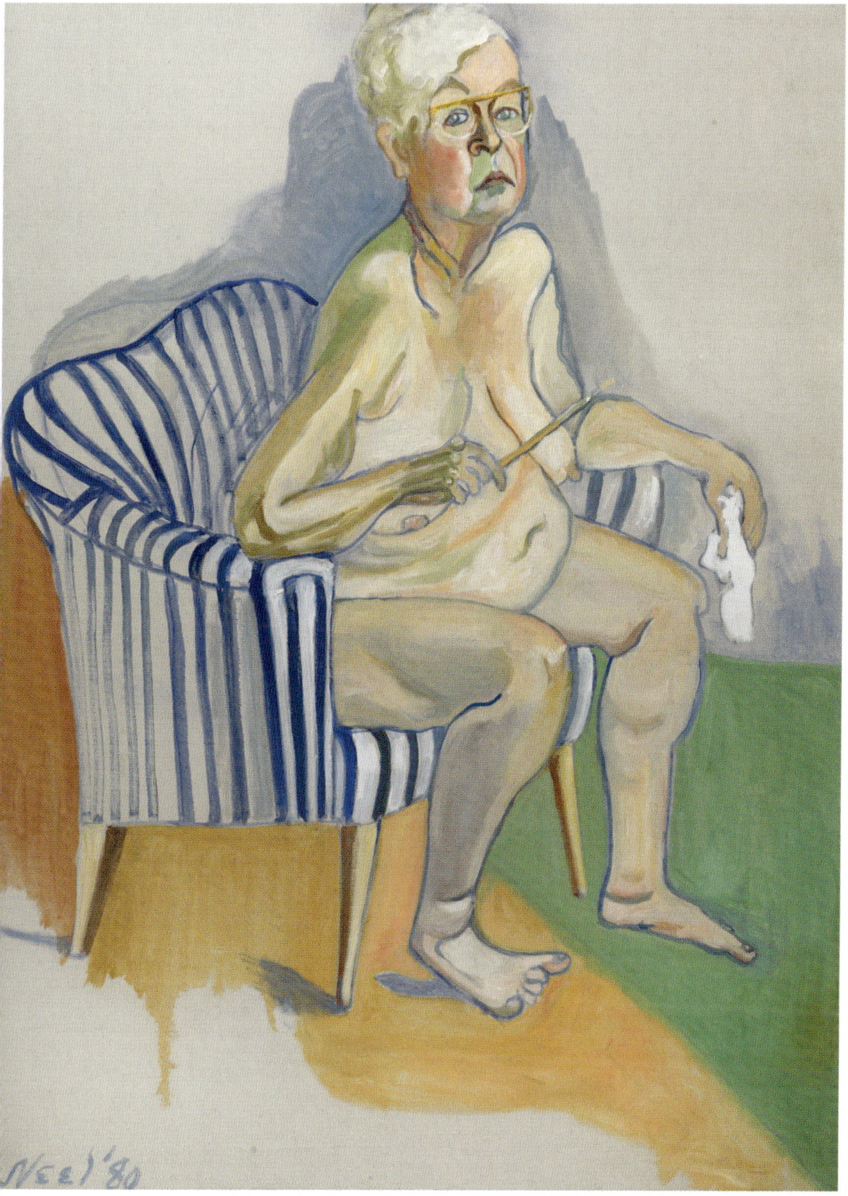

62 Alice Neel, *Self-Portrait*, 1980, oil on canvas.

the vitality and experience of Cunningham with her medium at the age of ninety.

In contrast to the polarity of youth and age in Imogen Cunningham's late self-portrait with her own earlier visage, Alice Neel (1900–1984) offers the ultimate candour of ageing in her daring self-portrait in the nude at age eighty (1980; illus. 62). Already known as a figural painter who specialized in expressive portraits of family, friends and art-world colleagues (such as Andy Warhol, topless and displaying his scar after a 1968 gunshot wound; 1970, New York, Whitney Museum), Neel never made any other self-portraits across her half-century career, but her unflinching observation of naked bodies finally turned to herself in old age. Here she shows steadfast gazing turned to herself in her later years, showing such visible bodily signs of old age as drooping breasts and a flabby stomach, complemented by white hair in a bun and the need to use eyeglasses in order to view herself in the mirror, brush in one hand and a cloth in the other. Neel rests on a blue chair and casts light blue shadows that bring her body forward against an otherwise neutral grey background. The shock effect of this image amounts to a conflation of Dater's photo of Imogen Cunningham with Twinka Thiebaud in the forest, as if Cunningham herself as an old woman were shown naked. This unprecedented display of what many older women attempt to hide marks a significant achievement in the representation of age in art and an overt rejection of the denial of ageing that Queen Elizabeth I maintained throughout her reign. Neel inverts and exposes the prejudice of traditional art in Europe, which so often depicted the female body by emphasizing both youth and beauty, often for the delectation of the male gaze. That this is a self-portrait, painted by a female artist

– and a portraitist in her own right – makes Alice Neel a radical revisionist and iconoclast as well as a champion of honesty in old age.

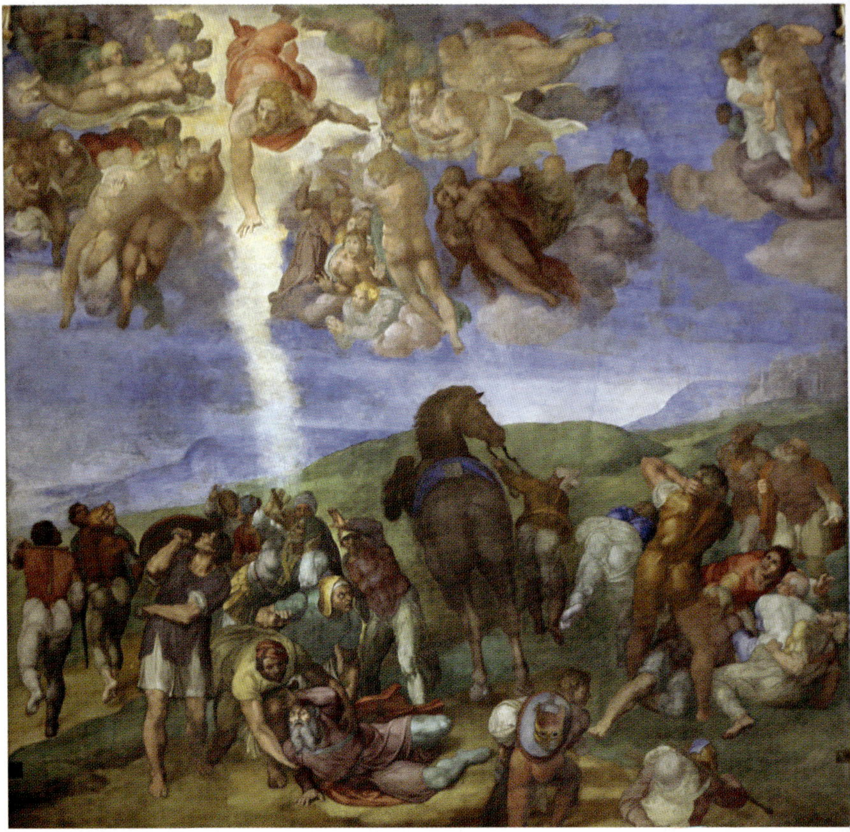

63 Michelangelo, *The Conversion of St Paul*, *c.* 1542–5, fresco, Pauline Chapel, Vatican City.

Five

Old-Age Style

It is evident that those who have retained their
creative powers into old age take a very poor view
of human life and develop as their only defence
a kind of transcendental pessimism.

KENNETH CLARK[1]

No one has full mastery before reaching the end
of his art and his life.

MICHELANGELO[2]

Let us cherish and love old age; for it is full of pleasure
if one knows how to use it.
Fruits are most welcome when almost over;
youth is most charming at its close.

SENECA, 'Letters to Lucillus', XII

When great artists have mastered their craft across decades but have also aged in the process, that combination of circumstances occasions new possibilities. Although the examples could be multiplied, this final chapter will consider the new turns of imagery, both in form and chosen content, for a group of long-lived artists, often masters of multiple media, to examine what innovations and personal challenges they adopted in their last decades.[3]

Michelangelo Buonarroti (1475–1564) mastered multiple media. In addition to his primary work in marble sculpture he achieved renown as both an architect and a painter, while also excelling in drawing and vernacular poetry.[4] His later years are normally gauged from after the 1534–41 completion of his massive *Last Judgement* fresco behind the altar in the Sistine Chapel. But the artist's remaining three decades were still productive, not least in architecture at St Peter's and elsewhere in Rome.[5] But in murals, sculpture and spare drawings Michelangelo continued to explore fundamental Christian themes with a new intensity. The years 1536–46 evoked his most prolific period of poetry and coincided with his well-known friendship with the noblewoman Vittoria Colonna (1490–1547). The spirituality of his religious poems (as well as those of Colonna) derives from consciousness of a direct personal relationship with God, reinforced by some serious brushes with mortal illness that he had in the mid-1540s.[6] Michelangelo's late work focuses almost exclusively on death and salvation through the cross, concerns that emerge repeatedly in his poetry.

In the wake of that powerful spiritual renewal and at the demand of his greatest patron, Pope Paul III, Michelangelo in his seventies also painted a pair of frescoes in the private papal Pauline Chapel (1542–50), adjacent to the Sistine Chapel. Its subjects feature the Conversion of Saul into St Paul, the pope's namesake, as well as the Crucifixion of Peter, the first pope.[7] In the former scene (illus. 63) Christ, sharply foreshortened, hovers with his own troops of angels in the heavens, and the saint below has been struck blind, inspiring fear among his crowd of followers. With counterpoint in the latter narrative, a muscular Peter, crucified upside down, still lives; as his cross is hoisted, he stares sternly outward at the viewer, as if in appeal by the spiritual leader of the Church to keep the faith, while soldiers and witnesses ascend and descend the Roman mount. Both scenes dramatize their events through strong figural actions in space before a minimal background. But most striking of all in the Pauline Chapel is the representation of blind Saul not as youthful, but with the white-bearded features of Michelangelo himself, as if the artist was identifying personally with the notion of this moment of spiritual rebirth.[8] He also transposed Paul III's features onto St Peter, just as in the previous mural for the pope, the Sistine *Last Judgement*.

Even more strikingly personal is the artist's final carving contribution to Florence, his *Pietà* (*c.* 1547–55; illus. 64), likely intended for his own tomb and larger than life, his second-largest sculpture.[9] An ambitious attempt to fashion four figures instead of just the Virgin and Christ left the old carver so disappointed that he smashed off the slung leg of Christ (which also could have been read sexually), so the work was never finished. Significantly, he included his own features (illus. 65) for the standing aged male figure behind the Virgin (already reduced in size herself), who supports the massive body of Christ. He is usually identified as the Pharisee disciple Nicodemus (traditionally regarded as a sculptor),[10] but possibly could also be Joseph of Arimathea, the wealthy member of the Sanhedrin who called for the body of Christ and laid it in the tomb (Mark 15:43–6). In John 3:1–17 Nicodemus asks Jesus the crucial question about being born again to see the kingdom of God. Mary Magdalene,

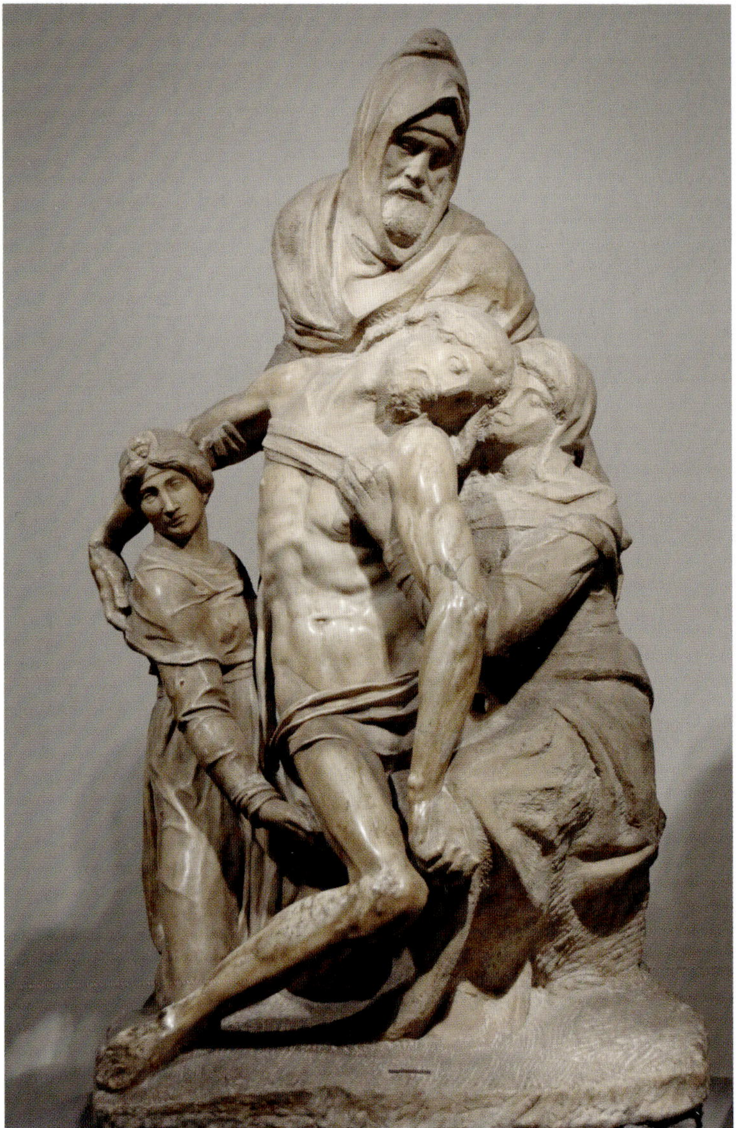

64 Michelangelo, *Pietà*, *c.* 1547–55, marble.

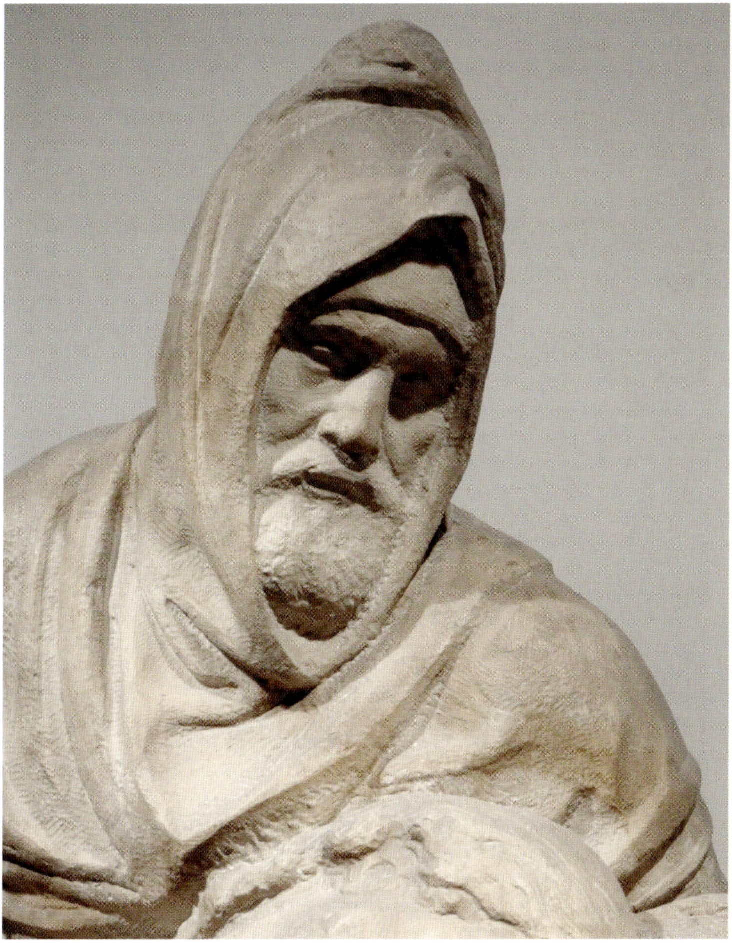

65 Michelangelo, self-portrait as Nicodemus, detail of illus. 64.

also included as a supporting figure, albeit in smaller scale, was the most fervent lover of Jesus and the first to discover him in his resurrected form (John 20:17). Thus Michelangelo's late sculpture – as much an Entombment as a Pietà – represents a kind of personal prayer that he can be the bearer of Christ's sacrificial body and a companion of the saints. The significance of this figure group and of his own inserted vertical likeness as Christ-bearer lies in its proposed placement over his own tomb.

Michelangelo's late drawings are spare in both form and content.[11] Many of them focus intently on the Crucifixion, with the minimal witness figures of the Virgin and St John the Evangelist below. These large drawings show signs of reworking, perhaps of a faltering hand but left as visible palimpsests, almost as if the artist wanted to show his own meditational revisits to this fundamental subject as a spiritual exercise (*c.* 1560–64; illus. 66). As Paul Joannides describes these 'transcendental' works: 'Physicality is subordinated to idea, the possibilities of pleasure eliminated.'[12] The use of black chalk as medium further blurs details of musculature and body structure, usually closely related to his sculptures. Michelangelo's earlier passion for bodily perfection and sensuous form has been replaced by religious concentration by means of the reductive flat and frontal focus on the merest figural essentials, akin to medieval precedents.

Titian (Tiziano Vecellio, *c.* 1488/90–1576) lied about his age, and in what was probably his late eighties in his latter years, he was credited with an age of almost one hundred. In any case, he was long-lived and productive throughout, with a career spanning seven decades.[13] To set off the painter's later style we might begin with the famous *poesie*, mythological subjects sent to King Philip II of Spain between 1551 and 1562. These works greatly influenced later painters, especially Rubens and Velázquez, with their increasingly assertive, broad brushstrokes that signal the artist and act of painting fully as much as the ambition to achieve pictorial illusion or verisimilitude. During the 1560s Titian's colour palette, a hallmark of his earlier pictures, narrowed, and

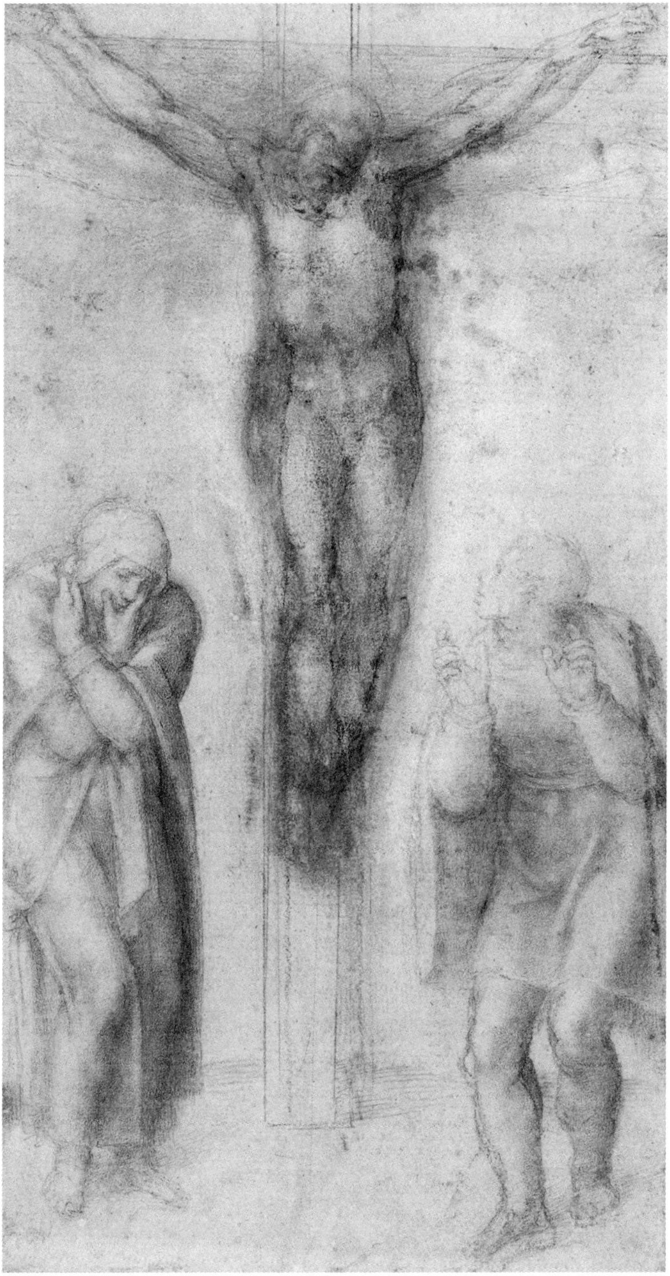

66 Michelangelo, *Crucifixion*, *c.* 1560–64, chalk drawing.

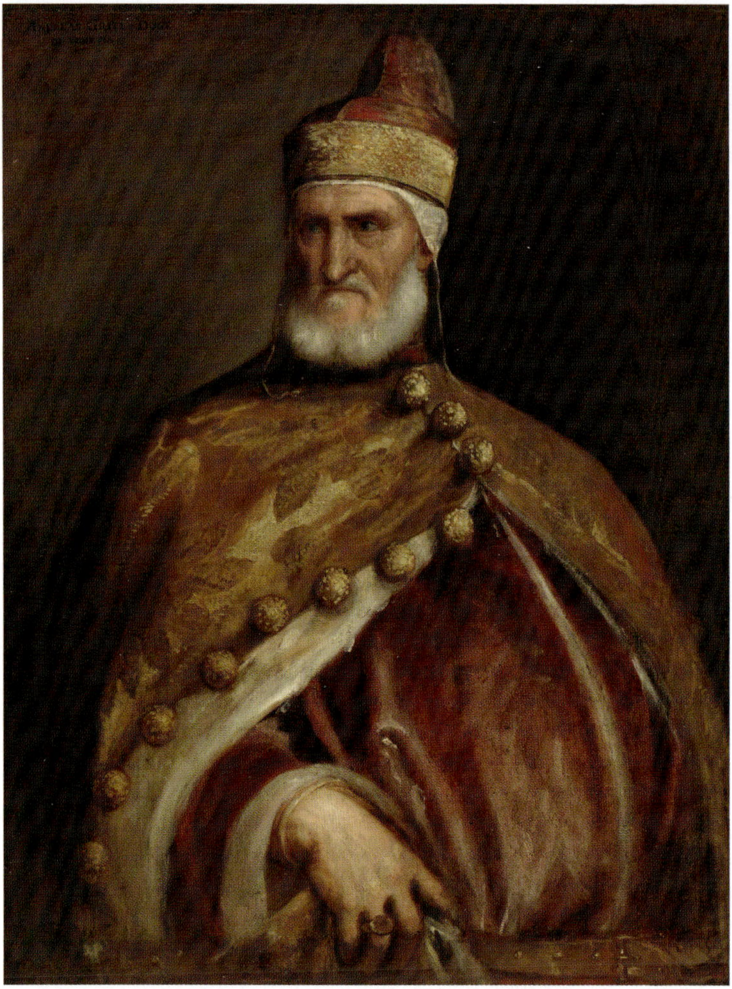

67 Titian, *Doge Andrea Gritti*, *c.* 1546–50, oil on canvas.

his brushstrokes became increasingly detached from representation while presenting pigment as substance; moreover, his subjects, even reprises of earlier subjects (such as *Crowning with Thorns*, *c.* 1572/6), often emphasized tragic and cruel actions and declined to pursue dominant Renaissance emphasis on bodily beauty and heroic deeds.[14] Like the contemporary critics of Impressionism, many observers have found that these works appear unfinished, or lacking in 'finish'. Once again, as with Michelangelo's late drawings, one can attribute this effect to age and declining fine motor dexterity with the brush, but this

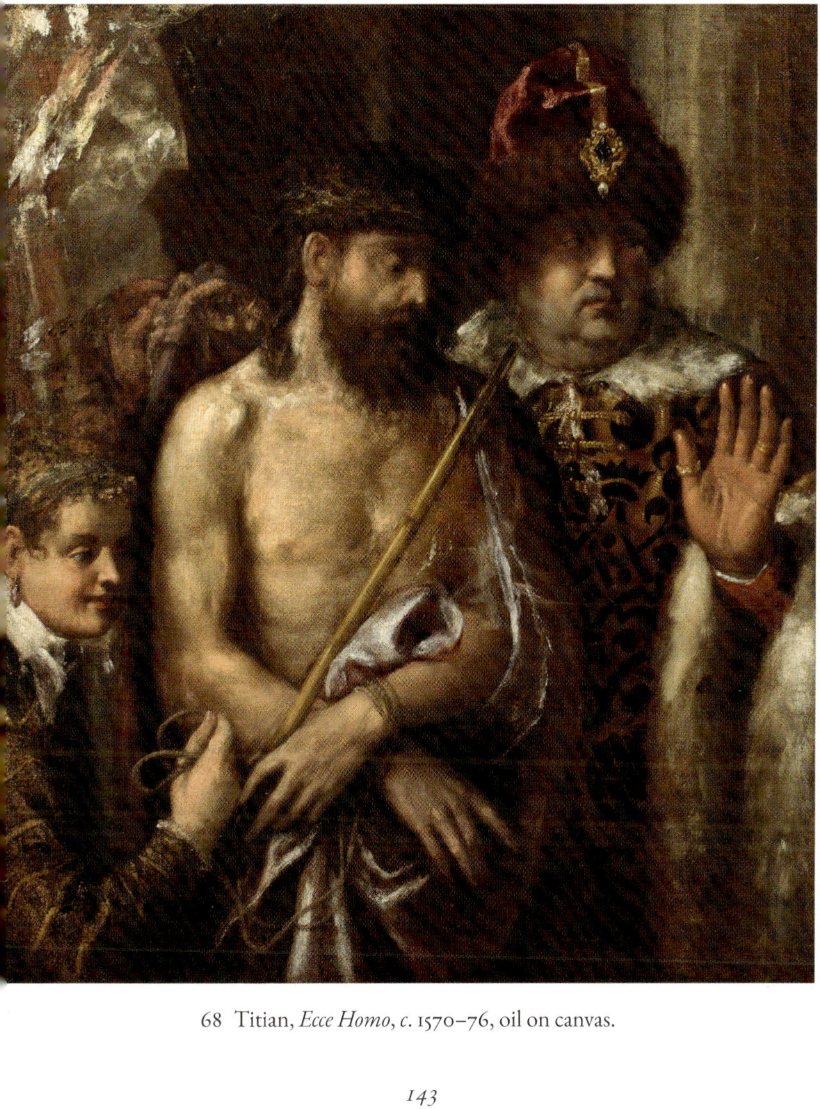

68 Titian, *Ecce Homo*, *c.* 1570–76, oil on canvas.

brushwork also suggests a gestural assertion born of experience and artistic self-confidence.[15]

A few examples will display Titian's marked departures in his late works. Already in his portrait *Doge Andrea Gritti* (*c.* 1546–50; illus. 67) the bulk of the sitter and the visibly layered brushwork of his golden cape of office suggest both physicality and power. Not only does the boundary of the canvas seem too narrow to contain this commanding figure, but his hand grasping his cape at the bottom of the painting expressly suggests even further extension, arbitrarily framed.

The same intensified interaction with a half-length figure of a portrait extends into an engaged suggestion of eyewitness proximity in a half-length narrative, such as the late *Ecce Homo* (*c.* 1570–76; illus. 68), one of the paintings that has been claimed to be unfinished owing to the sketchy brushwork for the torches in the upper left.[16] That flickering application, however, seems appropriate for the insubstantiality of fire itself in this nocturnal moment. Moreover, the degree of refinement of paint varies throughout the painting, from the careful rendering of Pilate's jewel to the contrast between his upraised hand in physical presence, silhouetted against his almost illegibly sketched ermine-trimmed sleeve. Attention by the artist to nuances of shadowy faces contrasts with the material surfaces of pigment elsewhere, especially on Jesus' bound hands and lighted shoulder, or his nearly transparent covering drapery. Focus remains clearly on the two main figures, Jesus and Pilate, as Titian adjusts his means to the purpose of his painting, just as in the *Gritti* portrait. Here the physical abjection of Christ in contrast to the luxury enjoyed by jowly Pilate underscores the pathos of the Passion. As Marcia B. Hall observes, Titian 'has placed himself between the text and the viewer as interpreter . . . and he does it with his unconventional compositions, moments of becoming, awkward poses, light, colour and above all brushstroke'.[17]

In mythological subjects such as the last image of Titian's *poesie*, his *Rape of Europa* (1562), the artist used unblended brushstrokes in the foreground, for the bull's fur and seafoam, alongside thin stretches of pigment for the distant shoreline. But Titian also explored the extremes of physicality in both manual execution and theme in his *Flaying of Marsyas* (*c.* 1570–76; illus. 69), another painting that has been debated as perhaps unfinished.[18] The subject (Ovid, *Metamorphoses* 6:384–400) is artistic arrogance, akin to Arachne's challenge to Minerva or, still more, to Apollo's contest with Pan and the ill-fated misjudgement of Midas. But this punishment produces gruesome physical torture. When the satyr Marsyas boasts of his superior reed-playing, Apollo punishes his presumption by tying him to a tree and flaying him alive. The god appears at the upper left, next to the offending pipes, which hang from the tree. Apollo wears his signature laurel wreath as he calmly bows on a contemporary *lira da braccio* (like his more usual classical lyre) during this unwatchable torment, which is inflicted on the satyr by a laurelled youthful assistant (or possibly the god himself) wielding a knife.[19] Marsyas hangs upside down from the tree, his goat feet suspended on top. Titian's thick layers of pigment that model the body, including red paint for blood, suggest layers of peeling skin like a carcass. Adding to the horror, a lapdog at the bottom slurps up the flowing blood. At right, a Midas-like greybeard sits in thought, a pose associated with melancholy (compare Dürer's *St Jerome,* illus. 18) and appropriate to this cruel tragedy. This old man echoes the aged painter himself in his final years, reflecting on the aspirations – but also on the final, material limitations – of his art.

But beyond Ovid's mythic world of transformations, Titian's ultimate testament, perhaps intended for his own tomb, was his *Pietà* (*c.* 1576; illus. 70).[20] As with Michelangelo's Florentine multi-figure sculpture, Titian did not limit his composition to just the Virgin with her dead son on her lap. Those protagonists, who appear isolated within a rusticated classical niche with gold mosaics of Byzantine-Venetian tradition with winged victories

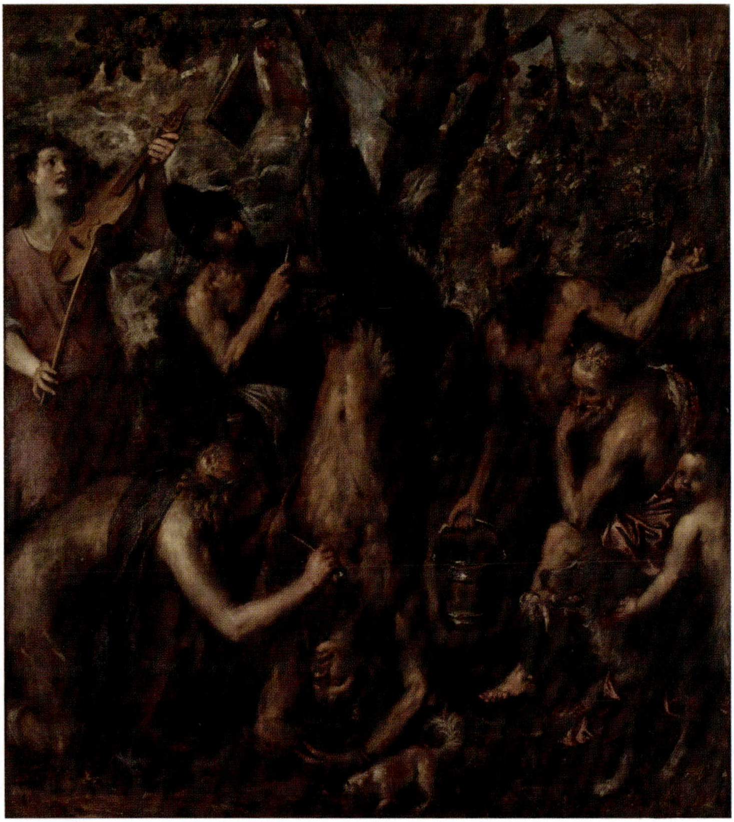

69 Titian, *Flaying of Marsyas*, *c.* 1570–76, oil on canvas.

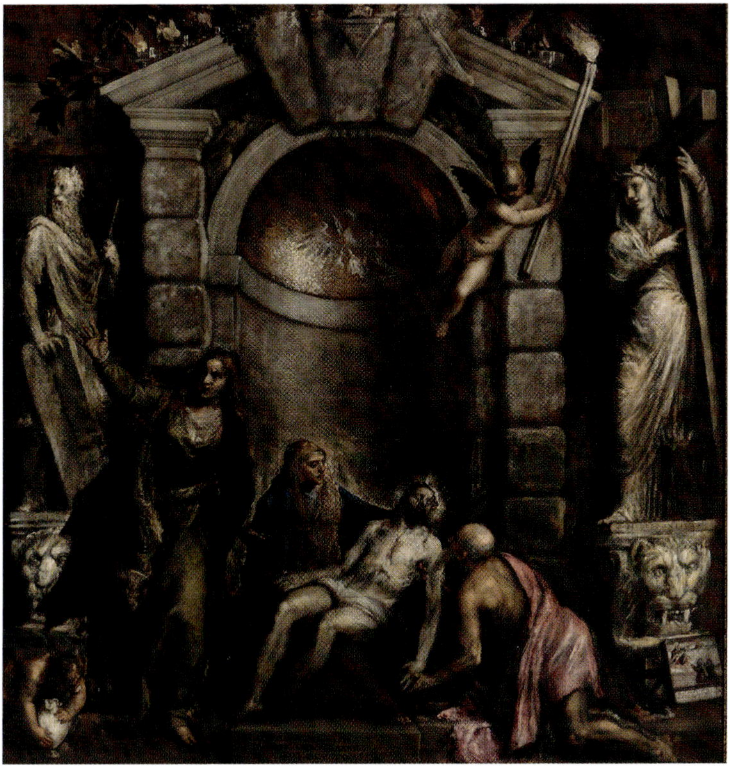

70 Titian, *Pietà*, *c.* 1576, oil on canvas.

in the spandrels, are flanked by statues of Moses with the Tablets of the Law and the Hellespontine Sibyl. The priestess bears the cross and crown of thorns, thus balancing Jewish and pagan, Law and Grace. The two carvings stand on bases with lions, the symbol of St Mark, the patron saint of Venice. Again Mary Magdalene appears at viewer left, standing with her arms outstretched in grief. At right, kneeling below and before Christ (rather than contemplating a crucifix, as in other Titian versions), is the penitent St Jerome, a recurrent subject for Titian during his later years.[21] But his white beard and profile link this figure to the likeness of aged Titian himself, in a final act of perpetual humility, prayer and hope of salvation.

The prolific and long-lived Gian Lorenzo Bernini (1598–1680) was Rome's greatest sculptor of the seventeenth century. His works, beginning as a prodigy with a sculptor father, spanned six productive decades.[22] Bernini was a highly public figure, patronized by all the popes of his lifetime and adept in architecture as well as sculpture, with occasional paintings and drawings, including a candid chalk self-portrait in old age (*c.* 1675–80; illus. 71). In keeping with the preoccupations that we have seen for both Michelangelo and Titian, Bernini's late works increasingly incorporate a heightened religiosity and occasional overt references to death.

When his final sponsoring pope, Alexander VII, born Fabio Chigi, commissioned two niche sculptures for the family chapel designed by Raphael in Santa Maria del Popolo in Rome, Bernini delivered two prophet figures.[23] Daniel (1655–7) kneels in prayer and stretches with hands upraised as he gazes upward to heaven; opposite him, Habakkuk (1656–61) startles and falls backwards when visited by an angel. Both figures are experiencing a spiritual epiphany. In similar fashion, for the Chigi Chapel in Siena Cathedral, two other Bernini saints (1661–3), Mary Magdalene and Jerome, wrap themselves in ecstatic rapture.[24] Mary's flowing garments cascade across her middle and fall to the floor in an objective correlative of her fervour. Jerome hugs a crucifix, which like his cloak extends beyond the confines of his niche. That all these single figures burst from their confines further indicates their spiritual animation and suggests a mystical experience.

For Alexander VII's tomb in St Peter's (1671–8; illus. 72), Bernini followed the model of his earlier work for Pope Urban

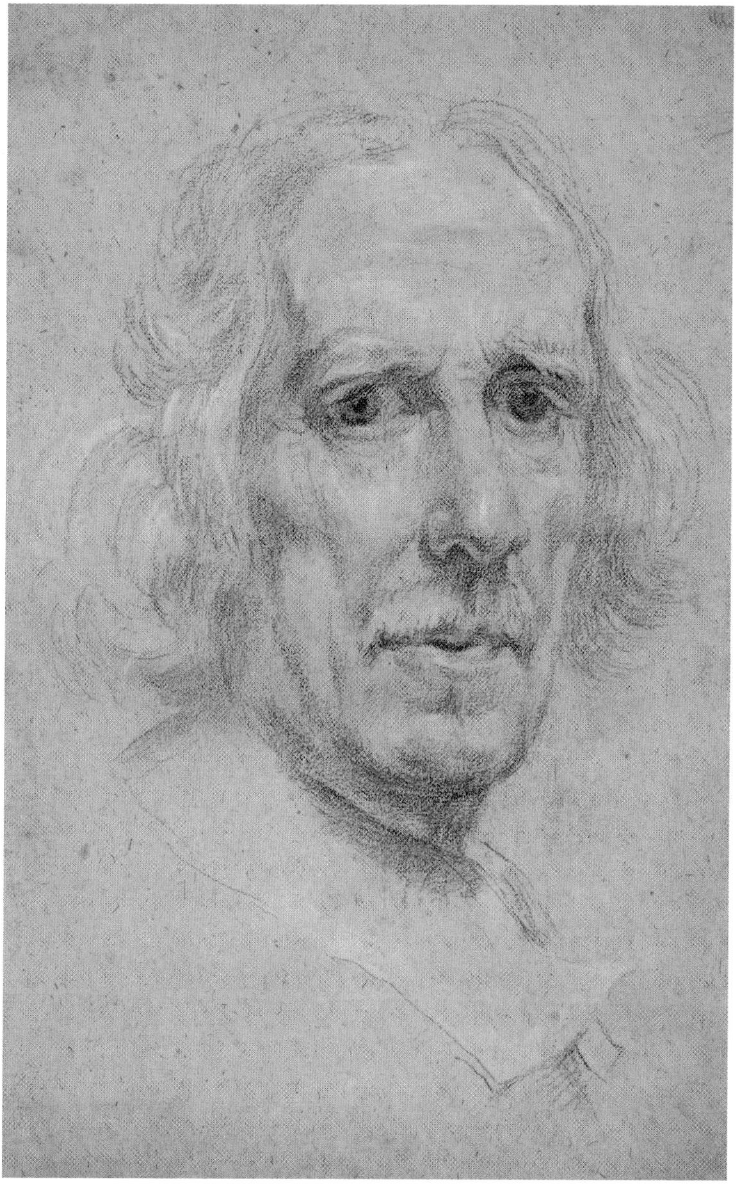

71 Gian Lorenzo Bernini, *Self-Portrait*, *c.* 1675–80, chalk drawing.

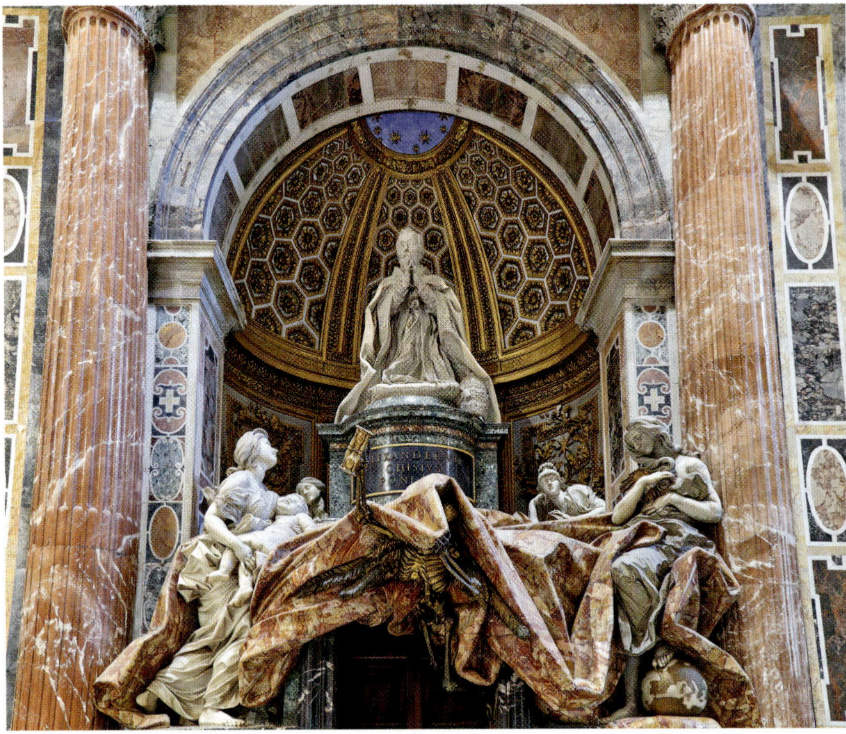

72 Gian Lorenzo Bernini, *Tomb of Pope Alexander VII*, 1671–8, marble.

VIII, born Maffeo Vincenzo Barberini (1628–47), a multi-figure pyramidal composition in both bronze and marble, with the deceased pope uppermost, still enthroned, crowned and powerful with his arm outstretched in benediction. His later concept, however, shows the Chigi pope kneeling, bareheaded, in humble yet serene prayer.[25] In the earlier tomb, flanked by allegories of Charity and Justice, the winged, skeletal figure of Death on the sarcophagus acts more in the role of Fame, inscribing Urban's name in letters of gold to ensure his immortality. For Alexander VII, in contrast, Bernini underscores the ephemeral nature of human life by showing Death in bronze, arising from under a fictive jasper drapery while brandishing an hourglass into foreground space. Once more, flanking female allegories appear, but Justice has been placed in the background behind Charity, to be replaced in the foreground by Truth, who modestly covers her nakedness with the drapery.

Bernini's ultimate representation of saintly ecstasy in death is his monument *Blessed Ludovica Albertoni* (1671–4; illus. 73.)[26] Revealed through an archway with hidden illumination, as if in a vision before the spectator, Bernini also enriched the reclining saint with a background painting by Jesuit artist Giovanni Battista Gaulli of the Virgin and Child with St Anne, framed by the sculpted heads of welcoming cherubs. The power of this religious image is best conveyed by its terracotta sketch, or *bozzetto* (*c.* 1672).[27] Lying on her couch, the saintly nun clasps

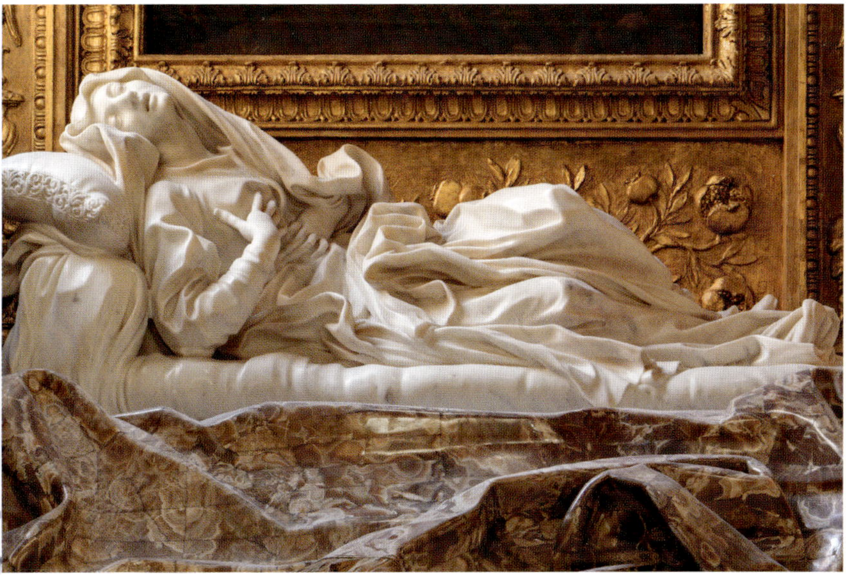

73 Gian Lorenzo Bernini, *Blessed Ludovica Albertoni*, 1671–4, marble and mixed media.

both hands tightly to her bosom with lips parted, as if she is drawing her last breath with a stricken heart. What both the sketch and the final marble sculpture emphasize is the wildly contorted drapery, especially at the saint's waist, which seems to come from within the figure or have a life of its own, conveying her ecstatic emotional state. Bernini's retention of carving ability is evident in the marble's contrasts between couch, drapery and smooth skin surfaces. As Shelley Perlove concludes,

> In the statue of the *beata*, Bernini fused Ludovica's mystical union with her death, establishing without equivocation that she triumphed over her mortality . . . The statue of Ludovica Albertoni, with its inherent promise of salvation, must have been a personal votive for the artist in his late years – a personal prayer of hope for himself and for humankind.[28]

Rembrandt van Rijn (1606–1669) spent the final decade and a half of his career in dire financial straits, which climaxed in his bankruptcy in 1656.[29] He made more self-portraits over his four-decade career than any of the artists mentioned previously, and he kept up the pace of such reflexive works until his last months.[30] One self-image (1661; Amsterdam) acts as a profession of faith: it shows the painter in an orientalizing turban looking up from reading an open gospel as he holds a sword under his arm, the martyrdom attribute of the evangelist St Paul.[31] Another shows a laughing Rembrandt at his easel painting the portrait of an ugly old woman (*c.* 1662; Cologne), in allusion to the classical legend of the painter Zeuxis (famous for taking the best features of five beautiful women to represent Helen of Troy), who literally died laughing at the assignment to paint such ugliness.[32] Perhaps

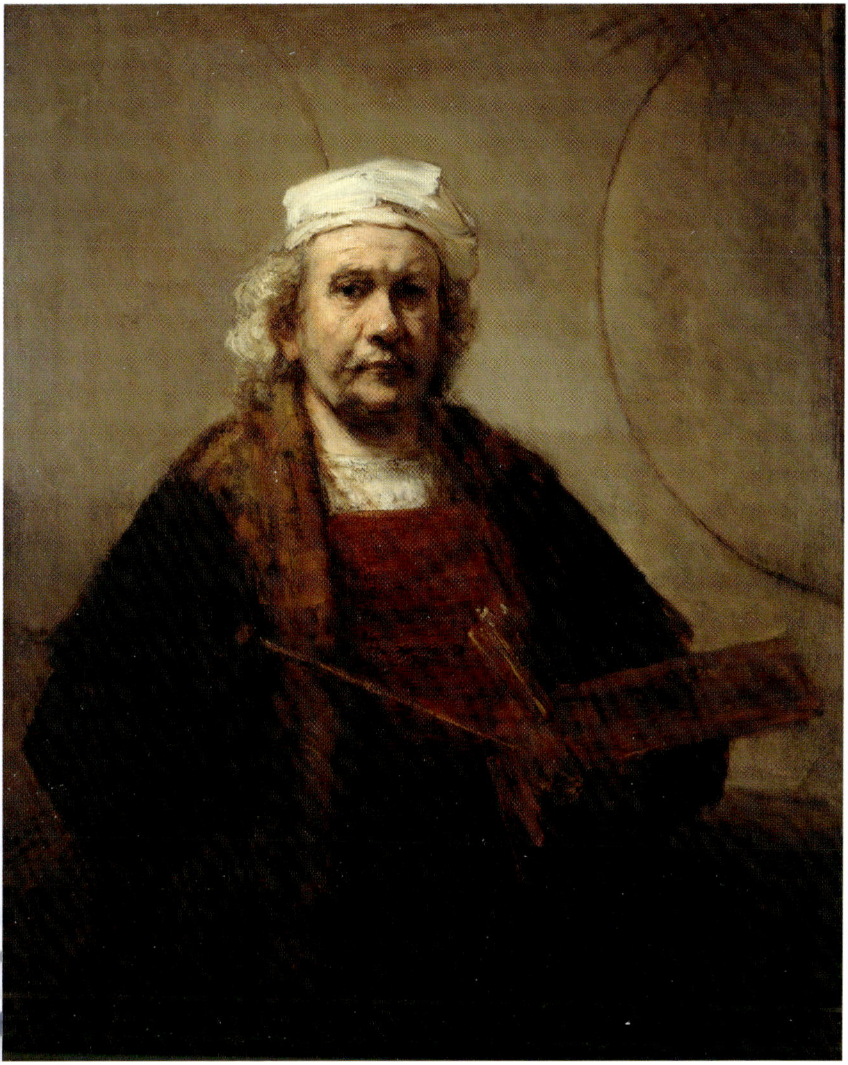

74 Rembrandt, *Self-Portrait*, *c.* 1665–9, oil on canvas.

the most candid late self-portrait is a large frontal half-length image with palette, maulstick and brushes in hand (*c.* 1665–9; illus. 74).[33] Like the self-portrait at the easel by Dirk Jacobsz. (see illus. 51), the painter is a craftsman dressed in his work clothes, with a broadly brushed white cap, applied wet-in-wet, above his unruly grey curls. His left hand is depicted as a sketchy blur that merges with the palette, and his cloak's fur trim and edges are only roughly suggested. Thick impasto strokes define Rembrandt's shadowed face as he stares outward towards the viewer. These touches – impasto, visible brushwork and relative lack of attention to finish – all characterize the textured surfaces of late Rembrandt images, much as in late Titians. A mysterious large pair of circle segments inflects the monochrome background. These have been variously interpreted, but the most plausible explanation is that they outline dual-hemisphere global maps in contemporary Dutch atlases and wall hangings, visible in the backgrounds of paintings. But they might also imply virtuoso brush control by an artist able to produce perfect circles without a compass. (According to legends about the early Renaissance painter Giotto, his talent was demonstrated precisely when the artist produced freehand circles for the pope.)[34]

In an over-life-sized multi-group narrative, *The Return of the Prodigal Son* (1663–5; illus. 75), shadowy figures at the side and rear bear silent witness to the ragged, barefoot penitent, seen from behind, who kneels and buries his shadowy profile face in the bosom of a frontal, grey-bearded father. The elder man tenderly caresses his son's shoulders, and strong overhead lighting of the protagonists adds to the pathos, suggesting ultimate divine forgiveness according to the parable (Luke 15:11–32). Like *The Denial of Peter* (see illus. 37), this quiet staging of a momentous religious narrative invites contemplation and reflection from a pious Christian viewer about proper spiritual behaviour.

The late Rembrandt also had what Kurt Bauch has called a distinctive 'iconographic style'.[35] Late subjects by Rembrandt

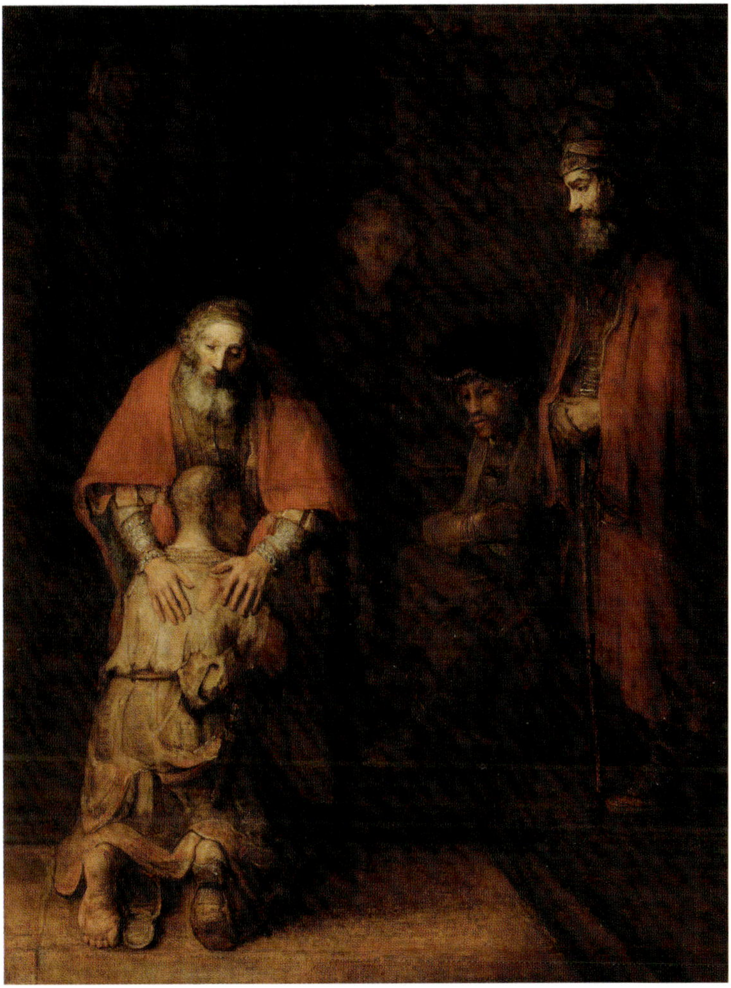

75 Rembrandt, *The Return of the Prodigal Son*, 1663–5, oil on canvas.

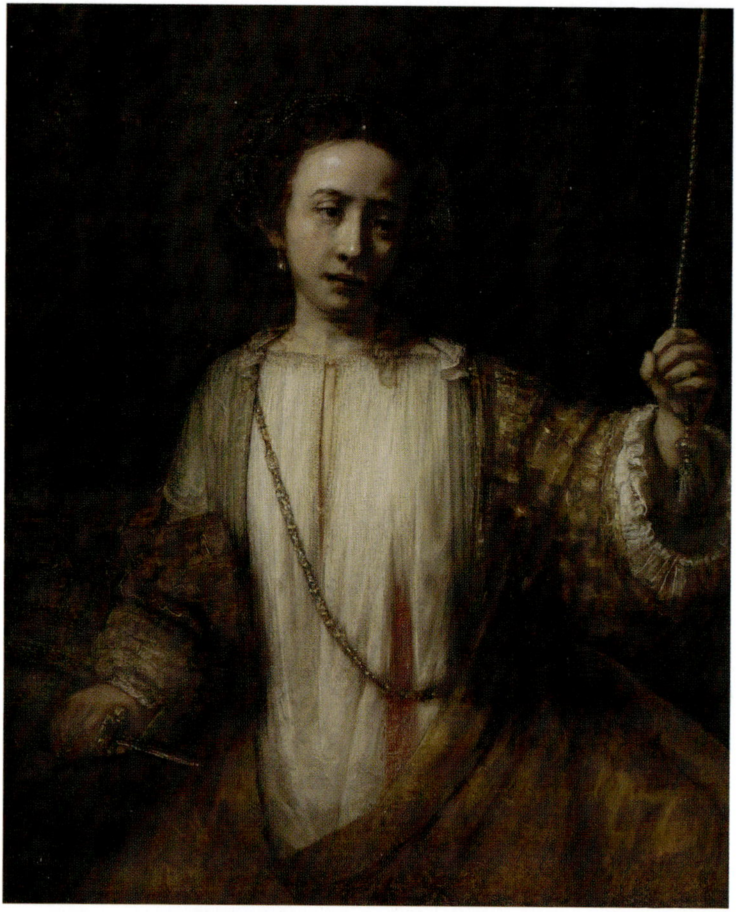

76 Rembrandt, *Lucretia*, 1666, oil on canvas.

transform conventional representations into close-up studies of individuals, reacting with a kind of stilled emotion of inner conflict in situations of tragedy.[36] Two life-sized late paintings also depict the suicide of Lucretia, the ancient Roman heroine whom Livy describes as avenging her brutal rape by placing 'death before dishonour'. Her self-denying virtue and suicide by knife-point sparked a revolt that led to the overthrow of kings of

Rome in favour of the Republic. Rembrandt shows Lucretia in isolation in both the prelude to (1664) and the aftermath of (1666; illus. 76) her stabbing. The latter moment shows her still calm, eyes averted and dagger in hand, while clinging to a rope as her wound seeps blood onto her chemise. Late techniques, such as an impasto chain and a series of gold patches for her sleeves, applied with the palette knife, add richness of modelling, while the deeply shadowed face of the heroine conveys her tragic end as she passes from life.

One of Rembrandt's later paintings (*c.* 1668–9; illus. 77), surely left unfinished, once again returns to the subject of aged Simeon holding the Christ Child (see illus. 38), a recurrent theme of spiritual engagement throughout his career. Here, however, only three figures appear, with the Virgin, almost lost in shadow, placed behind the shoulder of the prophet. No setting or other accessories intrude on this close-up half-length, which reveals Simeon's prayerful hands outstretched in the lower right corner. The old man's eyes are half-closed, almost in blindness, but suggestive of an interior religious experience, conveyed in earlier works through brilliant lighting. In this case, a pervasive rough handling of impasto paint evokes a more primal sensation, as much of touch as sight, like the prophet's physical contact and fulfilment by holding the promised Child.[37]

Francisco de Goya, like Rembrandt, was a virtuoso painter, draughtsman (in preserved albums) and printmaker, chiefly as an innovative etcher, making use of the recent technique of aquatint for additional tone.[38] Rendered deaf in 1798 and obliged to leave his native Spain in self-imposed exile to the French border city of Bordeaux for political reasons during his final years (1824–8), Goya's art often shows a bitter cynicism about the

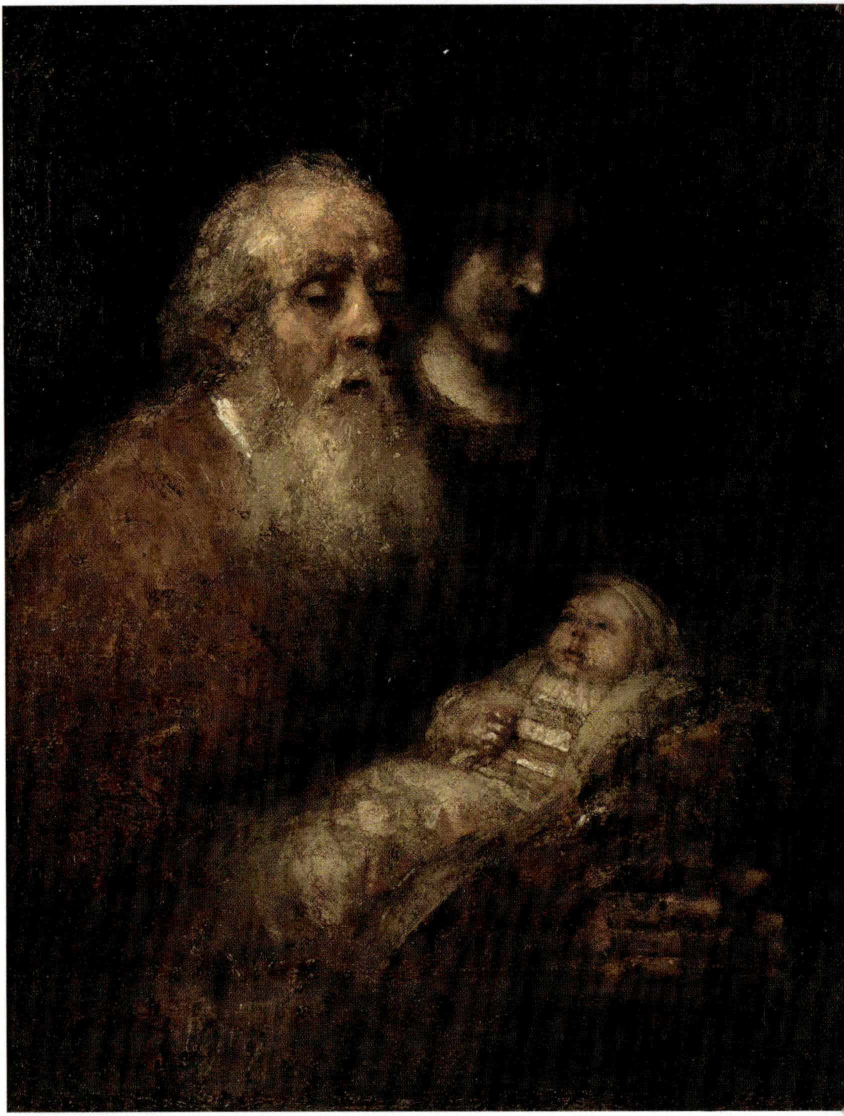

77 Rembrandt, *Simeon Holding the Christ Child*, *c.* 1668–9, oil on canvas.

presence of evil in human nature. We have already met his distinctive imagery: the paintings of carnivorous Saturn (see illus. 42) and two grotesque old women (see illus. 32), and several etchings about witchcraft (for example, illus. 31) and other follies from his 1799 *Caprichos* series. His isolation in Madrid and retreat to France showed little abatement of the artist's sardonic creativity, particularly in etched series, the imaginative *Disparates* (Follies) and the horrific *Disasters of War* (published posthumously) along with several caustic drawing albums (D–F, G–I stem from Bordeaux), either in ink and wash or chalk.[39]

Like Picasso after him, another Spaniard active in France, Goya turned in later years to imagery of bullfighting, both in paintings and prints. He etched one series, *La Tauromaquia* (1816), already late, but he produced another series during his eighties in the novel medium of lithography, *Bulls of Bordeaux* (1825). At the same time, one of his last paintings was a loosely brushed colourful scene depicting the opening ritual on horseback of the combat, *Suerte de Varas* (1824).[40] Goya relished both the cruelty and the artistry of this quintessential Spanish pastime.

A recurrence of serious illness in 1819 led Goya to paint the most vulnerable of all self-portraits, offered in gratitude to his healer, also portrayed, *Self-Portrait with Dr Arrieta* (1820; illus. 78).[41] That painting, offered as an act of friendship, bears a lengthy inscription, akin to the testimonials attached to ex-votos offered in churches as a token of gratitude for spiritual aid in healing. This self-portrait shows a weak and weary Goya, eyes rolled up, sitting up with a blanket while supported by his physician, who offers him a glass of medicine. Behind him, however, several ominous heads emerge from the inky background darkness;

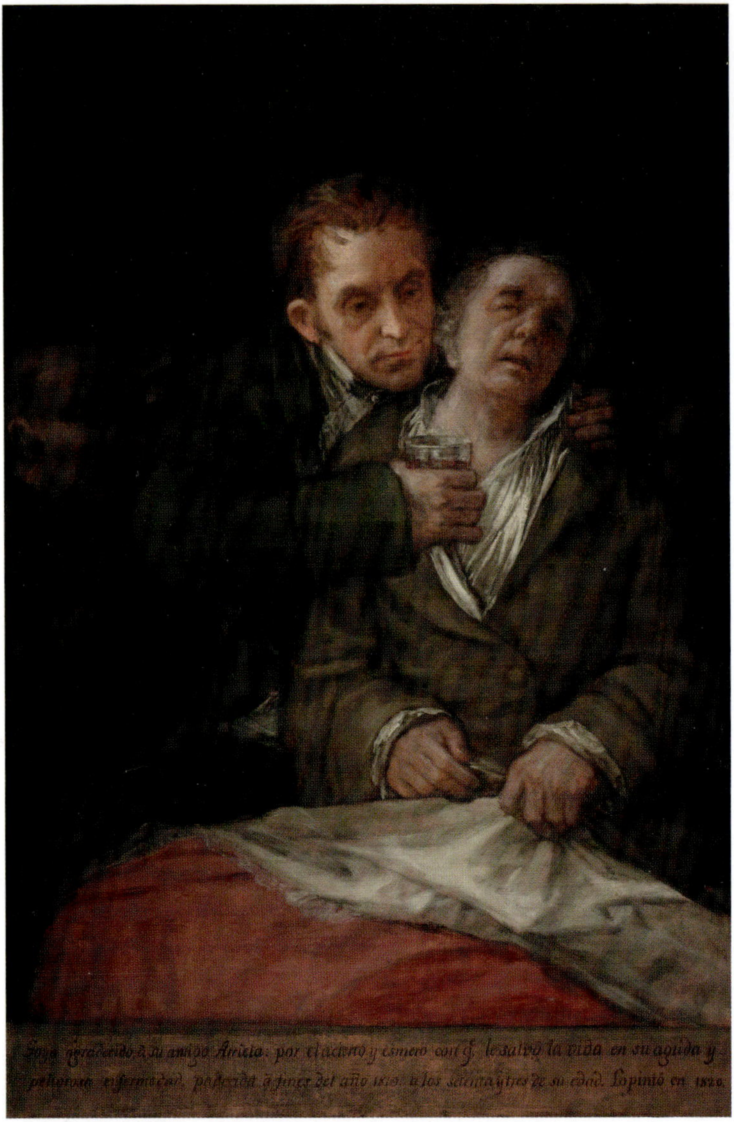

78 Francisco Goya, *Self-Portrait with Dr Arrieta*, 1820, oil on canvas.

they seem more demonic than sympathetic to the painter's situation, though they have been variously interpreted. Their forms echo the nightmarish *Black Paintings*, including *Saturn*, painted around the same time on the walls of Goya's Madrid house, the Quinta del Sordo (Deaf Man's Country House).

A tiny, late etching with aquatint, *Old Man on a Swing*, shows a grinning old man kicking up his bare feet (*c.* 1826–8; illus. 79).[42] It closely resembles a drawing of the same subject from Album H, which shows a similar elderly figure, also barefoot and flying even higher in his swing. Swings were associated with Carnival behaviour in Spain, and the jollity of this aged man defies the dignity of growing old and, like the bare feet, suggests basic frivolity.[43] But early impressions of the etching add another element, akin to the *Self-Portrait with Dr Arrieta*, showing dimly visible additional heads emerging from the dense background. These figures are mysterious, raising questions about both the space beneath and beyond the swing and whether they should be seen as either menacing or frivolous.

Joseph Mallord William Turner (1775–1851) enjoyed a long career across six full decades, but his final decade deeply disturbed and puzzled his contemporaries, only to thrill twentieth-century viewers as a major step towards abstraction through diffuse landscapes.[44] Already renowned as a leading practitioner of watercolours, in later years Turner increasingly applied similar sweeping brushwork in oils, notorious in their last-minute application before Royal Academy exhibitions, as he melded the two media. One critic lamented that in the contest between imagination and reality in his art, Turner's imagination won out. His subjects focused increasingly on air and water, conveyed through washes of colour. The painter strove continually to

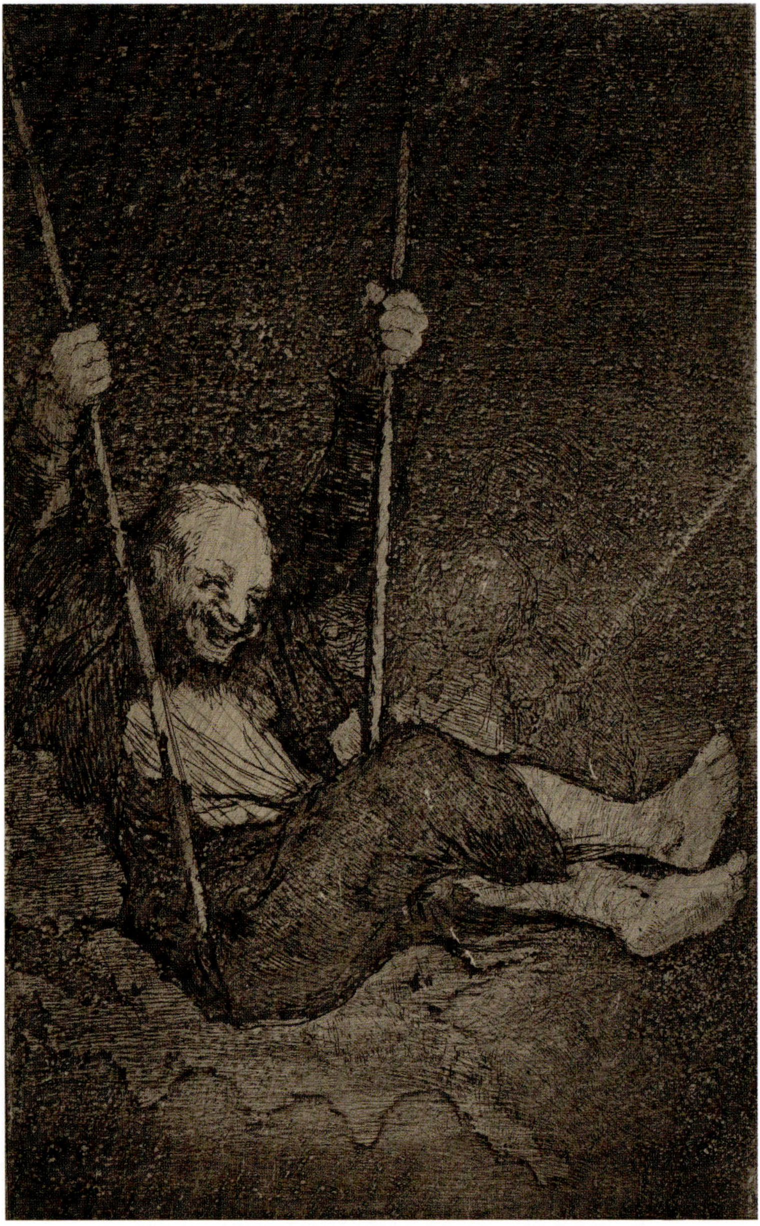

79 Francisco Goya, *Old Man on a Swing*, *c*. 1826–8, etching with aquatint.

achieve both the poetic and the sublime in his landscapes, and often he appended his original verses to his pictures.

The late Turner also responded to social changes as subjects of some of his ambitious large works. His transition to the late style was sparked, literally, by his watercolour sketches and final paintings (1835) that documented the traumatic burning of the Houses of Parliament. Turner then went on to commemorate another epochal change, the advent of steam engine transport. *The Fighting Temeraire Tugged to Her Last Berth to be Broken Up* (1838; illus. 80) shows the last voyage of that old, sailed warship, a veteran of the 1805 Battle of Trafalgar, now towed by a smaller paddlewheel steamship that belches fiery smoke from a black

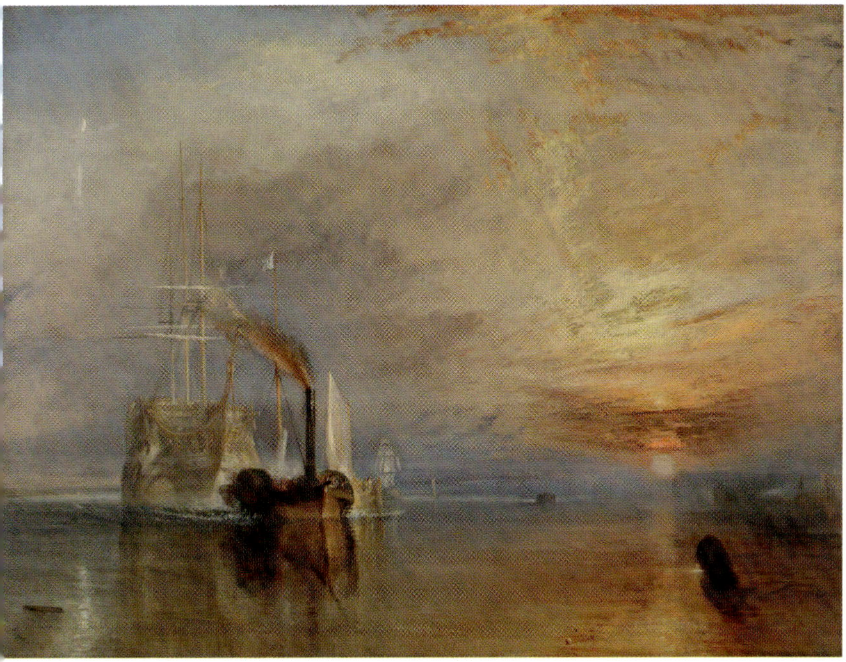

80 J.M.W. Turner, *The Fighting Temeraire Tugged to Her Last Berth to Be Broken Up*, 1839, oil on canvas.

stack. The event appears against a daubed, glowing yellow-orange sunset and dusky cityscape, principal features in other late Turners.

A year later he editorialized about the savage cruelty of slavery while also indulging in both sunset and stormy skies in *The Slave Ship*, originally titled *Slavers Throwing Overboard the Dead and Dying – Typhoon Coming On* (1840; Boston).[45] Lurid vignettes of human limbs and shackles amid swarming predatory fish punctuate the foreground billows; meanwhile the ship itself is dwarfed by a rising squall, awash in a spectrum of colours that stains its masts blood red. Here Turner climaxes a lifelong preoccupation with the dialogue between ships and powerful seas as he unleashes a new freedom of dynamic, coloured strokes.

Perhaps no other late Turner painting better encapsulates his dual sense of the new sublime, using the immaterial to show the power of human artifice, than *Rain, Steam, and Speed – The Great Western Railway* (1844; illus. 81). This symbol of the new Industrial Revolution emerges from a diffuse mist to rush along its railway bridge into viewer space. Its visual counterpoint of a dark boiler and smokestack contrasts with the placid river below and even with a tiny hare by the tracks, nature's image of speed. Even rain and mist are complemented here by the steam that provides unprecedented new force, captured by the surface energy of late Turner.

Other long-lived artists during the twentieth century made significant changes in their later decades. Claude Monet (1840–1926) withdrew to his gardens at Giverny and almost exclusively devoted himself to large-scale painted panels of *nymphéas* (water lilies), such as *The Water Lily Pond (Clouds)* (1903; illus. 82).[46]

Like Turner's late work, Monet's final phase of two decades also received renewed acclaim in the wake of abstract painting. His bold brushwork and striking colours dissolve into forms on a surface, which simulate but still defy reading simply as floating water plants with pink and white flower bursts. Instead Monet freely mixes his palette to produce opaque blends rather than transparent depths, complicated further here by floating white reflections of clouds.

The protean figure Pablo Picasso (1881–1973) was constantly shifting his forms and reinventing his art, working in virtually every medium, but especially painting and prints, so his seven-decade career incorporated many phases. Most commonly his late work is defined as beginning after the Second World War, but particularly from the mid-1950s until his death two decades later.[47] Unusually – in comparison to the old-age styles of other artists under discussion here – Picasso acted on his consciousness of his prominence and place in the overall history of art. Thus he reworked compositions of his predecessors, in series that acted like musical themes and variations: paintings and drawings after Delacroix's *Women of Algiers* (1955), Velázquez's *Las Meninas* (1957) or Manet's *Luncheon on the Grass* (1960–61), but also prints, such as several lithographs after Lucas Cranach. Moreover, in Picasso's swan song series of etchings, the *347 Series* (1968), named for the imposing number of compositions, he often portrays himself interacting with varied earlier admired artists, particularly Rembrandt, El Greco and Velázquez, arrayed in period costumes, as well as with erotic female nudes – as if in open defiance of death during his own eighth decade. Picasso seemed to be swallowing their works and absorbing them to give him inspiration and strength for his own creativity. He did,

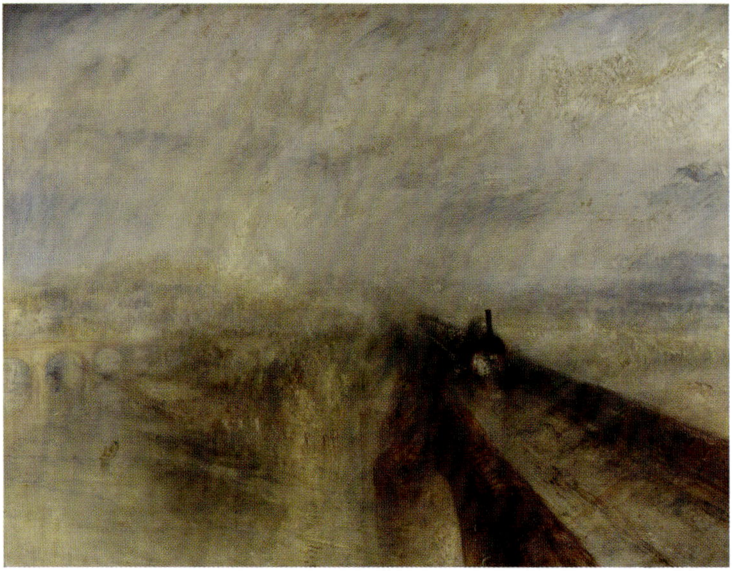

81 J.M.W. Turner, *Rain, Steam and Speed – The Great Western Railway*, 1844, oil on canvas.

however, produce a haunted and haunting frontal bust self-portrait in 1972; he faces old age frankly, showing himself as a living skull with sunken cheeks and staring eyes in enlarged sockets. Just as the novelist Philip Roth turned in short final novels (*The Humbling*, 2009; *Nemesis*, 2010) from *Eros* to *Thanatos*, so at the very end did Pablo Picasso.

Infirmity marked the final decades of Henri Matisse (1869–1954), whose five-decade career started somewhat later than that of his rival, the precocious Picasso.[48] Increasingly bedridden after repeated surgery in 1941, but still preoccupied with the intense colour that characterized his breakthrough works in the first decade of the century, Matisse turned to pure shaped colour as *papiers découpés*, or cut-outs. Beginning with his wartime *Icarus* (1943), a black silhouette against a blue ground with yellow shell bursts, the artist developed a series of vibrant cut-out images that he assembled into a 1947 book, *Jazz*. His contrasting colour shapes had edges but remained fundamentally planar rather than illusions of depth. He also returned to the idylls of his first decade with mural-sized tropical imagery with exotic names, *Océanie* (1946) and *Polynésie* (1946), as well as *Memory of Oceania* (1953). Finally, the series *Blue Nudes* (1952) climaxed in a nine-panel mural ensemble, *La piscine* (1952), with the same enfolding panorama as Monet's *grandes décorations* canvases of water lilies for the Orangerie of the Tuileries in Paris. Thus did Matisse successfully rejuvenate himself in old age, finding bright new bottles for his own distinctive vintage wine.

While the examples could be multiplied, these great masters of art from the Renaissance through to the twentieth century

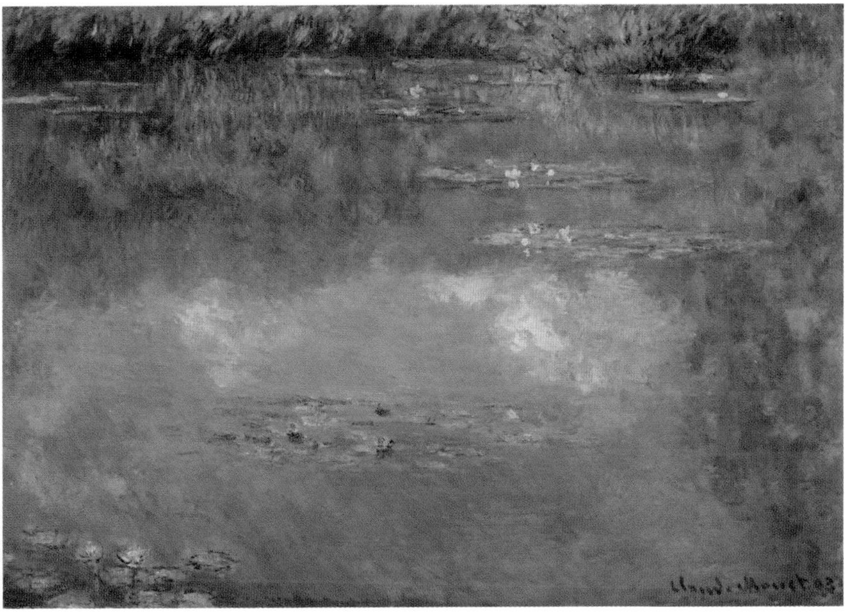

82 Claude Monet, *The Water Lily Pond* (*Clouds*), 1903, oil on canvas.

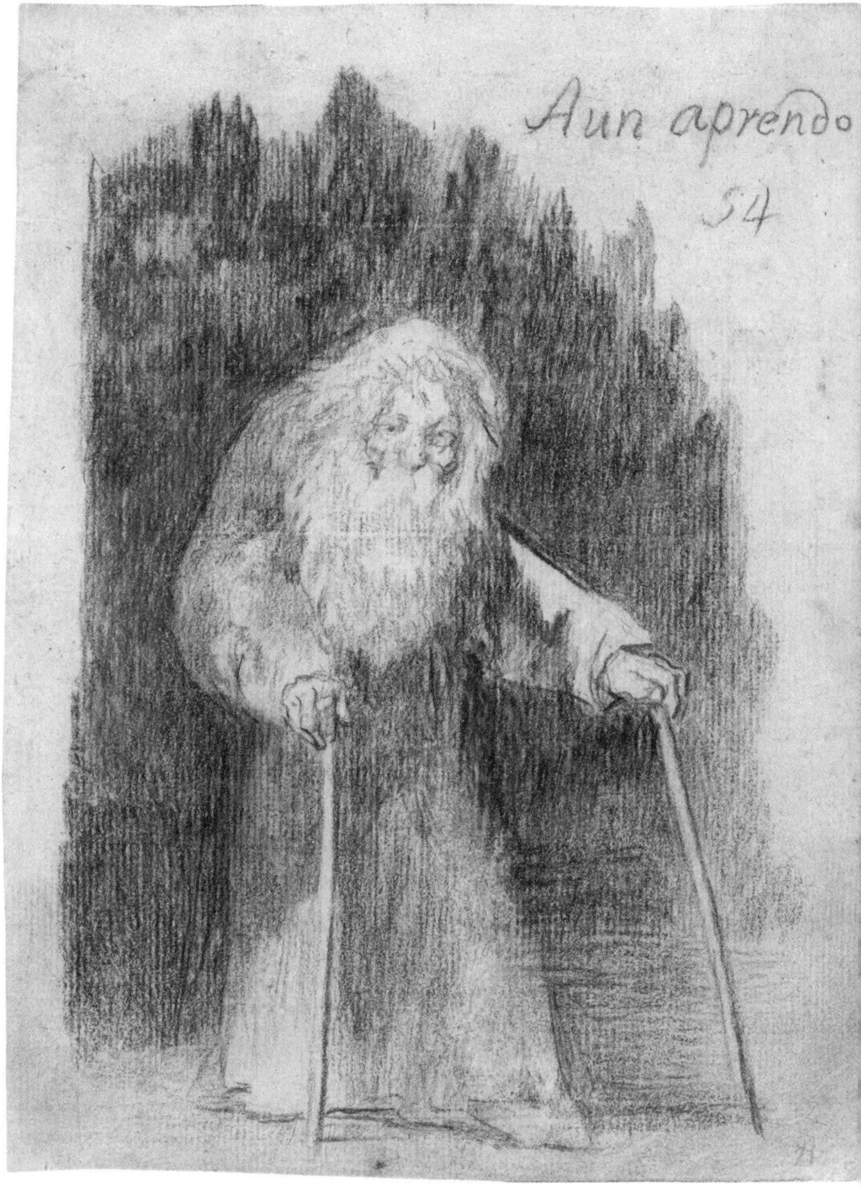

83 Francisco Goya, 'I am still learning', from the *Bordeaux Sketchbook G*, *c.* 1825–8, black crayon drawing.

all display something that we might call an 'old-age style'. Their experience, accumulated over decades, could combine with the new detachment and independence afford by advanced age to produce something truly distinctive and meaningful (even if not always embraced until later). Often accused of producing works that seemed 'unfinished' or radical compared to those of contemporaries or to their earlier accomplishments, these artists produced works of powerful energy, using their hard-won licence to defy inevitable loss of fine motor skills and physical dexterity – not to mention any debilitating health issues. Bold brushwork and reduced form, with other novel experimentation, mark the productive final decades of these long careers.

Picasso exclaimed, 'I stand for life against death.'[49] And, appropriately, the deaf and halting figure of Goya could still make the same claim visually, even in his last years of exile in Bordeaux (*c.* 1825–8; illus. 83).[50] In black crayon he depicts an old man with a long white beard, walking with a stoop on a pair of crutches by sheer force of will, but the old artist also appends the phrase *Aún aprendo* (I am still learning). No more vivid declaration of creativity in the face of infirmity and advanced age could be imagined.

References

Preface: **Ars longa, vita brevis**

1 Robert Harrison Pogue, *Juvenescence: A Cultural History of Our Age* (Chicago, IL, 2014), p. x: 'a species younger in looks, behavior, mentality, lifestyles, and, above all, desires'. This book has stimulated some of these remarks.

2 James H. Sweet, President of the American Historical Association, 'Is History History?', *Perspectives on History* (September 2022), following up on Lynn Hunt, 'Against Presentism', ibid. (May 2002).

3 Pogue, *Juvenescence*, p. xi.

4 Ibid., p. 44; also p. 131: 'If the young are to inherit the future they must hold to a path . . . that descends into the past, away from the tanglements of the present.'

5 A rich, brilliant resource for the history and range of attitudes towards ruins is Susan Stewart, *The Ruins Lesson: Meaning and Material in Western Culture* (Chicago, IL, 2020), with references: 'A castle or monument acquires age value because it speaks to the resistance of human effort against nature – a resistance that inverts and follows on the ontology of the structure itself as wrested from nature' (p. 17).

6 Edmund Spenser's translation, quoted by Stewart, *Ruins Lesson*, pp. 100–101.

7 Ovid, *Metamorphoses*, XV, 234–5. This work can be seen in Stewart, *Ruins Lesson*, p. 126, pl. 5; Nicole Dacos, 'Hermannus Posthumus pingebat 1536', *Roma Quanta Fuit: Tre pittori fiamminghi nella Domus Aurea* (Rome, 1995), pp. 15–20.

8 Aloïs Riegl, 'The Modern Cult of Monuments: Its Character and Its Origin', trans. Kurt Forster and Diane Ghirardo, *Oppositions*, 25 (1982), pp. 21–51.

9 Soumya Karlamangla, 'In California, Where Trees Are King, One Hardy Pine Has Survived for 4,800 Years', *New York Times*, 8 October 2022, www.nytimes.com: 'Before the Egyptians built the Pyramids, before Jesus was born, before the Roman Empire formed or collapsed, the trees were here.'

10 See Stewart, *Ruins Lesson*, pp. 83–5, 102–17, on imagery of virginity and prostitution in terms of human agency.

11 On the subject of place, cognate with such urban sites as *Platz* or *piazza/plaza*, see the entry by Carl Darling Buck, *A Dictionary of Selected Synonyms in the Principal Indo-European Languages* (Chicago, IL, 1949), pp. 830–31. Yi-Fu Tuan, *Space and Place: The Perspective of Experience* (Minneapolis, MN, 2001); Charles Withers, 'Place and the "Spatial Turn" in Geography and History', *Journal of the History of Ideas*, LXX/4 (2009), pp. 637–58.

12 Anouk Janssen, 'The Good, the Bad, and the Elderly: The Representation of Old Age in Netherlandish Prints (ca. 1550–1650)', in *Old Age in the Middle Ages and the Renaissance*, ed. Albrecht Classen (Berlin, 2007), pp. 437–83; Wayne Franits, 'Zwischen Frömmigkeit und Geiz: Das Alter in Genredarstellungen', in *Bilder vom alten Menschen in der niederländischen und deutschen Kunst 1550–1750*, ed. Thomas Döring, exh. cat., Herzog Anton-Ulrich Museum (Braunschweig, 1993), pp. 78–86. See also Pat Thane, *Old Age in English History: Past Experiences, Present Issues* (Oxford, 2000); Thane, ed., *The Long History of Old Age* (London, 2005).

One: Old Age Is Relative: Age and Stage as Concepts from Antiquity to the Renaissance

1 C. S. Lewis, 'Imagination and Thought in the Middle Ages', *Studies in Medieval and Renaissance Literature* (Cambridge, 1998), pp. 41–63; quote on p. 44.

2 Concise introductions to these conceptual relations can be found in synthetic overviews: S. K. Heninger, *The Cosmographical Glass: Renaissance Diagrams of the Universe* (San Marino, CA, 1977); C. S. Lewis, *The Discarded Image: An Introduction to Medieval and Renaissance Literature* (Cambridge, 1964); Jean Seznec, *The Survival of the Pagan Gods: The Mythological Tradition and Its Place in Renaissance Humanism and Art* (New York, 1953).

3 Elizabeth Sears, *The Ages of Man: Medieval Interpretations of the Life Cycle* (Princeton, NJ, 1986); J. A. Burrow, *The Ages of Man: A Study in Medieval Writing and Thought* (Oxford, 1988); Samuel C. Chew, *The Pilgrimage of Life* (New Haven, CT, 1962), pp. 144–73; still useful is Franz Boll, 'Die Lebensalter. Ein Beitrag zur antiken Ethologie und zur Geschichte der Zahlen', *Neue Jahrbücher für das klassische Altertum, Geschichte und deutsche Literatur und für Pädagogik*, XVI/31 (1913), pp. 89–145.

4 Cornelia Harcum, 'The Ages of Man: A Study Suggested by Horace, *Ars poetica*, Lines 153–78', *Classical Weekly*, VII/15 (1914), pp. 114–18.

5 Hans-Martin Kaulbach, ed., *'Der Welt Lauf'. Allegorische Graphikserien des Manierismus*, exh. cat., Staatsgalerie Stuttgart (1997), pp. 93–5, nos 19, 1–4. An earlier De Vos cycle of the Four Ages (1591) focused on activities: love, labour, honour and sorrows. A later cycle, engraved by Nicolaes de Bruyn in 1599, has nine sheets at ten-year intervals up to the age of one hundred.

6 Erwin Panofsky, 'Father Time', in *Studies in Iconology: Humanistic Themes in the Art of the Renaissance* (New York, 1962), pp. 69–93.
7 *De generatione animalium* V, 3, cited by Sears, *Ages of Man*, p. 9 n. 1; see Sears, *Ages of Man*, pp. 9–37 for 'Seasons of Life'. See also Heninger, *Cosmographical Glass*, pp. 99–115.
8 Also published by Goltzius, but engraved after his design by his stepson Jacob Matham; Ilja Veldman, 'Seasons, Planets and Temperaments in the Work of Maarten van Heemskerck: Cosmo-Astrological Allegory in Sixteenth-Century Netherlandish Prints', *Simiolus*, XI/3/4 (1980), pp. 149–76, esp. pp. 154–5, figs 5–8 (translation of verses by Franciscus Estius, ibid., p. 155, n. 27); Kaulbach, ed., '*Der Welt Lauf*', pp. 122–4, nos 30, 1–4.
9 Gert von der Osten, *Hans Baldung Grien. Gemälde und Dokumente* (Berlin, 1983), pp. 237–46, no. 87b. Baldung had painted a similar small panel with four figures, including Death (ibid., pp. 58–62, no. 10), but that work shows a playful infant holding up a transparent veil.
10 On heavenly glows above earthly landscapes in German painting and prints, see Larry Silver, 'Nature and Nature's God: Landscape and Cosmos of Albrecht Altdorfer', *Art Bulletin*, LXXXI/2 (1999), pp. 194–214.
11 David Jaffé, ed., *Titian*, exh. cat., National Gallery (London, 2003), pp. 88–9, no. 8; Paul Joannides, *Titian to 1518* (New Haven, CT, and London, 2001), pp. 193–201; Erwin Panofsky, *Problems in Titian: Mostly Iconographic* (New York, 1969), pp. 94–6.
12 Pictured as a suspended wreath in Lorenzo Lotto's *Venus and Cupid* (*c.* 1525). Myrtle wreaths were worn by brides in Venetian weddings; Rona Goffen, *Titian's Women* (New Haven, CT, and London, 1997), pp. 35, 43, 146, fig. 28.
13 Erwin Panofsky, '*Et in Arcadia ego*: Poussin and the Elegiac Tradition', in *Meaning in the Visual Arts* (Chicago, IL, 1982), pp. 295–320.
14 Joseph Koerner, 'The Epiphany of the Black Magus circa 1500', in *The Image of the Black in Western Art*, vol. III/1: *From the 'Age of Discovery' to the Age of Abolition*, ed. David Bindman and Henry Gates Jr (Cambridge, MA, 2010), pp. 7–92. Eventually the European discovery of the Americas would add the Four Continents to the tetrads, which in turn would inspire print series, such as the allegories on mounts designed by Maarten de Vos and engraved by Adriaen Collaert; Kaulbach, *Der Welt Lauf*, pp. 113–16, nos 27, 1–4.
15 David Alan Brown and Sylvia Ferino-Pagden, eds, *Bellini, Giorgione, Titian, and the Renaissance of Venetian Painting*, exh. cat., National Gallery (Washington, DC, 2006), pp. 164–7, 293–5, no. 30; Salvatore Settis, *Giorgione's 'Tempest': Interpreting the Hidden Subject* (Chicago, IL, 1990), pp. 14–47; however, this inexplicit subject has been variously interpreted; see also, Ludwig von Baldass, *Giorgione* (New York, 1964), pp. 134–49, no. 13.
16 Sears, *Ages of Man*, pp. 25–31; Lewis, *Discarded Image*, pp. 169–74; Nancy Siraisi, *Medieval and Early Renaissance Medicine* (Chicago, IL, 1990), pp. 102–10.

17 Kaulbach, *Der Welt Lauf*, pp. 111–13, no. 26.4.
18 Heninger, *Cosmographical Glass*, pp. 108–9, fig. 66; Bruno Reudenbach, 'Ein Weltbild als Hieroglyphe. Das Signet des Warburg Institute', in *Porträt aus Büchern. Bibliothek Warburg und Warburg Institute*, ed. Michael Diers (Hamburg, 1993), pp. 145–55.
19 Seznec, *Survival of Pagan Gods*, pp. 42–69; Aby Warburg, 'Pagan-Antique Prophecy in Words and Images in the Age of Luther', *The Renewal of Pagan Antiquity* [1918] (Los Angeles, CA, 1999), pp. 598–697; Robin B. Barnes, *Astrology and Reformation* (Oxford, 2016).
20 Sears, *Ages of Man*, pp. 38–53; Seznec, *Survival of Pagan Gods*, pp. 70–83; for planets, see Lewis, *Discarded Image*, pp. 102–12, where he notes that each planet also had an associated metal, ranging from the gold of the Sun and the silver of the Moon to the lead of Saturn. For liberal arts, see Lewis, ibid., pp. 185–97.
21 Raymond Klibansky, Erwin Panofsky and Fritz Saxl, *Saturn and Melancholy: Studies in the History of Natural Philosophy, Religion, and Art* (London, 1964). On Children of the Planets, see Dieter Blume, *Regenten des Himmels. Astrologische Bilder in Mittelalter und Renaissance* (Berlin, 2000).
22 Kaulbach, ed., *Der Welt Lauf*, pp. 76–92, nos 15–18; Veldman, 'Seasons, Planets and Temperaments', pp. 149–76; Veldman, 'From Allegory to Genre', in *Images for the Eye and Soul: Function and Meaning in Netherlandish Prints* (Leiden, 2006), pp. 193–222. The principal early Italian series (*c*. 1465) was made by the Florentine printmaker Baccio Baldini, possibly after a Northern woodblock series.
23 Jan Piet Filedt Kok, ed., *Livelier than Life: The Master of the Amsterdam Cabinet or the Housebook Master*, exh. cat., Rijksmuseum (Amsterdam, 1985), pp. 218–24, fol. 11r–17r; Christoph Graf zu Waldburg Waldegg, *Venus and Mars: The World of the Medieval Housebook* (Munich, 1998), pp. 24–43.
24 Kaulbach, *Der Welt Lauf*, pp. 83–8, no. 17.8; Ilja Veldman, 'De macht van de planeten over het mensdom in prenten naar Maarten de Vos', *Bulletin van het Rijksmuseum*, XXXI/1 (1983), pp. 21–53.
25 Translation based on the concise summary from the Latin by Veldman, 'Macht van planeten', p. 31, n. 41 (full text with Dutch translation). See also Kaulbach, *Der Welt Lauf*, pp. 84–5. For a general overview, see Kibansky, Panofsky and Saxl, *Saturn and Melancholy*.
26 Larry Silver, *Europe Views the World, 1500–1700* (London, 2022), pp. 56–70.
27 In his *Etymologiae* 11:2, Isidore of Seville divided human life into six unequal sections: infancy, childhood, adolescence, youth, senescence and old age. Panofsky, *Problems in Titian*, p. 94.
28 Sears, *Ages of Man*, pp. 144–51, figs 86–92.
29 London, British Library, MS Arundel 83, fo. 126v. Sears, *Ages of Man*, pp. 146–8, fig. 87; Chew, *Pilgrimage of Life*, p. 150, fig. 104.

30 Holger Jacob-Friesen, ed., *Hans Baldung Grien. Heilig/Unheilig*, exh. cat., Staatliche Kunsthalle Karlsruhe (2019), pp. 479–81, no. 252. An unusual feature of Breu's woodcut is animals who occupy the niches under each step; these are symbols of each decade, according to an Augsburg songbook of 1471.
31 Christine Armstrong, *The Moralizing Prints of Cornelis Anthonisz* (Princeton, NJ, 1990), pp. 81–4, fig. 32; the Breu woodcut is fig. 92. She describes the animal symbolism of the decades as follows: 'Children were like playful kids and adolescents like awkward calves; young men were recklessly strong like bulls, while mature men were noble and wise like lions. As they grew older, men became crafty like foxes, avaricious and greedy like wolves, contentious like dogs, indolent like cats, and finally foolish like asses' (p. 82). Cornelis Anthonisz. made an earlier woodcut, *Allegory of Transience* (1537), which features a skeleton and an hourglass framing an infant and a grown man with warning texts in both Dutch and Latin derived from Ecclesiastes II (ibid., pp. 79–81, fig. 14).

Two: **Wisdom and Folly**

1 Susan B. Matheson and J. J. Pollitt, *Old Age in Greek and Roman Art* (New Haven, CT, and London, 2022), esp. pp. 19–22; Mary Beard, *Classical Art from Greece to Rome* (Oxford, 2001), pp. 205–38.
2 Roberta Panzanelli, 'Compelling Presence', in *Ephemeral Bodies: Wax Sculpture and the Human Figure*, ed. Panzanelli (Los Angeles, CA, 2008), pp. 15–17.
3 Pliny, *Natural History* 35.2, translation from John Bostock, ed. (London, 1855), vol. VI, p. 25. See Georges Didi-Huberman, 'The Molding Image: Genealogy and the Truth of Resemblance in Pliny's *Natural History*, Book 35, 1–7', in *Law and the Image: The Authority of Art and the Aesthetics of Law*, ed. Costas Douzinas and Lynda Nead (Chicago, IL, 1999), pp. 77–80.
4 Matheson and Pollitt, *Old Age in Greek and Roman Art*, pp. 123–31; Richard Brilliant, *Roman Art: From the Republic to Constantine* (London, 1974), pp. 165–87.
5 Matheson and Pollitt, *Old Age in Greek and Roman Art*, pp. 91–100.
6 Peter Kurmann, *La façade de la cathédrale de Reims: architecture et sculpture des portails* (Lausanne, 1987).
7 Claire Richter Sherman, *The Portraits of Charles V of France, 1338–1380* (New York, 1969), esp. pp. 51–5; on the continuity of basic types admixed with naturalistic features, see Stephen Perkinson, *The Likeness of the King: A Prehistory of Portraiture in Late Medieval France* (Chicago, IL, 2009), esp. pp. 135–48.
8 Paul Binski, *Medieval Death: Ritual and Representation* (Ithaca, NY, 1996), pp. 139–52; Kathleen Cohen, *Metamorphoses of a Death Symbol: The Transi Tomb in the Late Middle Ages and the Renaissance* (Berkeley, CA, 1973).

9 Gertrud Schiller, *Iconography of Christian Art*, vol. II: *The Passion of Christ* (Greenwich, CT, 1972), pp. 219–24, n. 55: 'the representation of God the Father did not become possible or usual in this manner until the 14th century . . . also for the Trinity image.' Georg Troescher, 'Die "Pitiè de Nostre-Seigneur" oder die "Not Gottes"', *Wallraf-Richartz Jahrbuch*, 9 (1936), pp. 148–68; Fides Buchheim, *Der Gnadenstuhl. Darstellung der Dreifaltigkeit* (Würzburg, 1984).

10 Edgar Wind, 'Michelangelo's Prophets and Sibyls', *Proceedings of the British Academy*, LI (1965), pp. 47–84; George Hersey, *High Renaissance Art in St. Peter's and the Vatican: An Interpretive Guide* (Chicago, IL, 1993), pp. 187–8, 198–204. Besides Jeremiah, other prophets are shown with bald pates and white beards: Zechariah, Joel and Ezekiel, whereas most of the sibyls are youthful in contrast to wrinkled Cumaea.

11 Marcia B. Hall, ed., *Raphael's 'School of Athens'* (Cambridge, 1997); Matthias Winner, 'Projects and Execution in the Stanza della Segnatura', in *Raphael in the Apartments of Julius II and Leo X* (Milan, 1993).

12 Astrid Harth and Maximiliaan Martens, 'Albrecht Dürer's Iconic Image of Saint Jerome: Making, Meaning, and Reception', in *Dürer's Journeys: Travels of a Renaissance Artist*, ed. Susan Foister and Peter van den Brink, exh. cat., National Gallery (London, 2021), pp. 252–65.

13 For the early modern increase of the St Joseph cult, see Joseph Chorpenning, 'St. Joseph as Guardian Angel, Artisan, and Contemplative: Christophorus Blancus's Engravings for the *Summary of the Excellencies of St. Joseph* (1597)', in *Joseph of Nazareth through the Centuries*, ed. Chorpenning (Philadelphia, PA, 2011), pp. 103–30; Cynthia Hahn, '"Joseph Will Perfect, Mary Enlighten, and Jesus Save Thee": The Holy Family as Marriage Model in the Mérode Triptych', *Art Bulletin*, LXVIII/1 (1986), pp. 54–66; Carolyn C. Wilson, *St. Joseph in Italian Renaissance Society and Art* (Philadelphia, PA, 2001).

14 Jonathan Brown et al., *El Greco of Toledo*, exh. cat., Toledo Museum of Art (Boston, MA, 1982), pp. 240–41, no. 28. A larger version is in the Museo Nacional del Prado, Madrid, whose St Joseph is a younger man who replaces an earlier version of the saint as an old man.

15 Brown et al., *El Greco of Toledo*, p. 239, no. 26. For the tradition of the Virgin and St Anne, Kathleen Ashley and Pamela Sheingorn, eds, *Interpreting Cultural Symbols: Saint Anne in Late Medieval Society* (Athens, GA, 1990), esp. pp. 169–98; Virginia Nixon, *Mary's Mother: Saint Anne in Late Medieval Europe* (University Park, PA, 2004), esp. pp. 133–64.

16 Jeffrey M. Muller, *Rubens: The Artist as Collector* (Princeton, NJ, 1989), pp. 21, 45–6, 151, no. III.7. Two closely related busts survive; they can be found at Rubens House in Antwerp, and the Ashmolean Museum in Oxford. For the reuse of the bust in the *Four Philosophers* painting, see Wolfram Prinz, 'The *Four Philosophers* by Rubens and the Pseudo-Seneca in Seventeenth-Century Painting', *Art Bulletin*, LV/3 (1973), pp. 410–28.

17 Anne-Marie Logan, *Peter Paul Rubens: The Drawings*, exh. cat., Metropolitan Museum of Art (New York, 2005), pp. 112–15; Elizabeth McGrath, *Subjects from History: Corpus Rubenianum Ludwig Burchard XIII* (London, 1997), pp. 108–12, 282–94, no. 54, fig. 195. The preserved original sculpture, now called *Old Fisherman*, is Roman (second century CE), after a Greek original of the late third century BCE; Matheson and Pollitt, *Old Age in Greek and Roman Art*, pp. 133–4, fig. 79.

18 Matheson and Pollitt, *Old Age in Greek and Roman Art*, pp. 141–4; Paul Zanker, *Die Trunkene Alte. Das Lachen der Verhöhnten* (Frankfurt, 1989).

19 R. Bulbeck, 'The Doubt of St. Joseph', *Catholic Biblical Quarterly*, X/3 (1948), pp. 296–309; Joseph Lienhard, 'St Joseph in Early Christianity: Devotion and Theology', in *Joseph through the Centuries*, ed. Chorpenning, pp. 15–46. According to Jacobus de Voragine's *The Golden Legend* (mid-thirteenth century), St Bernard gives three reasons for Joseph's marriage to Mary, primarily for appearances sake: 'because thereby the mystery was hidden from the demons; Mary's virginity was confirmed by her spouse; and her modesty and good name were preserved'. Translation by William Granger Ryan, *The Golden Legend: Readings on the Saints* (Princeton, NJ, 1993), p. 197. Johan Huizinga, *The Waning of the Middle Ages* (New York, 1954), pp. 168–70, underscores that in literature Joseph becomes a 'caricature' and a 'drudging husband'. He quotes the late medieval poet Eustache Deschamps in translation (nn. 12–13): 'He served his wife gloomily and mournfully . . . And so he never had any amusement in this world.' Also: 'The good man is painted quite exhausted . . . Old spent and broken . . . But of him people say "That is Joseph the fool."'

20 Diane Wolfthal, *Household Servants and Slaves: A Visual History, 1300–1700* (New Haven, CT, 2022), pp. 43–4; Anne L. Williams, *Satire, Veneration, and St. Joseph in Art, c. 1300–1500* (Amsterdam, 2019).

21 E. H. Gombrich, 'The Grotesque Heads', in *The Heritage of Apelles* (London, 1976), pp. 57–75; Mark Clayton, 'Leonardo's Grotesques', in *The Ugly Duchess: Beauty and Satire in the Renaissance*, ed. Emma Capron, exh. cat., National Gallery (London, 2023), pp. 33–41.

22 Emma Capron, 'Quinten Massys and the Art of Satire', in *The Ugly Duchess*, ed. Capron, pp. 11–31.

23 David Alan Brown and Sylvia Ferino-Pagden, eds, *Bellini, Giorgione, Titian, and the Renaissance of Venetian Painting*, exh. cat., National Gallery (Washington, DC, 2006), pp. 212–15, no. 39; Ludwig von Baldass, *Giorgione* (New York, 1964), pp. 159–60, pl. 24.

24 Nancy Thomson de Grummond, 'VV and Related Inscriptions in Giorgione, Titian, and Dürer', *Art Bulletin*, LVII/3 (1975), pp. 346–56.

25 Larry Silver, *Hieronymus Bosch* (New York, 2006), pp. 239–73.

26 Claudia Swan, '*The Preparation for the Sabbath* by Jacques de Gheyn II', *Print Quarterly*, XVI/4 (1999), pp. 327–39. De Gheyn, paradoxically, was also

one of the keenest observers of natural life, with close studies of small animals and plants; Swan, *Art, Science, and Witchcraft in Early Modern Holland: Jacques de Gheyn II* (Cambridge, 2005), esp. pp. 123–94. She cites inscriptions in Latin and Dutch on an anonymous witchcraft print (*c.* 1580) that point to the evil and satanic delusions of these women: 'It is but dream and illusion, what the impious sows here./ He abandons God and heeds only evil (Dutch); the seeds of the godless are mere spells and tricks/ Having relinquished their god they summon Evil (Latin)'. More generally on images of witches, see Linda C. Hults, *The Witch as Muse* (Philadelphia, PA, 2005); Charles Zika, *The Appearance of Witchcraft* (New York, 2007).

27 Mariët Westermann, *The Amusements of Jan Steen* (Zwolle, 1997), esp. pp. 159–66; Wayne Franits, *Dutch Seventeenth-Century Genre Painting* (New Haven, CT, and London, 2004), pp. 203–14; for Maes, see ibid., pp. 149–56.

28 Hults, *Witch as Muse*, pp. 217–62, fig. 7.4.

Three: **Old-Age Stories**

1 Dagmar Eichberger and Shelley Perlove, eds, *Visual Typology in Early Modern Europe* (Turnhout, 2018), pp. 55, 63–4, 78–9, 162–3, figs 1.10, 2.3, 3.1, 7.5. The *Biblia pauperum* woodcut (*c.* 1460–65) declares that 'Abraham signifies the heavenly Father, who sacrificed his son (that is, Christ)'.

2 Shelley Perlove and Larry Silver, *Rembrandt's Faith* (University Park, PA, 2009), pp. 76–92, for Abraham subjects.

3 Christiaan Vogelaar et al., eds, *Lucas van Leyden en de Renaissance*, exh. cat., De Lakenhal (Leiden, 2011), pp. 254–5, no. 52; Ellen S. Jacobowitz and Stephanie Loeb Stepanek, eds, *The Prints of Lucas van Leyden and His Contemporaries*, exh. cat., National Gallery of Art (Washington, DC, 1983), pp. 188–9, no. 69.

4 Mary D. Garrard, *Artemisia Gentileschi* (Princeton, NJ, 1989), pp. 183–209; see also Garrard, 'Artemisia and Susanna', in *Feminism and Art History: Questioning the Litany*, ed. Norma Broude and Garrard (New York, 1982), pp. 146–71; Eric Jan Sluijter, *Rembrandt and the Female Nude* (Amsterdam, 2006), pp. 113–41.

5 Perlove and Silver, *Rembrandt's Faith*, pp. 197–202, 206–13, 217–25, 327–31.

6 Horst Ziermann, *Matthias Grünewald* (Munich, 2001), pp. 74–152, esp. pp. 149–50. A Grünewald drawing of an old man likely served as the model for the face of St Paul, akin to Dürer's drawing study of 'a 93-year-old man' for his *St Jerome* (1521; illus. 18).

7 For the fullest discussion of the Anthony legend through the Hieronymus Bosch *St Anthony Triptych*, now see Eric de Bruyn, 'Hieronymus Bosch's Lisbon "Temptations of St. Anthony Triptych" and Its Written Sources',

in *Between Hell and Paradise: The Enigmatic World of Hieronymus Bosch*, ed. Bernadette Tóth, exh. cat., Szépmüvészéti Múzeum (Budapest, 2022), pp. 22–43.

8 Rüdiger Klessmann, ed., *Adam Elsheimer, 1578–1610*, exh. cat., Städel Museum (Frankfurt, 2006), pp. 36, 170–73, 187; nos 35, 52; Keith Andrews, *Adam Elsheimer: Paintings, Drawings, Prints* (New York, 1977), pp. 34–5, 153–4, nos 24.

9 Aneta Georgievska-Shine and Larry Silver, *Rubens, Velázquez, and the King of Spain* (Farnham, 2014), pp. 33–4, pl. 3. Svetlana Alpers, *The Decoration of the Torre de la Parada* (London, 1971), pp. 200–201, no. 17; the workshop painting by J. Cossiers (?) is lost.

10 Georgievska-Shine and Silver, *Rubens, Velázquez, and the King of Spain*, pp. 161–5, pl. 35; Alpers, *Torre*, pp. 259–61, no. 55. Saturn had already dispossessed his own father, Uranus, through castration with this scythe attribute.

11 Robert Hughes, *Goya* (London, 2004), pp. 383–4; Fred Licht, *Goya: The Origins of the Modern Temper in Art* (New York, 1979), pp. 167–71. Goya would have seen Rubens's precedent in the Spanish royal collections.

12 Elizabeth McGrath, *Rubens Subjects from History* (London, 1997), vol. II, pp. 282–97, no. 54, fig. 195; Konrad Renger and Claudia Denk, *Flämische Malerei des Barock* (Munich and Cologne, 2002), pp. 386–9, no. 305, there dated 1612/13.

13 Perrin Stein, ed., *Jacques Louis David: Radical Draftsman*, exh. cat., Metropolitan Museum of Art (New York, 2022), esp. pp. 143–9; Claudia Einecke, *Peyron, David, and the 'Death of Socrates'*, exh. cat., Joslyn Art Museum (Omaha, NE, 2002); Thomas Crow, *Emulation: Making Artists for Revolutionary France* (New Haven, CT, 1995), pp. 93–102; Albert Boime, *Art in an Age of Revolution, 1750–1800* (Chicago, IL, 1987), pp. 407–11.

14 Winifred H. Friedman, *Boydell's Shakespeare Gallery* (New York, 1976); Walter Pape and Frederick Burwick, eds, *The Boydell Shakespeare Gallery* (Essen, 1996). For West's religious paintings, see Nancy Pressly, *Revealed Religion: Benjamin West's Commissions for Windsor Castle and Fonthill Abbey*, exh. cat., San Antonio Museum of Art (1983). For Fuseli narratives drawn from Shakespeare, classics, Milton, Dante and the Bible, see Gert Schiff, *Henry Fuseli, 1741–1825*, exh. cat., Tate Gallery (London, 1975), esp. pp. 58–104.

15 Anne Poulet, *Jean-Antoine Houdon*, exh. cat, National Gallery of Art (Washington, DC, 2003), pp. 246–50, no. 43, made when Franklin was 73 years old. The marble Franklin bust, dated 1779, is in the Philadelphia Museum of Art. The painting is a sketch for a never-executed, large-scale portrait in tribute to Franklin, destined for the Philadelphia Hospital. See also Brandon Brame Fortune, ed., *Franklin and His Friends: Portraying the Man of Science in Eighteenth-Century America*, exh. cat., Smithsonian National Portrait Gallery (Washington, DC, 1999).

16 Edgar Wind, *Hume and the Heroic Portrait: Studies in Eighteenth-Century Imagery* (Oxford, 1986), pp. 1–52; David Mannings, 'Reynolds, Garrick, and the Choice of Hercules', *Eighteenth-Century Studies*, XVII/3 (1983–4), pp. 259–83; Richard Wendorf, 'Reynolds and the Genius of Life', in *The Elements of Life: Biography and Portrait-Painting in Stuart and Georgian England* (Oxford, 1990), pp. 226–60.

Four: Portraits - Self and Others

1 Craig Clunas, *Chinese Painting and Its Audiences* (Princeton, NJ, 2017), pp. 91–103; *Portrayals from a Brush Divine: A Special Exhibition on the Tricentennial of Giuseppe Castiglione's Arrival in China*, exh. cat., National Palace Museum (Taipei, 2015).

2 Susan Doran, ed., *Elizabeth*, exh. cat., National Maritime Museum (Greenwich, 2003); John N. King, *Tudor Royal Iconography: Literature and Art in an Age of Religious Crisis* (Princeton, NJ, 1989); Roy Strong, *The Cult of Elizabeth: Elizabethan Portraiture and Pageantry* (London, 1977).

3 Angela Vanhaelen, *The Moving Statues of Seventeenth-Century Amsterdam: Automata, Waxworks, Fountains, Labyrinths* (University Park, PA, 2022), pp. 129–32; Giovanni Ricci, 'Masks of Power: Funeral Effigies in Early Modern Europe', in *Waxing Eloquent: Italian Portraits in Wax*, ed. Andrea Daninos (Milan, 2012), pp. 61–7; Ralph E. Giesey, *The Royal Funeral Ceremony in Renaissance France* (Geneva, 1960), pp. 61–2, 80–85.

4 Angela Vanhaelen, *Moving Statues*, pp. 130–31, fig. 34.

5 Farah Nayeri, 'Lucian Freud's Self-Portraits: But What Do They Mean?', *New York Times*, 5 October 2019, www.nytimes.com. See also Adam Gopnik, 'Lucian Freud and the Truth of the Body', *New Yorker*, 8 February 2021.

6 Courtney Graham Donnell et al., *Ivan Albright*, exh. cat., Art Institute of Chicago (1997).

7 Michael Roth, *Dürers Mutter. Schönheit, Alter und Tod im Bild der Renaissance*, exh. cat., Kupferstichkabinett (Berlin, 2006), esp. pp. 24–8, 30–31, nos 1–2, 4; Jeffrey Chipps Smith, 'Dürer's Losses and the Dilemmas of Being', in *Enduring Loss in Early Modern Germany: Cross Disciplinary Perspectives*, ed. Lynne Tatlock (Leiden, 2010), pp. 74–7.

8 Manuel Teget-Welz, ed., *Michael Wolgemut. Mehr als Dürers Lehrer*, exh. cat., Museen der Stadt Nürnberg (Regensberg, 2019), esp. pp. 155–7, no. 1.

9 Quoted by Christopher White, *Dürer: The Artist and His Drawings* (London, 1971), pp. 152–3, no. 63; Erwin Panofsky, *The Life and Art of Albrecht Dürer* (Princeton, NJ, 1995), pp. 170–71. Diagnosing her disease as stomach cancer, see Wolfgang Pirsig, '"Dürers Mutter" – aus ärtztlicher Sicht', in Roth, *Dürers Mutter*, pp. 17–22.

10 Daantje Meuwissen, ed., *Jacob Cornelisz Van Oostsanen, ca. 1475–1533*, exh. cat., Amsterdam Museum and Stedelijk Museum Alkmaar (2014), pp. 282–4, no. 60. Richard Dorment and Margaret MacDonald, eds, *James McNeill Whistler*, exh. cat., Tate Gallery, London (1994).

11 Quoted by Daniel Sutherland, *Whistler: A Life for Art's Sake* (New Haven, CT, 2014), p. 109, from an 1868 letter by Whistler to the French artist Fantin-Latour.

12 Keith Christiansen and Stefan Weppelman, eds, *The Renaissance Portrait from Donatello to Bellini*, exh. cat., Metropolitan Museum of Art (New York, 2011), pp. 59–162, no. 43; L. M. Sleptzoff, *Men or Supermen? The Italian Portrait in the Fifteenth Century* (Jerusalem, 1978), esp. pp. 36–74.

13 John Pope-Hennessy, *Italian Renaissance Sculpture* (New York, 1985), pp. 45–52, 289–91.

14 Christiansen and Weppelman, *Renaissance Portrait*, pp. 129–32, nos 23–4, documented by Strozzi as a 'lifelike marble bust of me' (*testa di marmo . . . al mio naturale da Benedetto da Maiano*). See Weppelman, 'Some Thoughts on Likeness in Early Renaissance Portraits', pp. 64–76; and Rudolf Preimesberger, '"The face that is known draws the eyes of all spectators . . ."', pp. 77–84.

15 Roberta Panzanelli, 'Compelling Presence', in *Ephemeral Bodies: Wax Sculpture and the Human Figure*, ed. Panzanelli (Los Angeles, CA, 2008), pp. 15–17; Andrea Daninos, 'Wax Figures in Italy: A Brief History', in *Waxing Eloquent: Italian Portraits in Wax*, ed. Daninos (Milan, 2012), pp. 13–42; Megan Holmes, 'Ex-votos: Materiality, Memory and Cult', in *The Idol in the Age of Art: Objects, Devotions and the Early Modern World*, ed. Michael Cole and Rebecca Zorach (Aldershot, 2009), pp. 165–88; Aby Warburg, 'The Art of Portraiture and the Florentine Bourgeoisie', in *The Renewal of Pagan Antiquity* [1918] (Los Angeles, CA, 1999), pp. 191, 206.

16 Daantje Meuwissen, ed., *Jacob Cornelisz Van Oostsanen, ca. 1475–1533*, exh. cat., Amsterdam Museum and Stedelijk Museum Alkmaar (2014), pp. 282–4, no. 60.

17 Susan B. Matheson and J. J. Pollitt, *Old Age in Greek and Roman Art* (New Haven, CT, and London, 2022), pp. 123–31.

18 Christiansen and Weppelman, *Renaissance Portrait*, pp. 190–93, nos 60–61; see also medals of Guarino Guarini da Verona and Vittorinoi da Feltre, ibid., pp. 210–11, 232–4, nos 72, 88; Sleptzoff, *Men or Supermen?*, pp. 75–96.

19 Anne Poulet, *Jean-Antoine Houdon: Sculptor of the Enlightenment*, exh. cat., National Gallery of Art (Washington, DC, 2003). The list is extensive and includes, among others, Gluck, Molière, Jean de La Fontaine, Larive, Diderot, Rousseau, d'Alembert, Buffon and American intellectuals who also served as diplomats in France: Franklin and Jefferson.

20 Poulet, *Houdon*, pp. 152–70, nos 23–6.

21 Ibid., pp. 246–50, no. 43.

22 Allen Staley, *Copley and West in England, 1775–1815* (London, 2021), fig. 2. Franklin also appears prominently seated at table in Benjamin West's unfinished documentary painting *The American Commissioners of the Preliminary Peace Negotiations with Great Britain* (1783); Paul Staiti, *Of Arms and Artists: The American Revolution through Painters' Eyes* (New York, 2016), pp. 63–96, pl. 4.
23 Lillian Miller, ed., *The Peale Family: Creation of a Legacy, 1770–1870*, exh. cat., Philadelphia Museum of Art (1996), pp. 261–75. Among its highlights was a mastodon skeleton unearthed in 1801 (pls 10, 135).
24 Ibid., pp. 130–32, fig. 2.15.
25 'That Gentleman, Dallas Museum of Art', http://browse.americanartcollaborative.org, accessed 4 May 2023.
26 Will Stapp, 'The Nineteenth-Century Portrait', in *The Art of Photography, 1839–1989*, ed. Mike Weaver, exh. cat., Royal Academy (London, 1989), pp. 44–6.
27 Joel Snyder, 'Inventing Photography, 1839–1879', in *On the Art of Fixing a Shadow: One Hundred and Fifty Years of Photography*, exh. cat., National Gallery of Art (Washington, DC, 1989), p. 23.

Five: Old-Age Style

1 Kenneth Clark, 'The Artist Grows Old', *Daedalus*, CXXXV/1 (Winter 2006), pp. 77–90; quotation on p. 80.
2 James M. Saslow, *The Poetry of Michelangelo: An Annotated Translation* (New Haven, CT, 1991), no. A35.
3 Clark, 'The Artist Grows Old'; David Rosand, 'Old Age Style', *Art Journal*, XLVI/2 (Summer 1987), pp. 91–133. Catherine Soussloff, 'Old Age and Old Age Style in the *Lives* of Artists: Gianlorenzo Bernini', *Art Journal*, XLVI/2 (1987), pp. 115–21. See also Gordon McMullan and Sam Smiles, eds, *Late Style and its Discontents: Essays in Art, Literature, and Music* (Oxford, 2016); Nicholas Delbanco, *Lastingness: The Art of Old Age* (New York, 2011).
4 Entire libraries discuss this artist. Among important monographs, see William E. Wallace, *Michelangelo: The Artist, the Man, and His Times* (Cambridge, 2010); Howard Hibbard, *Michelangelo* (New York, 1974); Herbert von Einem, *Michelangelo* (London, 1973). For the late period, see Wallace, *Michelangelo, God's Architect* (Princeton, NJ, 2019) and Charles de Tolnay, *Michelangelo: The Final Period* (Princeton, NJ, 1960).
5 Wallace, *God's Architect*, pp. 75–94, 184–214; James Ackerman, *The Architecture of Michelangelo* (Harmondsworth, 1971), pp. 131–277.
6 Wallace, *Michelangelo*, pp. 210–21; Una Roman D'Elia, 'Drawing Christ's Blood: Michelangelo, Vittoria Colonna, and the Aesthetics of Reform', *Renaissance Quarterly*, LIX/1 (2006), pp. 90–129; Alexander Nagel,

'Observations on Michelangelo's Late *Pietà* Drawings and Sculptures', *Zeitschrift für Kunstgeschichte*, LIX/4 (1996), pp. 548–71; Nagel, 'Gifts for Michelangelo and Vittoria Colonna', *Art Bulletin*, LXXIX/4 (1997), pp. 647–68. Note the artist's sonnet (Saslow, *The Poetry of Michelangelo*, no. 288), which begins, 'The vanities of the world have robbed me/ the time allotted for contemplating God.'

7 Wallace, *God's Architect*, pp. 95–8, 106–10; Wallace, 'Narrative and Religious Expression in Michelangelo's Pauline Chapel', *Artibus et historiae*, X/19 (1989), pp. 107–22; Margaret Kunz, 'A Ceremonial Ensemble: Michelangelo's *Last Judgment* and the Cappella Paolina Frescoes', in *Michelangelo's 'Last Judgment'*, ed. Marcia B. Hall (Cambridge, 2005), pp. 150–82; Leo Steinberg, *Michelangelo's Last Paintings* (New York, 1975).

8 Paul Barolsky, *Michelangelo's Nose: A Myth and Its Maker* (University Park, PA, 1990), pp. 37–52: 'Michelangelo's identification in old age with the saint . . . is evocative in the spiritual sense of Saint Paul's preaching on the death of the old man as the prelude to rebirth' (p. 39). Of course, in the Sistine *Last Judgement*, Michelangelo attached his features to the flayed skin held by St Bartholomew in heaven, suggesting that it is the discarded worldly shell of someone who found salvation in answer to his prayers; see Barolsky, ibid., p. 31; Steinberg, *Last Paintings*, pp. 37–41.

9 Wallace, *God's Architect*, pp. 131–43; Wallace, 'Michelangelo, Tiberio Calcagni, and the Florentine *Pietà*', *Artibus et historiae*, XXI/42 (2000), pp. 81–99; Jack Wasserman, *Michelangelo's Florentine 'Pietà'* (Princeton, NJ, 2003); Leo Steinberg, 'Michelangelo's Florentine *Pietà*: The Missing Leg', *Art Bulletin*, L/4 (1968), pp. 343–53; Steinberg, 'Animadversions: Michelangelo's Florentine *Pietà:* The Missing Leg Twenty Years After', *Art Bulletin*, LXXI/3 (1989), pp. 480–505.

10 Barolsky, *Michelangelo's Nose*, pp. 65–7; Wolfgang Stechow, 'Joseph of Arimathea or Nicodemus?', *Studien zur toskanischen Kunst. Festchrift für Ludwig Heinrich Heydenreich* (Munich, 1963), pp. 289–302; Corine Schleif, 'Nicodemus and Sculptores: Self-Reflexivity in Works by Adam Kraft and Tilman Riemenschneider', *Art Bulletin*, LXXV/4 (1993), pp. 599–626; Michelangelo's Florentine figure is on p. 612, fig. 19.

11 Paul Joannides, '"Primitivism" in the Late Drawings of Michelangelo: The Master's Construction of an Old-Age Style', in *Michelangelo Drawings*, ed. Craig Hugh Smyth (Washington, DC, 1992), pp. 244–61; Alexander Nagel, *Michelangelo and the Reform of Art* (Cambridge, 2000), pp. 143–85; Carmen Bambach, 'Art and Personal Spirituality in an Age of Reform', in *Michelangelo Drawings*, ed. Bambach, exh. cat., Metropolitan Museum of Art (New York, 2017), pp. 190–231, esp. pp. 222–31.

12 Johannides, 'Late Drawings', p. 247.

13 No authoritative, comprehensive volume on Titian exists in English, though there is a biography, Sheila Hale, *Titian: His Life* (New York, 2012). Brief,

authoritative overviews in Maria Loh, *Titian's Touch: Art, Magic and Philosophy* (London, 2019); Tom Nichols, *Titian and the End of the Venetian Renaissance* (London, 2013), esp. Chapter Four; Charles Hope, *Titian* (London, 1980). For his later works, see Jodi Cranston, *The Muddied Mirror: Materiality and Figuration in Titian's Later Paintings* (University Park, PA, 2010); Francesco Valcanover, 'Le dernier Titien et la fin du siècle à Venise', in *Le siècle de Titien*, ed. Gilles Fage, exh. cat., Grand Palais (Paris, 1993), pp. 595–625. Specifically for the late religious works, Marcia B. Hall, *The Sacred Image in the Age of Art* (New Haven, CT, and London, 2011), pp. 144–71, esp. 164–71.

14 Other examples include *Entombment* (1559), the large *Martyrdom of St Lawrence* (1567), *Tarquin and Lucretia* (1571), *Ecce Homo* (*c.* 1570) and *St Sebastian* (*c.* 1575); see David Jaffé, ed., *Titian*, exh. cat., National Gallery (London, 2003), pp. 151–79, nos 31, 36, 41, 43.

15 David Rosand, 'Titian and the Eloquence of the Brush', *Artibus et historiae*, II/3 (1981), pp. 85–96; Paula Carabel, '*Finito* and *non-finito* in Titian's Last Paintings', *RES: Anthropology and Aesthetics*, XXVIII (1995), pp. 77–93.

16 Valcanover, 'Le dernier Titien', pp. 620–21, no. 261. Sixten Ringbom, *Icon to Narrative: The Rise of the Dramatic Close-Up in Fifteenth-Century Devotional Painting* (Åbo, 1965).

17 Hall, *Sacred Image*, p. 170: 'The painter's hand, made so evident with the loose brushwork, is a metaphor for the artist as interpreter.'

18 Valcanover, 'Le dernier Titien', pp. 623–4, no. 265; *Titian, Prince of Painters*, exh. cat., National Gallery, Washington, DC, and Palazzo Ducale, Venice (1990), pp. 370–72, no. 76; Cranston, *Muddied Mirror*, pp. 47–73, pl. 3: 'A series of antinomies structures the story, including divine and mortal, rational and bestial, mind and body, Apollonian and Dionysian, living and dead' (p. 50). The picture was still in Titian's estate when he died.

19 Emanuel Winternitz, 'The Curse of Pallas Athena', in *Musical Instruments and Their Symbolism in Western Art* (New Haven, CT, 1979), pp. 150–65, esp. pp. 155–6, n. 3.

20 Leonard Barkan, *The Gods Made Flesh: Metamorphosis and the Pursuit of Paganism* (New Haven, CT, 1986), esp. pp. 171–242; *Titian, Prince of Painters*, pp. 373–5, no. 77; Rona Goffen, *Piety and Patronage in Renaissance Venice* (New Haven, CT, and London, 1986), pp. 151–4.

21 *Titian, Prince of Painters*, pp. 350–51, no. 68 (*c.* 1570/75; Madrid, Museo Thyssen-Bornemisza).

22 Still fundamental is Rudolf Wittkower, *Bernini* (London, 1961); for the late works, see Howard Hibbard, *Bernini* (Harmondsworth, 1965), pp. 185–229. See also Soussloff, 'Old Age *Lives* of Artists', pp. 115–21.

23 Wittkower, *Bernini*, pp. 232–4, no. 58.

24 Ibid., pp. 241–2, no. 63. For terracotta preliminary studies, *bozzetti*, of *Jerome*, see C. D. Dickerson III, Anthony Sigel and Ian Wardropper, *Bernini*

Sculpting in Clay, exh. cat., Metropolitan Museum of Art (New York, 2012), pp. 257–65, nos 30–31.

25 Wittkower, *Bernini*, pp. 21–3, 259–60, no. 77.

26 Ibid., pp. 11, no. 76. Fullest analysis by Shelley Perlove, *Bernini and the Idealization of Death: The 'Blessed Ludovica Albertoni' and the Altieri Chapel* (University Park, PA, 1990).

27 Dickerson, Sigel and Wardropper, *Sculpting in Clay*, pp. 206–15, nos 20–21.

28 Perlove, *Ludovica Albertoni*, pp. 37, 50. She also evokes comparison to Bernini's earlier image of pious ecstasy, *St Teresa* (*c*. 1647).

29 Paul Crenshaw, *Rembrandt's Bankruptcy: The Artist, His Patrons, and the Art Market in Seventeenth-Century Netherlands* (Cambridge, 2006). Rembrandt literature is also abundant. For his paintings, see Gary Schwartz, *Rembrandt: His Life, His Paintings* (New York, 1985), to be supplemented with Schwartz, *The Rembrandt Book* (New York, 2006); Bob Haak, *Rembrandt: His Life, His Work, His Time* (New York, 1969); Christian and Astrid Tümpel, *Rembrandt: Images and Metaphors* (London, 2006). The standard reference to the paintings is Ernst van de Wetering, *Rembrandt's Paintings Revisited: A Complete Survey* (Dordrecht, 2015), and a catalogue by Volker Manuth, *Rembrandt: The Complete Paintings* (Cologne, 2019). For late works, see Jonathan Bikker et al., eds, *Rembrandt: The Late Works*, exh. cat., National Gallery and Rijksmuseum (London and Amsterdam, 2014). On late painting technique, see Ernst van de Wetering, *Rembrandt: The Painter at Work* (Amsterdam, 1997), pp. 155–90. On late drawings, see Nicola Courtright, 'Origins and Meanings of Rembrandt's Late Drawing Style', *Art Bulletin*, LXXVIII/3 (1996), pp. 484–510.

30 H. Perry Chapman, *Rembrandt's Self-Portraits* (Princeton, NJ, 1990); Christopher White and Quentin Buvelot, *Rembrandt by Himself*, exh. cat., National Gallery and Mauritshuis (London and The Hague, 1999).

31 Chapman, *Self-Portraits*, pp. 120–27; White and Buvelot, *Rembrandt by Himself*, pp. 213–15, no. 81; Arthur K. Wheelock, ed., *Rembrandt's Late Religious Portraits*, exh. cat., National Gallery of Art (Washington, DC, 2005), pp. 108–10, no. 11.

32 Chapman, *Self-Portraits*, pp. 101–4; White and Buvelot, *Rembrandt by Himself*, pp. 216–19, no. 82. Albert Blankert, 'Rembrandt, Zeuxis, and Ideal Beauty', in *Album amicorum J. G. van Gelder*, ed. J. Bruyn et al. (The Hague, 1973), pp. 32–9. A very early Rembrandt self-portrait (*c*. 1628); Ernst van de Wetering, 'Rembrandt Laughing, *c*. 1628 – A Painting Resurfaces', *Kroniek van het Rembrandthuis* (2007), pp. 18–40. Another interpretation of the picture sees Rembrandt as enacting the traditional role of Democritus, the laughing philosopher, amused by the follies of humanity, in contrast to the scowling profile of Heraclitus, the dour philosopher regarding the world.

33 Chapman, *Self-Portraits*, pp. 97–101; White and Buvelot, pp. 220–22, no. 83.

34 B.P.J. Broos, 'The "O" of Rembrandt', *Simiolus*, IV/3 (1971), pp. 150–84.

35 Kurt Bauch, 'Ikonographischer Stil', *Studien zur Kunstgeschiichte* (Berlin, 1967), pp. 123–51; see also J. Bialostocki, 'Ikonographische Forschungen zu Rembrandt's Werk', *Still und Ikonographie* (Cologne, 1981), pp. 173–213.

36 Gregor J. M. Weber, 'Inner Conflict' and 'Reconciliation', in *Rembrandt: The Late Works*, ed. Jonathan Bikker and Weber, exh. cat., National Gallery and Rijksmuseum (London and Amsterdam, 2014), pp. 235–69.

37 A related late drawing, also seemingly unfinished, was added by Rembrandt for the *album amicorum* for Jacobus Heyblocq (1661). It also shows a rough-hewn *Simeon in the Temple* with broken linework; he is accompanied only by Mary and Joseph. Courtright, 'Rembrandt's Late Drawing Style', pp. 488–9, fig. 3.

38 Rena Hoisington, *Aquatint: From Its Origins to Goya*, exh. cat., National Gallery of Art, Washington, DC (Princeton, NJ, 2021), pp. 209–27; Eleanor Sayre, *The Changing Image: Prints by Francisco Goya*, exh. cat., Boston Museum of Fine Arts (1974). José Manuel Matilla and Manuela Mena Marqués, eds, *Only My Strength Will Remain: Goya Drawings*, exh. cat., Museo Nacional del Prado (Madrid, 2019). General: Janis Tomlinson, *Goya: A Portrait of the Artist* (Princeton, NJ, 2020), esp. pp. 265–319; Robert Hughes, *Goya* (London, 2003), esp. pp. 320–402; Alfonso Pérez Sánchez and Eleanor Sayre, eds, *Goya and the Spirit of Enlightenment*, exh. cat., Museo del Prado, Museum of Fine Arts and Metropolitan Museum of Art (Madrid, Boston, MA, and New York, 1989), esp. pp. 264–393, nos 118–79; Pierre Gassier and Juliet Wilson, *The Life and Complete Work of Francisco Goya* (New York, 1971), pp. 227–372.

39 Pérez Sánchez and Sayre, *Spirit of Enlightenment*, pp. 279–393, nos 125–79; Matilla and Mena Marqués, *Goya Drawings*, pp. 185–271, nos 111–81; Jonathan Brown, *Goya's Last Works*, exh. cat., Frick Collection (New York, 2006).

40 Sayre, *Changing Image*, pp. 197–250, 310–14, nos 162–99, 257–8; Hughes, *Goya*, pp. 350–65.

41 Pérez Sánchez and Sayre, *Spirit of Enlightenment*, pp. 270–73, no. 121; Hughes, *Goya*, pp. 373–5.

42 Sayre, *Changing Image*, pp. 317–20, nos 262–4, there identified as a 'warlock'; Pérez Sánchez and Sayre, *Spirit of Enlightenment*, pp. 392–3, no. 179.

43 Swings held erotic connotations in eighteenth-century French paintings; see Donald Posner, 'The Swinging Women of Watteau and Fragonard', *Art Bulletin*, LXIV/1 (1982), pp. 75–88.

44 A breakthrough Museum of Modern Art exhibition led the revisionist reconsideration of late Turner's achievement: Lawrence Gowing, *Turner: Imagination and Reality*, exh. cat., Museum of Modern Art (New York, 1966). See also David Blayney Brown, Amy Concannon and Sam Smiles, eds, *J.M.W. Turner: Painting Set Free*, exh. cat., Getty Museum (Los Angeles, CA, 2015). For a general overview, see Andrew Wilton, *J.M.W. Turner:*

His Art and Life (New York, 1979), esp. pp. 193–248; John Gage, *J.M.W. Turner: 'A Wonderful Range of Mind'* (New Haven, CT, 1987).

45 John McCoubrey, 'Turner's *Slave Ship*, Abolition, Ruskin, and Reception', *Word and Image*, XIV/4 (1998), pp. 319–53.

46 *Monet's Years at Giverny: Beyond Impressionism*, exh. cat., Metropolitan Museum of Art (New York, 1978); Christian Geelhaar, ed., *Claude Monet: Nymphéas, Impression, Vision*, exh. cat., Kunstmuseum Basel (1986); Jean-Dominique Rey and Denis Rouart, *Monet: Water Lilies: The Complete Series* (Paris, 2008). For a general overview, see Virginia Spate, *Claude Monet: Life and Work* (New York, 1992), pp. 253–316.

47 For a general overview, see William Rubin, ed., *Pablo Picasso: A Retrospective*, exh. cat., Museum of Modern Art (New York, 1980), esp. pp. 378–458. For his later work, see Jean Sutherland Boggs, 'The Last Thirty Years', in *Picasso in Retrospect*, ed. Roland Penrose and John Golding (New York, 1973), pp. 127–59; Gert Schiff, *Picasso: The Last Years, 1963–1973*, exh. cat., Guggenheim Museum (New York, 1983).

48 John Elderfield, *Henri Matisse: A Retrospective*, exh. cat, Museum of Modern Art (New York, 1992), pp. 413–69; Elderfield, *The Cutouts of Henri Matisse* (New York, 1978); Lawrence Gowing, *Matisse* (New York, 1979), pp. 176–97.

49 Quoted by Sutherland Boggs, 'Last Thirty Years', p. 127. See also the remarks from ancient Rome by Pliny the Elder, *Natural History*, 35:145, as quoted by David Rosand, 'Style and the Aging Artist', p. 91: 'The latest works of artists and the pictures left unfinished at their death are valued more than their finished pictures . . . The reason is that in these we see traces of the design and the original conception of the artists, while sorrow for the hand that perished at its work beguiles us into the bestowal of praise.'

50 Matilla and Mena Marqués, *Goya Drawings*, pp. 366–7, no. 251.

Bibliography

Ackerman, James, *The Architecture of Michelangelo* (Harmondsworth, 1971)
Alpers, Svetlana, *The Decoration of the Torre de la Parada* (London, 1971)
Andrews, Keith, *Adam Elsheimer: Paintings, Drawings, Prints* (New York, 1977)
Armstrong, Christine, *The Moralizing Prints of Cornelis Anthonisz* (Princeton, NJ, 1990)
Ashley, Kathleen, and Pamela Sheingorn, eds, *Interpreting Cultural Symbols: Saint Anne in Late Medieval Society* (Athens, GA, 1990)
Baldass, Ludwig von, *Giorgione* (New York, 1964)
Bambach, Carmen, 'Art and Personal Spirituality in an Age of Reform', in *Michelangelo Drawings*, ed. Bambach, exh. cat., Metropolitan Museum of Art (New York, 2017), pp. 190–231
Barkan, Leonard, *Nature's Work of Art: The Human Body as Image of the World* (New Haven, CT, 1975), pp. 8–60
—, *The Gods Made Flesh: Metamorphosis and the Pursuit of Paganism* (New Haven, CT, 1986), pp. 171–242
Barnes, Robin B., *Astrology and Reformation* (Oxford, 2016)
Barolsky, Paul, *Michelangelo's Nose: A Myth and Its Maker* (University Park, PA, 1990)
Bauch, Kurt, 'Ikonographischer Stil', *Studien zur Kunstgeschiichte* (Berlin, 1967), pp. 123–51
Beard, Mary, *Classical Art from Greece to Rome* (Oxford, 2001)
Bialostocki, Jan, 'Ikonographische Forschungen zu Rembrandt's Werk', *Still und Ikonographie* (Cologne, 1981), pp. 173–213
Bikker, Jonathan, et al., eds, *Rembrandt: The Late Works*, exh. cat., National Gallery and Rijksmuseum (London and Amsterdam, 2014)
Binski, Paul, *Medieval Death: Ritual and Representation* (Ithaca, NY, 1996)
Blankert, Albert, 'Rembrandt, Zeuxis, and Ideal Beauty', in *Album amicorum J. G. van Gelder*, ed. J. Bruyn et al. (The Hague, 1973), pp. 32–9
Blayney Brown, David, Amy Concannon and Sam Smiles, eds, *J.M.W. Turner: Painting Set Free*, exh. cat., Getty Museum (Los Angeles, CA, 2015)

Blume, Dieter, *Regenten des Himmels. Astrologische Bilder in Mittelalter und Renaissance* (Berlin, 2000)
Boime, Albert, *Art in an Age of Revolution, 1750–1800* (Chicago, IL, 1987)
Boll, Franz, 'Die Lebensalter. Ein Beitrag zur antiken Ethologie und zur Geschichte der Zahlen', *Neue Jahrbücher für das klassische Altertum, Geschichte und deutsche Literatur und für Pädagogik*, XVI/31 (1913), pp. 89–145
Brilliant, Richard, *Roman Art: From the Republic to Constantine* (London, 1974)
Broos, B.P.J., 'The "O" of Rembrandt', *Simiolus*, IV/3 (1971), pp. 150–84
Brown, David Alan, and Sylvia Ferino-Pagden, eds, *Bellini, Giorgione, Titian, and the Renaissance of Venetian Painting*, exh. cat., National Gallery of Art (Washington, DC, 2006)
Brown, Jonathan, *Goya's Last Works*, exh. cat., Frick Collection (New York, 2006)
—, et al., *El Greco of Toledo*, exh. cat., Toledo Museum of Art (Boston, MA, 1982)
Buchheim, Fides, *Der Gnadenstuhl. Darstellung der Dreifaltigkeit* (Würzburg, 1984)
Bulbeck, R., 'The Doubt of St. Joseph', *Catholic Biblical Quarterly*, X/3 (1948), pp. 296–309
Burrow, J. A., *The Ages of Man: A Study in Medieval Writing and Thought* (Oxford, 1988)
Capron, Emma, 'Quinten Massys and the Art of Satire', in *The Ugly Duchess: Beauty and Satire in the Renaissance*, ed. Capron, exh. cat., National Gallery (London, 2023), pp. 11–31
Carabel, Paula, '*Finito* and *non-finito* in Titian's Last Paintings', *RES: Anthropology and Aesthetics*, XXVIII (1995), pp. 77–93
Chapman, H. Perry, *Rembrandt's Self-Portraits* (Princeton, NJ, 1990)
Chew, Samuel C., *The Pilgrimage of Life* (New Haven, CT, 1962)
Chorpenning, Joseph, 'St. Joseph as Guardian Angel, Artisan, and Contemplative: Christophorus Blancus's Engravings for the *Summary of the Excellencies of St. Joseph* (1597)', in *Joseph of Nazareth through the Centuries*, ed. Chorpenning (Philadelphia, PA, 2011), pp. 103–30
Christiansen, Keith, and Stefan Weppelman, eds, *The Renaissance Portrait from Donatello to Bellini*, exh. cat., Metropolitan Museum of Art (New York, 2011)
Clark, Kenneth, 'The Artist Grows Old', *Daedalus*, CXXXV/1 (Winter 2006), pp. 77–90
Clayton, Mark, 'Leonardo's Grotesques', in *The Ugly Duchess: Beauty and Satire in the Renaissance*, ed. Emma Capron, exh. cat., National Gallery (London, 2023), pp. 33–41
Clunas, Craig, *Chinese Painting and Its Audiences* (Princeton, NJ, 2017)
Cohen, Kathleen, *Metamorphoses of a Death Symbol: The Transi Tomb in the Late Middle Ages and the Renaissance* (Berkeley, CA, 1973)
Cranston, Jodi, *The Muddied Mirror: Materiality and Figuration in Titian's Later Paintings* (University Park, PA, 2010)

Crenshaw, Paul, *Rembrandt's Bankruptcy: The Artist, His Patrons, and the Art Market in Seventeenth-Century Netherlands* (Cambridge, 2006)
Crow, Thomas, *Emulation: Making Artists for Revolutionary France* (New Haven, CT, 1995)
Courtright, Nicola, 'Origins and Meanings of Rembrandt's Late Drawing Style', *Art Bulletin*, LXXVIII/3 (1996), pp. 484–510
Daninos, Andrea, 'Wax Figures in Italy: A Brief History', in *Waxing Eloquent: Italian Portraits in Wax*, ed. Daninos (Milan, 2012), pp. 13–42
De Bruyn, Eric, 'Hieronymus Bosch's Lisbon "Temptations of St. Anthony Triptych" and Its Written Sources', in *Between Hell and Paradise: The Enigmatic World of Hieronymus Bosch*, ed. Bernadette Tóth, exh. cat., Szépmüvészéti Múzeum (Budapest, 2022), pp. 22–43
De Grummond, Nancy Thomson, 'VV and Related Inscriptions in Giorgione, Titian, and Dürer', *Art Bulletin*, LVII/3 (1975), pp. 346–56
D'Elia, Una Roman, 'Drawing Christ's Blood: Michelangelo, Vittoria Colonna, and the Aesthetics of Reform', *Renaissance Quarterly*, LIX/1 (2006), pp. 90–129
De Tolnay, Charles, *Michelangelo: The Final Period* (Princeton, NJ, 1960)
Delbanco, Nicholas, *Lastingness: The Art of Old Age* (New York, 2011)
Dickerson, C. D. III, Anthony Sigel and Ian Wardropper, *Bernini Sculpting in Clay*, exh. cat., Metropolitan Museum of Art (New York, 2012)
Didi-Huberman, Georges, 'The Molding Image: Genealogy and the Truth of Resemblance in Pliny's *Natural History*, Book 35, 1–7', in *Law and the Image: The Authority of Art and the Aesthetics of Law*, ed. Costas Douzinas and Lynda Nead (Chicago, IL, 1999), pp. 77–80
Donnell, Courtney Graham, et al., *Ivan Albright*, exh. cat., Art Institute of Chicago (1997)
Doran, Susan, ed., *Elizabeth*, exh. cat., National Maritime Museum (Greenwich, 2003)
Dorment, Richard, and Margaret MacDonald, eds, *James McNeill Whistler*, exh. cat., Tate Gallery (London, 1994)
Eichberger, Dagmar, and Shelley Perlove, eds, *Visual Typology in Early Modern Europe* (Turnhout, 2018)
Einem, Herbert von, *Michelangelo* (London, 1973)
Einecke, Claudia, *Peyron, David, and the 'Death of Socrates'*, exh. cat., Joslyn Art Museum (Omaha, NE, 2002)
Elderfield, John, *The Cutouts of Henri Matisse* (New York, 1978)
—, *Henri Matisse: A Retrospective*, exh. cat., Museum of Modern Art (New York, 1992), pp. 413–69
Erikson, Erik H., *Identity: Youth and Crisis* (New York, 1968)
Filedt Kok, Jan Piet, *Livelier than Life: The Master of the Amsterdam Cabinet or the Housebook Master*, exh. cat., Rijksmuseum (Amsterdam, 1985)

Filipczak, Zirka, *Hot Dry Men, Cold Wet Women: The Theory of Humors in Western European Art, 1575–1700*, exh. cat., American Federation of Arts (New York, 1997)
Fortune, Brandon Brame, ed., *Franklin and His Friends: Portraying the Man of Science in Eighteenth-Century America*, exh. cat., Smithsonian National Portrait Gallery (Washington, DC, 1999)
Franits, Wayne, *Dutch Seventeenth-Century Genre Painting* (New Haven, CT, and London, 2004)
Friedman, Winifred H., *Boydell's Shakespeare Gallery* (New York, 1976)
Gage, John, *J.M.W. Turner: 'A Wonderful Range of Mind'* (New Haven, CT, 1987)
Garrard, Mary D., 'Artemisia and Susanna', in *Feminism and Art History: Questioning the Litany*, ed. Norma Broude and Garrard (New York, 1982), pp. 146–71
—, *Artemisia Gentileschi* (Princeton, NJ, 1989)
Gassier, Pierre, and Juliet Wilson, *The Life and Complete Work of Francisco Goya* (New York, 1971), pp. 227–372
Geelhaar, Christian, ed., *Claude Monet: Nymphéas, Impression, Vision*, exh. cat., Kunstmuseum Basel (1986)
Georgievska-Shine, Aneta, and Larry Silver, *Rubens, Velázquez, and the King of Spain* (Farnham, 2014)
Giesey, Ralph E., *The Royal Funeral Ceremony in Renaissance France* (Geneva, 1960)
Goffen, Rona, *Piety and Patronage in Renaissance Venice* (New Haven, CT, and London, 1986)
—, *Titian's Women* (New Haven, CT, and London, 1997)
Gombrich, E. H., 'The Grotesque Heads', in *The Heritage of Apelles* (London, 1976), pp. 57–75
Gopnik, Adam, 'Lucian Freud and the Truth of the Body', *New Yorker*, 8 February 2021
Gowing, Lawrence, *Turner: Imagination and Reality*, exh. cat., Museum of Modern Art (New York, 1966)
Haak, Bob, *Rembrandt: His Life, His Work, His Time* (New York, 1969)
Hahn, Cynthia, '"Joseph Will Perfect, Mary Enlighten, and Jesus Save Thee": The Holy Family as Marriage Model in the Mérode Triptych', *Art Bulletin*, LXVIII/1 (1986), pp. 54–66
Hale, Sheila, *Titian: His Life* (New York, 2012)
Hall, Marcia B., ed., *Raphael's 'School of Athens'* (Cambridge, 1997)
—, *The Sacred Image in the Age of Art* (New Haven, CT, and London, 2011)
Harcum, Corneia, 'The Ages of Man: A Study Suggested by Horace, *Ars poetica*, Lines 153–78', *Classical Weekly*, VII/15 (1914), pp. 114–18
Harth, Astrid, and Maximiliaan Martens, 'Albrecht Dürer's Iconic Image of Saint Jerome: Making, Meaning, and Reception', in *Dürer's Journeys: Travels of*

a Renaissance Artist, ed. Susan Foister and Peter van den Brink, exh. cat., National Gallery (London, 2021), pp. 252–65

Heninger, S. K., *The Cosmographical Glass: Renaissance Diagrams of the Universe* (San Marino, CA, 1977)

Hersey, George, *High Renaissance Art in St Peter's and the Vatican: An Interpretive Guide* (Chicago, IL, 1993)

Hibbard, Howard, *Bernini* (Harmondsworth, 1965)

—, *Michelangelo* (New York, 1974)

Hoisington, Rena, *Aquatint: From Its Origins to Goya*, exh. cat., National Gallery of Art, Washington, DC (Princeton, NJ, 2021), pp. 209–27

Holmes, Megan, 'Ex-votos: Materiality, Memory and Cult', in *The Idol in the Age of Art: Objects, Devotions and the Early Modern World*, ed. Michael Cole and Rebecca Zorach (Aldershot, 2009), pp. 165–88

Homer, *The Iliad*, trans. Stanley Lombardo (Indianapolis, IN, 1997)

Hope, Charles, *Titian* (London, 1980)

Hughes, Robert, *Goya* (London, 2004)

Huizinga, Johan, *The Waning of the Middle Ages* (New York, 1954)

Hults, Linda C., *The Witch as Muse* (Philadelphia, PA, 2005)

Hutchinson, Ben, *The Midlife Mind: Literature and the Art of Ageing* (London, 2020)

Jacob-Friesen, Holger, ed., *Hans Baldung Grien. Heilig/Unheilig*, exh. cat., Staatliche Kunsthalle Karlsruhe (2019)

Jacobowitz, Ellen S., and Stephanie Loeb Stepanek, eds, *The Prints of Lucas van Leyden and His Contemporaries*, exh. cat., National Gallery of Art (Washington, DC, 1983)

Jaffé, David, ed., *Titian*, exh. cat., National Gallery (London, 2003)

Joannides, Paul, '"Primitivism" in the Late Drawings of Michelangelo: The Master's Construction of an Old-Age Style', in *Michelangelo Drawings*, ed. Craig Hugh Smyth (Washington, DC, 1992), pp. 244–61

—, *Titian to 1518* (New Haven, CT, and London, 2001)

Kaulbach, Hans-Martin, and Reinhart Schleier, eds, '*Der Welt Lauf*'. *Allegorische Graphikserien des Manierismus*, exh. cat., Staatsgalerie Stuttgart (1997)

King, John N., *Tudor Royal Iconography: Literature and Art in an Age of Religious Crisis* (Princeton, NJ, 1989)

Klessmann, Rüdiger, ed., *Adam Elsheimer, 1578–1610*, exh. cat., Städel Museum (Frankfurt, 2006)

Klibansky, Raymond, Erwin Panofsky and Fritz Saxl, *Saturn and Melancholy: Studies in the History of Natural Philosophy, Religion, and Art* (London, 1964)

Knipping, John, *Iconography of the Counter Reformation in the Netherlands* (Nieuwkoop, 1974)

Koerner, Joseph, 'The Epiphany of the Black Magus circa 1500', in *The Image of the Black in Western Art*, vol. III/1: *From the 'Age of Discovery' to the*

Age of Abolition, ed. David Bindman and Henry Gates Jr (Cambridge, MA, 2010), pp. 7–92

Kunz, Margaret, 'A Ceremonial Ensemble: Michelangelo's *Last Judgment* and the Cappella Paolina Frescoes', in *Michelangelo's 'Last Judgment'*, ed. Marcia Hall (Cambridge, 2005), pp. 150–82

Kurmann, Peter, *La façade de la cathédrale de Reims: architecture et sculpture des portails* (Lausanne, 1987)

Lestringant, Frank, *Cannibals: The Discovery and Representation of the Cannibal from Columbus to Jules Verne* (Berkeley, CA, 1997), pp. 1–111

Lewis, C. S., *The Discarded Image: An Introduction to Medieval and Renaissance Literature* (Cambridge, 1964)

—, 'Imagination and Thought in the Middle Ages', *Studies in Medieval and Renaissance Literature* (Cambridge, 1998), pp. 41–63

Licht, Fred, *Goya: The Origins of the Modern Temper in Art* (New York, 1979)

Lienhard, Joseph, 'St Joseph in Early Christianity: Devotion and Theology', in *Joseph of Nazareth through the Centuries*, ed. Joseph Chorpenning (Philadelphia, PA, 2011), pp. 15–46

Logan, Anne-Marie, *Peter Paul Rubens: The Drawings*, exh. cat., Metropolitan Museum of Art (New York, 2005)

Loh, Maria, *Titian's Touch: Art, Magic and Philosophy* (London, 2019)

McCoubrey, John, 'Turner's *Slave Ship*, Abolition, Ruskin, and Reception', *Word and Image*, XIV/4 (1998), pp. 319–53

McGrath, Elizabeth, *Subjects from History: Corpus Rubenianum Ludwig Burchard XIII* (London, 1997)

McMullan, Gordon, and Sam Smiles, eds, *Late Style and Its Discontents: Essays in Art, Literature, and Music* (Oxford, 2016)

Mannings, Edgar, 'Reynolds, Garrick, and the Choice of Hercules', *Eighteenth-Century Studies*, XVII/3 (1983–4), pp. 259–83

Manuth, Volker, *Rembrandt: The Complete Paintings* (Cologne, 2019)

Matheson, Susan B., and J. J. Pollitt, *Old Age in Greek and Roman Art* (New Haven, CT, and London, 2022)

Matilla, José Manuel, and Manuela Mena Marqués, eds, *Only My Strength Will Remain: Goya Drawings*, exh. cat., Museo Nacional del Prado (Madrid, 2019)

Meuwissen, Daantje, ed., *Jacob Cornelisz Van Oostsanen, ca. 1475–1533*, exh. cat., Amsterdam Museum and Stedelijk Museum Alkmaar (2014)

Miller, Lillian, ed., *The Peale Family: Creation of a Legacy, 1770–1870*, exh. cat., Philadelphia Museum of Art (1996)

Monet's Years at Giverny: Beyond Impressionism, exh. cat., Metropolitan Museum of Art (New York, 1978)

Muller, Jeffrey M., *Rubens: The Artist as Collector* (Princeton, NJ, 1989)

Nagel, Alexander, 'Observations on Michelangelo's Late *Pietà* Drawings and Sculptures', *Zeitschrift für Kunstgeschichte*, LIX/4 (1996), pp. 548–71

—, 'Gifts for Michelangelo and Vittoria Colonna', *Art Bulletin*, LXXIX/4 (1997), pp. 647–68
—, *Michelangelo and the Reform of Art* (Cambridge, 2000)
Nayeri, Farah, 'Lucian Freud's Self-Portraits: But What Do They Mean?', *New York Times*, 5 October 2019, www.nytimes.com
Nichols, Tom, *Titian and the End of the Venetian Renaissance* (London, 2013)
Nixon, Virginia, *Mary's Mother: Saint Anne in Late Medieval Europe* (University Park, PA, 2004)
Nuttall, Paula, *From Flanders to Florence: The Impact of Netherlandish Painting, 1400–1500* (New Haven, CT, and London, 2004)
Osten, Gert von der, *Hans Baldung Grien. Gemälde und Dokumente* (Berlin, 1983)
Panofsky, Erwin, 'Father Time', in *Studies in Iconology: Humanistic Themes in the Art of the Renaissance* (New York, 1962), pp. 69–93
—, *Problems in Titian: Mostly Iconographic* (New York, 1969)
—, '*Et in Arcadia ego*: Poussin and the Elegiac Tradition', in *Meaning in the Visual Arts* (Chicago, IL, 1982), pp. 295–320
—, *The Life and Art of Albrecht Dürer* (Princeton, NJ, 1995)
Panzanelli, Roberta, 'Compelling Presence', in *Ephemeral Bodies: Wax Sculpture and the Human Figure*, ed. Panzanelli (Los Angeles, CA, 2008), pp. 15–17
Pape, Walter, and Frederick Burwick, eds, *The Boydell Shakespeare Gallery* (Essen, 1996)
Partridge, Loren, and Randolph Starn, *A Renaissance Likeness: Art and Culture in Raphael's 'Julius II'* (Berkeley, CA, 1980)
Pérez-Sanchez, Alfonso, and Eleanor Sayre, eds, *Goya and the Spirit of Enlightenment*, exh. cat., Museo del Prado, Museum of Fine Arts and Metropolitan Museum of Art (Madrid, Boston, MA, and New York, 1989)
Perkinson, Stephen, *The Likeness of the King: A Prehistory of Portraiture in Late Medieval France* (Chicago, IL, 2009)
Perlove, Shelley, *Bernini and the Idealization of Death: The 'Blessed Ludovica Albertoni' and the Altieri Chapel* (University Park, PA, 1990)
—, and Larry Silver, *Rembrandt's Faith* (University Park, PA, 2009)
Pope-Hennessy, John, *Italian Renaissance Sculpture* (New York, 1985)
Portrayals from a Brush Divine: A Special Exhibition on the Tricentennial of Giuseppe Castiglione's Arrival in China, exh. cat., National Palace Museum (Taipei, 2015)
Poulet, Anne, *Jean-Antoine Houdon*, exh. cat., National Gallery of Art (Washington, DC, 2003)
Pressly, Nancy, *Revealed Religion: Benjamin West's Commissions for Windsor Castle and Fonthill Abbey*, exh. cat., San Antonio Museum of Art (1983)
Prinz, Wolfram, 'The *Four Philosophers* by Rubens and the Pseudo-Seneca in Seventeenth-Century Painting', *Art Bulletin*, LV/3 (1973), pp. 410–28
Renger, Konrad, and Claudia Denk, *Flämische Malerei des Barock in der Alten Pinakothek* (Munich and Cologne, 2002)

Reudenbach, Bruno, 'Ein Weltbild als Hieroglyphe. Das Signet des Warburg Institute', in *Porträt aus Büchern. Bibliothek Warburg und Warburg Institute*, ed. Michael Diers (Hamburg, 1993), pp. 145–55

Rey, Jean-Dominique, and Denis Rouart, *Monet: Water Lilies: The Complete Series* (Paris, 2008)

Ricci, Giovanni, 'Masks of Power: Funeral Effigies in Early Modern Europe', in *Waxing Eloquent: Italian Portraits in Wax*, ed. Andrea Daninos (Milan, 2012), pp. 61–7

Ringbom, Sixten, *Icon to Narrative: The Rise of the Dramatic Close-Up in Fifteenth-Century Devotional Painting* (Åbo, 1965)

Rosand, David, 'Titian and the Eloquence of the Brush', *Artibus et historiae*, II/3 (1981), pp. 85–96

—, 'Old Age Style', *Art Journal*, XLVI/2 (Summer 1987), pp. 91–133

Roth, Michael, *Dürers Mutter. Schönheit, Alter und Tod im Bild der Renaissance*, exh. cat., Kupferstichkabinett (Berlin, 2006)

Rubin, William, ed., *Pablo Picasso: A Retrospective*, exh. cat., Museum of Modern Art (New York, 1980)

Saslow, James M., *The Poetry of Michelangelo: An Annotated Translation* (New Haven, CT, 1991)

Sayre, Eleanor, *The Changing Image: Prints by Francisco Goya*, exh. cat., Boston Museum of Fine Arts (1974)

Schiff, Gert, *Henry Fuseli, 1741–1825*, exh. cat., Tate Gallery (London, 1975)

—, *Picasso: The Last Years, 1963–1973*, exh. cat., Guggenheim Museum (New York, 1983)

Schiller, Gertrud, *Iconography of Christian Art*, vol. II: *The Passion of Christ* (Greenwich, CT, 1972)

Schleif, Corine, 'Nicodemus and Sculptors: Self-Reflexivity in Works by Adam Kraft and Tilman Riemenschneider', *Art Bulletin*, LXXV/4 (1993), pp. 599–626

Schwartz, Gary, *Rembrandt: His Life, His Paintings* (New York, 1985)

—, *The Rembrandt Book* (New York, 2006)

Sears, Elizabeth, *The Ages of Man: Medieval Interpretations of the Life Cycle* (Princeton, NJ, 1986)

Seidenstein, Joanna Sheers, *Divine Encounter: Rembrandt's 'Abraham and the Angels'*, exh. cat., Frick Collection (New York, 2017)

Settis, Salvatore, *Giorgione's 'Tempest': Interpreting the Hidden Subject* (Chicago, IL, 1990)

Seznec, Jean, *The Survival of the Pagan Gods: The Mythological Tradition and Its Place in Renaissance Humanism and Art* (New York, 1953)

Sherman, Claire Richter, *The Portraits of Charles V of France, 1338–1380* (New York, 1969)

Silver, Larry, 'Nature and Nature's God: Landscape and Cosmos of Albrecht Altdorfer', *Art Bulletin*, LXXXI/2 (1999), pp. 194–214

—, *Hieronymus Bosch* (New York, 2006)

—, *Europe Views the World, 1500–1700* (London, 2022), pp. 56–70

Sleptzoff, L. M., *Men or Supermen? The Italian Portrait in the Fifteenth Century* (Jerusalem, 1978)

Sluijter, Eric Jan, *Rembrandt and the Female Nude* (Amsterdam, 2006)

Smith, Jeffrey Chipps, 'Dürer's Losses and the Dilemmas of Being', in *Enduring Loss in Early Modern Germany: Cross Disciplinary Perspectives*, ed. Lynne Tatlock (Leiden, 2010), pp. 74–7

Snyder, Joel, 'Inventing Photography, 1839–1879', in *On the Art of Fixing a Shadow: One Hundred and Fifty Years of Photography*, exh. cat., National Gallery of Art (Washington, DC, 1989)

Soussloff, Catherine, 'Old Age and Old-Age Style in the *Lives* of Artists: Gianlorenzo Bernini', *Art Journal*, XLVI/2 (1987), pp. 115–21

Spate, Virginia, *Claude Monet: Life and Work* (New York, 1992)

Staiti, Paul, *Of Arms and Artists: The American Revolution through Painters' Eyes* (New York, 2016)

Stapp, Will, 'The Nineteenth-Century Portrait', in *The Art of Photography, 1839–1989*, ed. Mike Weaver, exh. cat., Royal Academy (London, 1989), pp. 44–6

Staley, Allen, *Copley and West in England, 1775–1815* (London, 2021)

Stechow, Wolfgang, 'Joseph of Arimathea or Nicodemus?', *Studien zur toskanischen Kunst. Festchrift für Ludwig Heinrich Heydenreich* (Munich, 1963), pp. 289–302

Stein, Perrin, ed., *Jacques Louis David: Radical Draftsman*, exh. cat., Metropolitan Museum of Art (New York, 2022)

Steinberg, Leo, 'Michelangelo's Florentine *Pietà*: The Missing Leg', *Art Bulletin*, L/4 (1968), pp. 343–53

—, *Michelangelo's Last Paintings* (New York, 1975)

—, 'Animadversions: Michelangelo's Florentine *Pietà:* The Missing Leg Twenty Years After', *Art Bulletin*, LXXI/3 (1989), pp. 480–505

Strong, Roy, *The Cult of Elizabeth: Elizabethan Portraiture and Pageantry* (London, 1977)

Sutherland, Daniel E., *Whistler: A Life for Art's Sake* (New Haven, CT, 2014)

Sutherland Boggs, Jean, 'The Last Thirty Years', in *Picasso in Retrospect*, ed. Roland Penrose and John Golding (New York, 1973), pp. 127–59

Swan, Claudia, '*The Preparation for the Sabbath* by Jacques de Gheyn II', *Print Quarterly*, XVI/4 (1999), pp. 327–39

—, *Art, Science, and Witchcraft in Early Modern Holland: Jacques de Gheyn II* (Cambridge, 2005)

Tomlinson, Janis, *Goya: A Portrait of the Artist* (Princeton, NJ, 2020)

Troescher, Georg, 'Die "Pitiè de Nostre-Seigneur" oder die "Not Gottes"', *Wallraf-Richartz Jahrbuch*, 9 (1936), pp. 148–68

Tümpel, Christian and Astrid, *Rembrandt: Images and Metaphors* (London, 2006)

Valcanover, Francesco, 'Le dernier Titien et la fin du siècle à Venise', in *Le siècle de Titien*, ed. Gilles Fage, exh. cat., Grand Palais (Paris, 1993), pp. 595–625

Vandenbroeck, Paul, 'Bubo significans. Die Eule als Sinnbild von Schlechtigkeit und Torhiet, vor allem in der niederländischen und deutschen Bilddarstellung und bei Jheronimus Bosch', *Jaarboek Koninklijk Museum voor Schone Kunsten Antwerpen* (Antwerp, 1985), pp. 19–135

Vanhaelen, Angela, *The Moving Statues of Seventeenth-Century Amsterdam: Automata, Waxworks, Fountains, Labyrinths* (University Park, PA, 2022)

Veldman, Ilja, 'Seasons, Planets and Temperaments in the Work of Maarten van Heemskerck: Cosmo-Astrological Allegory in Sixteenth-Century Netherlandish Prints', *Simiolus*, XI/3/4 (1980), pp. 149–76

—, 'De macht van de planeten over het mensdom in prenten naar Maarten de Vos', *Bulletin van het Rijksmuseum* (1983), pp. 21–53

—, 'From Allegory to Genre', in *Images for the Eye and Soul: Function and Meaning in Netherlandish Prints* (Leiden, 2006), pp. 193–222

Vogelaar, Christiaan, et al., eds, *Lucas van Leyden en de Renaissance*, exh. cat., De Lakenhal (Leiden, 2011)

Waldburg Wolfegg, Christoph Graf zu, *Venus and Mars: The World of the Medieval Housebook* (Munich, 1998)

Wallace, William E., 'Narrative and Religious Expression in Michelangelo's Pauline Chapel', *Artibus et historiae*, X/19 (1989), pp. 107–22

—, 'Michelangelo, Tiberio Calcagni, and the Florentine *Pietà*', *Artibus et historiae*, XXI/42 (2000), pp. 81–99

—, *Michelangelo: The Artist, the Man, and His Times* (Cambridge, 2010)

—, *Michelangelo, God's Architect* (Princeton, NJ, 2019)

Warburg, Aby, 'The Art of Portraiture and the Florentine Bourgeoisie', in *The Renewal of Pagan Antiquity* [1918] (Los Angeles, CA, 1999), pp. 185–221

—, 'Pagan-Antique Prophecy in Words and Images in the Age of Luther', in *The Renewal of Pagan Antiquity* [1918] (Los Angeles, CA, 1999), pp. 598–697

Wasserman, Jack, *Michelangelo's Florentine 'Pietà'* (Princeton, NJ, 2003)

Weber, Gregor J. M., 'Inner Conflict' and 'Reconciliation', in *Rembrandt: The Late Works*, ed. Jonathan Bikker and Weber, exh. cat., National Gallery and Rijksmuseum (London and Amsterdam, 2014), pp. 235–69

Wendorf, Richard, 'Reynolds and the Genius of Life', in *The Elements of Life: Biography and Portrait-Painting in Stuart and Georgian England* (Oxford, 1990), pp. 226–60

Westermann, Mariët, *The Amusements of Jan Steen* (Zwolle, 1997)

Wetering, Ernst van de, *Rembrandt: The Painter at Work* (Amsterdam, 1997)

—, *Rembrandt's Paintings Revisited: A Complete Survey* (Dordrecht, 2015)

Wheelock, Arthur K., ed., *Rembrandt's Late Religious Portraits*, exh. cat., National Gallery of Art (Washington, DC, 2005)

White, Christopher, *Dürer: The Artist and His Drawings* (London, 1971)
—, and Quentin Buvelot, *Rembrandt by Himself*, exh. cat., National Gallery and Mauritshuis (London and The Hague, 1999)
Williams, Anne L., *Satire, Veneration, and St. Joseph in Art, c. 1300–1500* (Amsterdam, 2019)
Wilson, Carolyn C., *St. Joseph in Italian Renaissance Society and Art* (Philadelphia, PA, 2001)
Wilton, Andrew, *J.M.W. Turner: His Art and Life* (New York, 1979)
Wind, Edgar, 'Michelangelo's Prophets and Sibyls', *Proceedings of the British Academy*, LI (1965), pp. 47–84
—, *Hume and the Heroic Portrait: Studies in Eighteenth-Century Imagery* (Oxford, 1986)
Winner, Matthias, 'Projects and Execution in the Stanza della Segnatura', in *Raphael in the Apartments of Julius II and Leo X* (Milan, 1993)
Winternitz, Emanuel, 'The Curse of Pallas Athena', in *Musical Instruments and Their Symbolism in Western Art* (New Haven, CT, 1979), pp. 150–65
Wittkower, Rudolf, *Bernini* (London, 1961)
Wolfthal, Diane, *Household Servants and Slaves: A Visual History, 1300–1700* (New Haven, CT, 2022)
Zanker, Paul, *Die Trunkene Alte. Das Lachen der Verhöhnten* (Frankfurt, 1989)
Ziermann, Horst, *Matthias Grünewald* (Munich, 2001)
Zika, Charles, *The Appearance of Witchcraft* (New York, 2007)
Zucker, Mark, 'Raphael and the Beard of Julius II', *Art Bulletin*, LIX/4 (1977), pp. 524–33

Acknowledgements

Today most authors seem to situate themselves personally in relation to their topics of study. In this instance, I acknowledge that I am just a shade past 77 years of age, so this study of old age (written not long after completing another study, *Fools and Folly in Flemish Art*, especially featuring the folly of old people) surely has an autobiographical dimension. As I watch a lively quartet of pre-school grandchildren discovering a world of their own that differs so much from my own childhood and even from those of my children, I experience the powerful sensation of being a form of living history, arising unbidden. At the same time, I have reached a stage of life when the losses of loved ones and peers in age occur ever more frequently. Thus I find myself turning to the obituary pages of the daily newspaper (now more often online than in print form). There I note the celebrities or even personal acquaintances who have died recently. Awareness of mortality comes with old age.

I also vividly remember what was called the 'generation gap' of the 1960s. Then, my own peers began to differ so drastically in their lives and values from their parents, who had experienced both the Depression and a World War. Professionally, I have been retired now for nearly a decade as a professor from a leading American university programme in art history, so the visual turn of this book stems from old teaching habits and cumulative scholarship.

The impetus for visiting this subject with Reaktion Books came initially from a long-time friend and colleague, Professor Barbara Rosenwein, who is preparing a similar historical discussion of old age (from the standpoint of happiness and care) across the same vast time span. Warm thanks to Professor Rosenwein, who was kind enough to share a draft of her invaluable scholarship on this topic with me.

As for dedications, the most appropriate collective nod would have to be former classmates, mentors and colleagues of similar vintage from across my academic career, too numerous to list here, lest I omit (or forget) important individuals. But the most deserving dedicatee (not for the first time) of such a book is my life companion, who has grown old with me for almost half a century at this point, the ever-patient and forbearing Elizabeth Silver-Schack. She still makes it all possible. 'Grow old along with me, the best is yet to be.'

Photo Acknowledgements

The author and publishers wish to express their thanks to the below sources of illustrative material and/or permission to reproduce it. Some locations of artworks are also given below, in the interest of brevity:

© The Art Institute of Chicago, photo Art Resource, NY/Scala, Florence: 46; Bayerische Staatsbibliothek, Munich (Clm 14300, fol. 8r): 7; British Library, London (Arundel MS 83, fol. 126v): 10; Dallas Museum of Art, TX (The Eugene and Margaret McDermott Art Fund, Inc., bequest of Mrs Eugene McDermott in honor of Nancy Hamon, 2019.67.13.MCD), photo courtesy Dallas Museum of Art: 82; Duke of Sutherland Collection, on loan to the National Galleries of Scotland, Edinburgh, photo SuperStock/DeAgostini: 4; © The Estate of Alice Neel: 50 (Philadelphia Museum of Art, PA), 62 (National Portrait Gallery, Smithsonian Institution, Washington, DC); Centrale Montemartini, Musei Capitolini, Rome (photo Carole Raddato/Flickr, CC BY-SA 2.0): 12; Gallerie dell'Accademia, Venice: 26, 70; Germanisches Nationalmuseum, Nuremberg: 51; Glyptothek, Munich (photo Marcus Cyron/Wikimedia, CC BY-SA 3.0): 22; iStock.com: 14 (Siempreverde22); Kenwood House, London: 74; Kroměříž Archdiocesan Museum: 69; Kupferstichkabinett, Staatliche Museen zu Berlin/Jörg P. Anders: 52; Los Angeles County Museum of Art (LACMA): 57; Mauritshuis, The Hague: 30; The Metropolitan Museum of Art, New York: 5, 20, 28, 34, 43, 61; Minneapolis Institute of Art, MN: 31, 76, 78; Musée du Louvre, Paris: 15 (photo Shonagon/Wikimedia, public domain), 54; Musée de l'Œuvre Notre-Dame, Strasbourg: 23; Musée d'Orsay, Paris: 53; Musée Unterlinden, Colmar: 39; Musei Vaticani, Vatican City: 16 (photo Jörg Bittner Unna/Wikimedia, CC BY 3.0), 17, 63 (photo Sailko/Wikimedia, CC BY 3.0); Museo Nacional del Prado, Madrid: 3, 41, 42, 83; Museo Nazionale del Bargello, Florence, photo Bridgeman Images: 55; Museo dell'Opera del Duomo, Florence (photos Marie-Lan Nguyen/Wikimedia, CC BY 2.5): 64, 65; Museu Nacional de Arte Antiga, Lisbon: 18; photo © Nara National Museum, reproduced courtesy Tōdai-ji Temple, Nara: 47; The National Gallery, London: frontispiece, 80, 81; National Gallery of Art, Washington, DC: 2, 19, 25, 27, 29, 33, 67, 79; Nationalmuseum, Stockholm/Erik

Cornelius: 77; Norton Simon Museum, Pasadena, CA (M.2005.2.P), photo © Norton Simon Art Foundation: 35; The Palace Museum, Beijing: 48; Palais des Beaux-Arts de Lille: 32; Philadelphia Museum of Art, PA: 45, 58, 59; private collection: 8; Rijksmuseum, Amsterdam: 1, 6, 9, 11, 37, 38, 49; RISD Museum, Providence, RI: 44; Rodin Museum, Philadelphia, PA: 21; Royal Collection Trust/© His Majesty King Charles III 2022: 24, 66, 71; Saint Louis Art Museum, MO: 68; Schloss Weissenstein, Pommersfelden: 36; Shutterstock.com: 72 (marcobrivio.gallery), 73 (Renata Sedmakova); The State Hermitage Museum, St Petersburg: 75; Toledo Museum of Art, OH: 56; The Walters Art Museum, Baltimore, MD: 13; © Wyeth Foundation for American Art/ARS, NY and DACS, London 2024, photo courtesy Dallas Museum of Art, TX (Dallas Art Association Purchase, 1962.27): 60; Yale University Art Gallery, New Haven, CT: 40.

Index

Illustration numbers are indicated by *italics*